Bill 'Swampy' Marsh is an award-winning writer/performer of stories, songs and plays. He spent most of his youth in rural south-western New South Wales. Bill was forced to give up any idea he had of a 'career' as a cricketer when a stint at agricultural college was curtailed due to illness, and so began his hobby of writing. After backpacking through three continents and working in the wine industry, his writing hobby blossomed into a career.

His first collection of short stories, *Beckom Pop. 64*, was published in 1988, his second, *Old Yanconian Daze*, in 1995 and his third, *Looking for Dad*, in 1998. During 1999, Bill released *Australia*, a CD of his songs and stories. That was followed in 2002 by *A Drover's Wife* and *Glory, Glory: A Tribute to the Royal Flying Doctor Service* in 2008 and *Open Roads: The Songs and Stories of Bill Swampy Marsh* in 2017. He has written soundtrack songs and music for the television documentaries *The Last Mail from Birdsville: The Story of Tom Kruse*; *Source to Sea: The Story of the Murray Riverboats* and the German travel documentaries *Traumzeit auf dem Stuart Highway*, *Clinic Flights (Tilpa & Marble Bar)*, *Traumzeit in den Kimberleys* and *Einsatz von Port Hedland nach Marble Bar*.

Bill has won and judged many nationwide short-story and songwriting competitions and short-film awards as well as running writing workshops throughout Australia. He has performed his songs and stories from outback places such as Mount Dare (pop. 10), down the Birdsville Track, as part of the

Great Australian Cattle Drive; on the Ghan as part of Great Southern Rail's ANZAC Tribute Journey; and at the Transport Hall of Fame gala dinner in Alice Springs as a support act to Slim Dusty.

Great Australian Volunteer Firies Stories is part of Bill's very successful series of 'Great Australian' stories, including: *Great Australian Outback Trucking Stories* (2019), *Great Australian Bush Funeral Stories* (2018), *Great Australian Outback Nurses Stories* (2017), *Great Australian Outback Teaching Stories* (2016), *Great Australian Outback Police Stories* (2015), *Amazing Grace: Stories of Faith and Friendship from Outback Australia* (2014), *The Complete Book of Australian Flying Doctor Stories* and *Great Australian Outback School Stories* (2013), *Great Australian CWA Stories* (2011), *New Great Australian Flying Doctor Stories* and *The ABC Book of Great Aussie Stories for Young People* (2010), *Great Australian Stories – Outback Towns and Pubs* (2009), *More Great Australian Flying Doctor Stories* (2007), *Great Australian Railway Stories* (2005), *Great Australian Droving Stories* (2003), *Great Australian Shearing Stories* (2001) and *Great Australian Flying Doctor Stories* (1999). Bill's biography *Goldie: Adventures in a Vanishing Australia* was published in 2008 and his semi-autobiographical collection *Swampy: Tall Tales and True from Boyhood and Beyond* was published in 2012.

More information about the author can be found at
www.billswampymarsh.com
Facebook: Bill 'Swampy' Marsh

GREAT AUSTRALIAN VOLUNTEER FIRIES STORIES

BILL 'SWAMPY' MARSH

ABC
BOOKS

The ABC 'Wave' device is a trademark of the
Australian Broadcasting Corporation and is used
under licence by HarperCollins*Publishers* Australia.

HarperCollins*Publishers*
Australia • Brazil • Canada • France • Germany • Holland • Hungary
India • Italy • Japan • Mexico • New Zealand • Poland • Spain • Sweden
Switzerland • United Kingdom • United States of America

First published in Australia in 2021
by HarperCollinsPublishers Australia Pty Limited
Level 13, 201 Elizabeth Street, Sydney NSW 2000
ABN 36 009 913 517
harpercollins.com.au

A catalogue record for this book is available from the National Library of Australia.

ISBN 978 0 7333 4008 6 (paperback)
ISBN 978 1 4607 1137 8 (ebook)

Cover design by HarperCollins Design Studio
Front cover image by AAP Image/Dan Peled
Back cover image by shutterstock.com
Author photograph by Chris Carter
Typeset in ITC Bookman Light by Kirby Jones
Printed and bound in Australia by McPherson's Printing Group
The papers used by HarperCollins in the manufacture of this book are a natural, recyclable product
made from wood grown in sustainable plantation forests. The fibre source and manufacturing processes
meet recognised international environmental standards, and carry certification.

Dedicated to
our brave volunteer firies.

Special thanks to Publishing Director Brigitta Doyle, editors Lachlan McLaine and Rachel Dennis, Rights and Contracts Associate Nicolette Houben, along with Head of Business Development Guy Bensaul, Royalties Manager ANZ Brendon Redmond, and the promotions and sales staff at ABC Books–HarperCollins Australia, without whose support these stories may never have seen the light of day; and to my precious support crew of Kath Beauchamp, Craig Langley and Margaret Worth.

I would also like to thank Jamie McElroy, Media Officer, Volunteer Fire and Rescue Services Association of WA (Inc.), and Jess O'Reilly, Media Officer, Queensland Fire and Emergency Services, for their much-welcomed assistance.

Contents

Contributors

The stories contained in this book are written from interviews recorded by Bill 'Swampy' Marsh. The contributors are:

Larry & Therese Adams
Darlene Addy
Kevin Anderson
Vince Balanzategui
Matthew Bazzica
Kath & Noel Beauchamp
A J Beavis
Terry Beltrame
Allan 'Bronco' Brett
Christine Brown
Chris Carter
Peter Cartner
Emma Cole
Bill & Nita Coombs
Gareth Ellem
John Forbes
Norman 'Pickles' Fulmer
Alistair Grant
Bob & Pat Greenhill
Rex Hall
Margurite Hann-Syme
David & Christine Harris
Neil Hatt
Malcolm Hull
Ray Johnston
Rusty Kraut
Geoff Landwehr
Craig Langley
George & Gillian Lee
John Legione
Brad Lennon

Jeanette & Garry Mann
Annette Marner
Fran McAllen
Pauline McAllister
Jamie McElroy
Neville Middleton
Kent Morley
Peter Murphy
Brian Muxworthy
Paula O'Connor
Tracy O'Donnell
David O'Neill
Jessica O'Reilly
Ken O'Reilly
Brian 'Dinga' & Justine Outtram
Frank & Marie Partington
Karen & Susan Partington
John Price
Garry 'Gazza' & Pol Purcell
Bronwyn & Grant Rigby
Barry Simes
Len Simmons
Peter 'Simpy' Simpfendorfer
Malcolm Sinclair
Ian & Moira Sirett
Trevor Syme
Stephanie Whyte
Ray Wilton
Margaret Worth
Kerry Wyvill
... and many, many more

Introduction

As I write this introduction, bushfires have broken out in Western Australia. At last report, something like ninety homes in the Perth Hills may have been destroyed and over twenty-five thousand hectares of land burnt. Arson is suspected. And now storms are moving in to the north-east of the state, bringing with them a predicted one hundred millimetres – four inches – of rain and one hundred kilometre per hour winds.

In my own state of South Australia, within the last month a dozen buildings, including houses, were destroyed by fires in the Adelaide Hills, with one case of suspected arson. More than four hundred firefighters were involved in containing the blaze, which burnt through 2500 hectares of land. Particularly badly hit was Cherry Gardens, where I used to live when I first came to South Australia back in the mid-1970s. I have friends living around the Mylor-Bradbury area who evacuated during the fires.

It's a frightening situation. We all saw the footage of the catastrophic fires that burnt through New South Wales and Victoria during the 2019–20 fire season. How could we not? At the forefront of all these blazes stood our volunteer fire service personnel.

As part of the interviewing process for this collection of stories, during August and September of 2019, I travelled through outback South Australia, southern Queensland, New South Wales and the Australian Capital Territory. I was back on the road in late December 2019, travelling through Victoria. Then it was over to Tasmania during February and March 2020. In fact, I just managed to get the last boat out of Tasmania before their COVID-19 restrictions came in, and barely scraped back into South Australia before the South Australian–Victorian border closures came into force. I would like to thank all those people who housed and fed me along my travels.

Because of COVID-19 restrictions, my mid-year travels of 2020 didn't eventuate, leaving me with a gap in Western Australia, Northern Queensland and the Northern Territory. I'd very much like to thank Jamie McElroy, media officer, Volunteer Fire and Rescue Services Association of WA (Inc.) and Jess O'Reilly, media officer, Queensland Fire and Emergency Services, for their assistance in helping me find people to interview.

During the writing of this book I met and talked with near on a hundred people who have volunteered their time to fight bushfires and house fires, attend road accident rescues, help out in flooded areas, clean up after cyclones and hailstorms, as well as attend a myriad of other emergency services duties. Between the good laughs and friendly banter I must admit there were times I was brought to tears by some of their experiences, all of which have left me with nothing but utter admiration for these people – our brave volunteer firies.

Keep well, stay safe, and hopefully we'll meet up out on the road somewhere.

Bill 'Swampy' Marsh
January 2021

An Excerpt from
'The Fire at Ross's Farm'
by Henry Lawson (1911)

One Christmas time, when months of drought
Had parched the western creeks,
The bush-fires started in the north
And travelled south for weeks.
At night along the river-side
The scene was grand and strange –
The hill-fires looked like lighted streets
Of cities in the range.

The cattle-tracks between the trees
Were like long dusty aisles,
And on a sudden breeze the fire
Would sweep along for miles;
Like sounds of distant musketry
It crackled through the brakes,
And o'er the flat of silver grass
It hissed like angry snakes.

It leapt across the flowing streams
And raced o'er pastures broad;
It climbed the trees and lit the boughs
And through the scrub it roared.
The bees fell stifled in the smoke
Or perished in their hives,
And with the stock the kangaroos
Went flying for their lives.

Yes, one Christmas time, when months of drought
Had parched the western creeks,
The bush-fires started in the north

And travelled south for weeks.
At night along the river-side
The scene was grand and strange –
The hill-fires looked like lighted streets
Of cities in the range.

A Christmas Memory

I had the feeling that it was going to be a different sort of Christmas when my cousin Esmay and I ran into our lounge room early on Christmas morning to find Esmay's dad dressed up as Santa and lying comatose under the Christmas tree while clinging on to the half-emptied flagon of port we'd left out specially for Santa. When I asked Esmay what was going on, she told me that her father – my Uncle Bob – was a bit partial to the occasional drop and that he'd probably snuck into the lounge room late that night in the hopes of stealing a few drops for himself before Santa got to it.

We were just checking to see if Uncle Bob was still alive when the rest of the adults arrived on the scene. The adults being my mum and dad and Esmay's mother, Aunty Flo. Now, with Uncle Bob being a real lump of a man, it took the whole three of them to drag him out from under the Christmas tree and off to the bedroom, where Aunty Flo suggested it'd be best for all concerned to allow him to 'sleep things off'.

With Uncle Bob now indisposed, Mum was keen that we get to it and distribute the presents. When I asked her why we weren't going to wait for my sixteen-year-old sister, Jean, to make an appearance, Dad gave a disgruntled nod over his shoulder. And there, out through the missing wooden panel in the lounge room wall that Dad had promised Mum he was going to fix before our guests arrived for Christmas, I could see our old farm ute, stuck on its side in a table drain, just off the track that led from our front gate to our house. What I could gather from the discussion that followed was that Jean had borrowed the ute the previous night to go out and meet up with some of her friends from the various properties around the area and she obviously hadn't quite made it home, which explained why the ute was lying on its side in the table drain.

Anyhow, with Uncle Bob now unavailable, Dad begrudgingly took it upon himself to dish out the presents. And that's where I struck gold. Santa had heard my words and he'd got me a brand-spanking-new cricket bat, freshly smelling of willow and linseed. A kid couldn't have wished for more. Though I had an inkling that Dad, in particular, might've had something to do with it, because when I took the bat out of its newspaper wrapping, scribbled across the face of it were the words 'To Swampy from Sir Donald Bradman' in something that looked a bit like Dad's own scrawly handwriting.

As for the other gifts, it'd been a pretty lean season on the farm so they weren't as special. Mum had bought Dad some Old Spice aftershave and one of those brand-new electric shavers, which was guaranteed not to cut him up as much as the old cut-throat razor he'd been struggling with for the past twenty years. In turn Dad had bought Mum a feather duster because she'd broken the last one after she'd caught me smoking cigarettes down behind Dad's personal hideaway, that is, his work shed. Santa had bought Esmay a frilly dress so that she wouldn't look like she'd come from such a poor family when she went back to the posh girls-only boarding school up in Darwin that her parents had wrangled a bursary to send her to. The currently waylaid Uncle Bob had bought Aunty Flo a box of his favourite chocolates that had been infused with liqueur, and Aunty Flo had bought Uncle Bob a book that I was told was a three-step instruction manual to try and help him sort out his 'small drinking problem', as Aunty Flo called it.

After the gifts had been dished out, Esmay and I went off to play our favourite game – fly swatting – where we'd try and swat as many of the bush flies and blowies that had got inside from the various openings in the house that Dad had promised Mum he'd fix before our guests arrived for Christmas. While Esmay and I were hell-bent on swatting a hundred before lunch, Dad got the tractor out of its shed and went over to drag the farm ute out of the table drain, and Mum and Aunty Flo got stuck to it in the kitchen to finish off the roast and the special Christmas pudding in the hundred-degree heat.

By midday the table was set and Uncle Bob had risen from his previous night's mishap and we all gathered at the table for our Christmas dinner. We always had the same thing: roast mutton burnt to a tee, and boiled vegetables which were so well done that you couldn't distinguish the cabbage from the carrots. Plus there was the piping hot gravy that had snared the occasional bush fly who'd found its way in through the gaping hole in the kitchen's flyscreen windows which Dad had promised Mum he'd fix before our guests arrived for Christmas. To top off the main meal there was the ever eagerly awaited Christmas pudding into which Aunty Flo and Mum had mixed thruppences and sixpences for us kids to find and put into our piggy banks for our future education.

Halfway through the pudding, my big sister Jean made her first appearance of the day. She looked as white as a sheet and when Dad gave her a dirty look, Mum snapped, 'Save it for later, Father. She hasn't been too well of late.'

Of course, with Uncle Bob being on Mum's side of the family, Dad assumed that Jean had been out drinking all night with her friends and had come home in no-fit-condition and had inadvertently driven the farm ute into the table drain. With all that going through Dad's mind, he completely ignored Mum's advice. He gave Jean another real dirty look and said, 'You'd better watch it, my young girl, or you'll end up like him' – the 'him' meaning Uncle Bob.

It was at that point in time Jean broke down in tears. 'She hadn't been drinking, Father,' said Mum before she added, 'and if you'd've been paying more attention to your daughter, you would've noticed that she hasn't had a drink now for a couple of months.'

'Why the hell's that?' replied Dad, to which Jean blurted through her bubbling tears, 'Because I'm pregnant!'

This was news to me. It was apparently news to Dad as well because he called out, 'So who the hell's the bloody father then?'

Before Jean had a chance to answer that one, Mum interrupted and said, 'She thinks it might've been one of the Smith boys.'

Now, I knew that there were three Smith boys – Bobby, James and Teddy, aged sixteen, eighteen and twenty. So I was a bit confused about that, and so must've been Dad because he was just about to ask Mum for some sort of clarification when she added, 'Or she thinks it could've been young Teddy Simpson.' Then, while Dad was grappling with that one, Mum added, 'Or it could've been that young German feller you had working here on the farm last harvest.'

That's when Dad finally found his voice. 'Jesus fuckin' Christ!' he shouted, which I assumed must've had some sort of Christmas connection. Because, even at my age, I knew that Christmas was all to do with Jesus, and I knew that Jesus had something to do with Christ. But for the life of me I couldn't work out where the 'funkin'' came into it.

But before I had a chance to sort that one out, Esmay started going on like she was throwing a fit. Unlike me, who'd been glued to the outcome of who it was that'd got Jean up the duff, Esmay had taken the opportunity to scoff down as much of the Christmas pudding as she could in the hopes of accumulating enough thruppences and sixpences so that she could buy cigarettes in order to get favours from the older girls at the posh boarding school she went to in Darwin.

'Oh my God!' shouted Aunty Flo. 'She's choking on a sixpence.'

'Give her a swig of this; it'll help loosen her larynx,' called out Uncle Bob, suddenly coming to life and holding up the flagon of port that he'd hidden under his chair at the dinner table. The only trouble was that, by now, whatever port that'd been left over in the flagon after his last night's shenanigans must've evaporated and there was hardly a dribble left.

But there was something about Dad that I came to admire that day. And that was how he could work well under pressure. In an instant, he'd lifted Esmay completely upside down and he'd given her such a whack on the back that the offending sixpence came shooting out of her mouth and scooted across the table to add to my eagerly awaiting collection of coins.

For some strange reason, by this stage the Christmas dinner seemed to have reached its end. Mum helped Jean rush back to the toilet to be sick. Uncle Bob left the kitchen in search of some more sustenance. Dad stormed off to his outside work shed mumbling something about how he was going off to try and work out why his life had turned out to be the complete mess that it had. Which left Aunty Flo to attack the mountain of dishes in amongst the hundred-degree heat, while Esmay and I finished off the Christmas pudding.

After we'd knocked off the pudding, Esmay and I decided to take a break from all the excitement and retreat outside into the scorching heat of the day. That's when she asked if I'd ever made fire sticks. 'No,' I said. So we went around the back of Dad's work shed, into the shade, where she produced a box of matches. The idea, she said, was to hold a match onto the lighting part of the matchbox and, with your other hand, flick the match off its launching pad. In doing so, the match would ignite and it'd fly through the air in flame.

So, with Dad taking a hammer to the anvil in his work shed and banging it in rhythm to his call of 'Jesus fuckin' Christ', Esmay gave me final instructions. After three goes I was still struggling. But on the fourth it worked. The match skidded off the scratchy part of the matchbox. It ignited and up it went in the air, spinning like a spectacular firelight-top. The only trouble was that it landed in one of the many rats' nests under the eaves of Dad's work shed – the very same ones that he'd promised Mum he'd have cleaned up before our guests arrived for Christmas.

Before you could say 'Jack Robinson', the rat's nest had burst into flames and Dad's shed was set alight. So when he looked up from banging the hammer on the anvil in his frustration, he saw the flames bursting out above him.

As it turned out, we were lucky that Dad was the chief of our local volunteer fire brigade. Like a flash he was out of his work shed and he scooted over to the tractor shed where the fire ute was sitting, awaiting an emergency such as this. The problem was that he'd forgotten to put any water into the fire ute's tank like he'd promised Mum he'd do before our guests arrived for Christmas. So by the time he'd driven the fire ute down to the dam and had pumped water into the tank and had driven back to the scene of the accident, his work shed was a ball of flames.

And this is where Dad's ability to work well under pressure again came to the fore. Before the shed had completely burnt to the ground, he had the fire pretty much under control.

By this stage Esmay and I had decided to make ourselves as scarce as possible. So we snuck around to the back side of the house to take up a game of French cricket using the bat that Santa had got me for Christmas which had been personally signed by Sir Donald Bradman.

Note: This story has been adapted from a collection of Bill 'Swampy' Marsh's stories-in-progress.

Heat, Fuel and Oxygen

Okay, are we recording? Good. Well, I joined the Queensland firies back in '68 and I've served in both the vollie – volunteer – and metro – metropolitan – brigades. I started out as a rookie learning the simple stuff, like how to attach the hose to the coupling and the nozzle onto the end of the hose. Once I got the hang of that, I went on to the centrifugal pump, learning how to draw water out of creeks or dams or wherever and get it up to and onto the fire.

See, the thing about a centrifugal pump is that it's got to be primed before it can work. If you can imagine: the pump works sideways. So the suction hose goes into the inlet, which is at the side of the pump. Then you have to prime the pump till the chamber's full. Once that's done the water can then be drawn up through the eye of the impeller and into the outlet hose.

But what really fascinated me was the science of fire. The basic theory behind it is known as 'the triangle'. See, for a fire to begin you need three elements: you have to have heat, you have to have fuel and you have to have oxygen. If you can exclude any one of those elements, the fire will go out. Then by adding in a fourth element such as a chemical reaction, you'll have what's called a 'fire tetrahedron'. In that case it's still the same result: take away any one of the four elements and you'll either not have a fire or the fire will be extinguished.

A prime example was the 2003 Canberra bushfires. They started on a hot day in the bush outside Canberra, so the heat was there. Then due to the lack of a strict back-burning regime, a huge fuel load had built up over the years. And of course the oxygen in the atmosphere was there to feed it. So when it went up, it really went up. It was a virtual firestorm. You'd see the flames ripping through the eucalypt trees well in the distance. Then all of a sudden a fire would burst right in front of you or, worse still, behind you.

Now the science behind these eucalyptus fire-bursts is very interesting. What happens is, the heat from the fire vaporises the eucalyptus oil in the leaves of the trees and, because of the horrific wind conditions, the vapour gets blown through the air ahead of the inferno. Then, when the heat from the fire reaches the vapour – *kaboom!* – it ignites and sets off another fire. And don't ever underestimate the sort of heat that's generated in a fire like that. I've seen the sides of houses, forty or fifty yards away from a fire front, burst into flames. And that's fair dinkum.

Another thing that a lot of your readers mightn't know is that you'll usually die of asphyxiation before the fire incinerates you. That's due to the huge amount of oxygen a fire chews up. So if you get stranded too close to the fire front without a breathing apparatus, you'll die from a lack of oxygen before the fire finishes you off.

But look, there was nothing they could do about those Canberra fires. Even with the huge number of brigades that came to fight it and all the water and/or retardant they dropped on it, it was like throwing a snowball into a volcano. Because once a fire like that really gets going, there ain't no stopping it. It'll do exactly what it wants to do. You just have to try to save what you can; then, when the fire gets the better of you, you fall back and try and save whatever else you can before you fall back again. It's fight, retreat, fight, retreat till it more or less stops itself or the weather conditions change and it rains.

Same thing with the fires they've recently had down along the New South Wales South Coast and into Victoria. Once they got going, they just took everything that was in their way. So that's the bushfire side of things.

Then there's the house fires. And something that's always stuck with me was the motto 'Life then Property', as in we'd try and save the people first. Then we'd try and save their property and belongings. Again, it's all to do with the triangle of fire – heat, fuel and oxygen.

Now, have you heard about flashovers? They're a very interesting phenomenon. Say there's a house on fire. If everything's locked up, the fire's oxygen is starved – like, the fire's still going, but it's retarded. But the moment you open the door to go inside, the oxygen rushes in and all hell breaks loose. So the trick is to try and shut the door behind you as fast as you can before getting on with the job of attacking the fire. And that's when you have to keep a lookout for the signs of a flashover.

Actually, a flashover is a very pretty sight. You'll see all the colours of the rainbow, flickering above you. Yellows, greens and blues. But then, the moment you hear the windows starting to crackle, that's the time to hit the deck. Because, once the windows go, the oxygen whooshes in and – *whoom-pa!* – if you're not down on the deck, you'll get blown straight back out the door and onto your arse. Too right you will.

One time I had a young bloke with me, Timmy. It was his first big house fire. It was in a derelict building. The power and water had been cut off and the homeless and the down-and-outs were squatting there. Anyhow, we got in and we're putting the wet stuff on the hot stuff and I've got my eyes looking out. When I saw the beautiful colours appear above me and I heard the windows start to crackle, I yelled out to Timmy, 'Hit the deck!'

But being new to the game, Timmy just stood there mesmerised by the colours. 'What? What?'

'Hit the fuckin' deck!' Then, just as I went to throw him onto the floor – *woof!* – we were blown clean back out the front door. By the time we hit the ground, I can tell you, Timmy's eyes were sticking out a mile from his head. Then I shocked him back into action. 'Come on!' I shouted. 'Quick, we're goin' back in!'

And he's still looking like a stunned mullet. But see, that's the time to get back inside and hit the fire. Because, due to the blast from the flashover, the oxygen inside the house has been momentarily diminished. So if you get straight back in, you've got a better chance of getting on top of it. Anyway, 'Righto,' so we go back in and we eventually knocked it down. But now the place is full of smoke – smoke and water and shit everywhere. I said to Timmy, 'We'd bett'a check and see if there's any people.'

So we're down on our guts trying to get below the heavy cloud of smoke. We can't see much, hardly nothing at all, so we're reaching around. It was all by feel. Now normally, if someone thinks they're about to get incinerated, more often than not they'll try and hide under a table or something. Anyway, I'm fishing around and that's when I hit something. It's a dead dog. Nothing more than ash and bone.

I'm just about to show it to Timmy when there's this almighty flash and Timmy almost shits himself. He must've thought he'd been electrocuted or something. Oh, I tell you, he was in one hell of a state. Then I seen this stupid bloody cameraman from a newspaper, taking flashlight photos of us. And boy, didn't I tell him where to go. I won't tell you what I said because, if I did, your book will probably be banned due to bad language.

So then Timmy and me, we're back down on our guts, reaching out, fishing around. We gradually make our way to the seat of the fire, which was in a bedroom. And that's where we found him. A bloke. The poor bugger was almost burnt to a cinder. He had a charred foot on him like a yowie. Near him was a candelabra, so maybe that's what started it. It'd caught fire to the bed and that was the end of him. Mind you, he probably wouldn't have been too alert at the time; you know, he might've been out of it on the turps or drugs and so he had no chance. None at all.

And so that was that one. But on the other hand, I would've saved at least half a dozen people from house fires, maybe more.

But you've got to get to them real quick. Like, if a house is almost gone by the time you arrive, it's too late to save anyone. All you'll be able to do is ply water onto the fire. Save what you can. Pick up the pieces and try to save the exposures of any neighbouring buildings. Like I said, it's 'Life then Property'.

Something else we had to be wary of was our use of CO_2 – carbon dioxide – gas. There was a pub on fire just down the road from here. We rocked up and they didn't have the keys to let us in. Our captain was a bit of a rush-in man, very much like meself. So we kick the door down and went in, no breathing apparatus, nothing. Back then that was only for sissies. Anyhow, the source of the fire was in the kitchen. A chip cooker had caught alight. Fat going like a beauty. Again the three major elements were at play: heat, fuel and oxygen.

Now, back then, for enclosed area fires, we used CO_2 extinguishers. What CO_2 done was, it excluded the oxygen from the situation, which in turn put the fire out. The thing is, like any fire does, we humans also need oxygen to keep us alive. So we started extinguishing this fire with the CO_2 gas. Next thing I see is our captain starting to stagger. Anyhow, I just managed to grab him before he passed out and I dragged him outside. Once he got some air into him, he was right as rain. Oh, and another thing about the CO_2 gas that comes out of an extinguisher is that it's extremely cold. So just one squirt and it'll cool down a bottle of beer just perfect. Too right it will. I know that one for sure.

In those early days our gear was pretty basic. But then, after some catastrophic fires in the mid-'70s, the Queensland government started to put a lot of money into firefighting. And as the technology got better, our methods became safer. So from about the late '70s things started to improve. We went from wearing woollen coats as protection to more fireproof outfits. There were advances in helmets and flash hoods, face masks and breathing apparatus.

The first oxygen breathing apparatus we used was the pre–World War Two Proto. You could get two hours out of a Proto and, if you could relax and control your breathing, you could stretch it out a couple more. Of course, you might well be thinking that it'd be pretty hard to relax when you're in the middle of a blazing fire. But it's like anything. Take scuba diving. The first time you go down, you're so hyped up that you'll breathe your tank down real quick. But given more experience, you learn to relax, so your tank will last longer. Same in a fire situation: you learn how to pace yourself.

But see, there's a lot more to it than just fighting fires. Outside of the larger centres the vollies have to do the lot. We've attended suicides where people wanted to jump off buildings and so forth. So we'd go up the ladder and try and talk them down. Vehicle accidents were a big one. Oh my God, they were. I can tell you, we became very familiar with the jaws of life – how to cut a door off, rip out the dashboard, get the seats back, then try and get whoever it was out of the vehicle and deliver them to the ambos.

One particular accident comes to mind. It happened near the National Heritage place, just up the hill. You might've seen it on your way into town. It involved two boys and three girls. Just youngsters, the whole lot of them. Only about sixteen or seventeen. Something like that. They'd pinched a car and the coppers spotted them. When they saw the cops, they took off up the hill. Going too fast, of course. The car spun out of control. Around and around it went till – *smash!* – smack-bang into the wall. No seatbelts I don't think because, when we got there, one of the boys had been flung out onto the road. I think the other boy had bolted. He got out unscathed. He might've been the driver. I said to my offsider, 'Get the oxygen mask onto the kid that's lying outside the car and see if you can revive him.'

Then I ran to the car. The engine was still going. But the petrol tank had been punctured and so fuel was running out underneath. At that stage I couldn't get inside to turn the ignition off. So I ripped the battery terminals off and that stopped it. Then I put our hose on full spray under the car to keep the fuel moving off the road. That done I got into the back seat to check on the girls. The bigger one was screaming her head off, yelling and carrying on. When I saw the state of the little one, I called out to my offsider, 'Quick, bring the oxygen down here.' Which he did.

But it was too late. I was holding the oxygen mask to her face when she died. Just like that, she died in my arms. The third girl wasn't faring much better. But we did get her out of the vehicle and we got her to the ambos. Then later on I found out that she'd died on the way to the hospital. So that was a tough one, really tough.

But by the time I was sixty-three, I'd had enough. I'd done forty years and by then I'd been in the Metro for quite a while. But I was lucky in that, unlike what's happened to a lot of other firies, I've never suffered from memory flashbacks about some of the worst things I saw. I think the reason for that is, different from me, we had a lot of young married blokes with kids of their own. And they'd been to fires where they'd seen children who'd been burnt to death. Like, I'd seen adults, but never a child. So that was some sort of a blessing.

But the mateship and the jokes amongst us were something special. And by gee there were some jokers amongst us. And the beauty of it was that we had blokes from all walks of life. Other than your usual suspects we had schoolteachers and tradies. At one stage we even had a solicitor. And some of us still get together. Most of them are younger than me. I could well be their grandfather, but we'd been out on jobs together. So we'd shared a lot of stuff, and like they'll ring me up and say, 'Hey, we're goin' out for a drink. Want'a come?'

'Righto. Okay.' And they'll drive over and pick me up and get me home after our session. Yes, so here's to all the great firies

I worked with during my time and all the funny fellers – the comedians – who kept me entertained during the tough times. There was never a dull moment, I can tell you. Never a dull moment.

Note: As of March 2020, the bushfires through New South Wales and Victoria had burnt through approximately 186,000 square kilometres of property, destroying near on six thousand buildings – including near on three thousand homes – and killing at least thirty-four people.

Albert

Well, as they say, I've been around a bit; fought a fire or two. After my early droving years in and around the Riverina area of New South Wales, I spent a few years as a patrol officer in New Guinea. Following that I worked in the federal public service for ten years, then there was ten years of farming in the United Kingdom.

Anyhow, for various reasons which I will not go into here, my wife and I found ourselves back in Australia where we had a farm named Gaia, on a 200-acre block, near Craven. Never heard of it? Well, not too many people have. Craven was about sixty miles or so – a hundred kilometres – west of Newcastle, and about five miles – eight kilometres – out from Gloucester. Why I say 'was' is because it doesn't exist any more. It's now disappeared into an open-cut coal mine.

Back in its day, Craven was a collection of half a dozen or so small farms and cottages, with a population of roughly 2550. It was fairly grassy country – good for stock – surrounded by lots of trees and scrub. Now, as I pen this letter from my home in the UK, I am fully aware that Australia is suffering the worst bushfires in its history. I feel for the country and its people. Because in the 1980s, when we were on our block at Craven, bushfires were fairly rare.

Though mind you, we were always at the good and ready. Though there was no formal firefighting service, each hamlet had its own volunteer brigade, which had been supplied with the basics from the state government. We, the volunteers, were supplied with ill-fitting orange overalls, with massive arm badges that conferred a status far beyond our competency. Nevertheless, it made us feel important. We had also been given hoses, a petrol engine pump and a sort of Furphy. Those old enough to remember will know that a Furphy's a large drum for carrying water. It was originally equipped with slats so that it could be drawn by a horse and was later modified to be towed by a tractor or ute. In addition, we had a couple of kerosene dispensers – drip torches – with wicks to set fires for back-burning.

And so now for the human element of our brigade. Our volunteers numbered around twelve – both male and female – and were aged from fourteen to their mid-seventies. Our leader was Albert, a close neighbour of ours who worked for the Department of Agriculture. Albert was our fire captain. He liked to be a leader and was well fitted for it. We met every six weeks or so and Albert would always begin with his mantra, 'Yer fight fire with fire!'

Then he'd drum into us how at all times we must be mindful of the direction of the wind. We must be prepared for the unpredictable. We must communicate with our neighbours and we must obey fire restrictions. When that was done he'd set about demonstrating the use of our archaic equipment. That would be followed by a refresher first-aid lesson. To end the training session, we'd have tea and biscuits, which were prepared by the more elderly lady members of our brigade while the younger members would act as gofers, keeping up the supply to us 'oldies'.

So it was all good fun until one evening someone spotted black smoke rising from the bush at the back of the nearby hamlet of Ward's River. In an instant Albert had us assembled and on our way. By now it was getting dark and, with the fire creating its own convection currents, it had spread rapidly. But good old Albert knew the area like the back of his hand – as he did everybody else's business – and he had soon sussed out a natural firebreak. It was a spot where there was a creek and, over the other side, a short distance away, roughly parallel to the creek, was a road.

Albert then assessed the prevailing wind direction and he got us to set a string of smaller fires along this natural firebreak. By doing that, the combustible material that we lit burnt back towards the advancing fire front. It's known as a back-burn. The reasoning was that when the fire front reached the break, there'd be nothing left to burn. Ingenious! And that's what Albert meant when he spruiked his well-worn mantra, 'Yer fight fire with fire!'

And it worked. We got the fire under control and, after about five hours of dousing out the still-burning stumps and so forth, the older local lady volunteers helped douse our thirst with much-appreciated tea and biscuits that were goffered to us oldies by the younger of the brigade. That done, we finally made our way home in the wee hours of the morning. Except Albert, that is, who remained vigilant and stayed behind, just to make absolutely sure that the fire didn't sprout wings and take off again.

So that's just one experience. And that was Albert. Then there was the fire on our farm, Gaia. I must take ownership of that one because it was my own bloody fault. We'd had an extremely wet season and so the grass and scrub had grown like a forest. Then the rainy season was followed by a severe drought.

Now, just as an aside, during this drought, our neighbours were short of feed and so they had to buy it in from the irrigation farmers. For as long as I could remember, the going rate had always been one dollar per bale for lucerne hay. That was a standard bale. But as the drought worsened, though the price per bale remained the same, the bales themselves vastly reduced in size. Human nature I suppose. Though I do hasten to add that most rural communities are like large families and, whenever there was any hint of trouble, they really pulled together and helped one another out.

Anyway, back to the fire on Gaia. Seeing that our once-lush back paddock was now overgrown with dried-out grass and scrub, Clever-Dick me decided to do a back-burn out of season. My thinking was that this would avoid the possible risks of a catastrophic fire later on in the season, caused by a rogue lightning strike or whatever. So I decided to plough a ten-metre firebreak around the intended fire zone. Which I did. Then, when I saw that the wind was coming from the north, I set my back-burn going from the southern break.

All good, but then the friggin' wind changed direction, didn't it? In a flash it had picked up the fire and *whoosh!* away it went.

I had no way of controlling it, so I rushed back to the homestead and called out to my wife to ring Albert. Then I rushed back out to move my stock into the night paddock. It had been pretty much eaten out by that stage, so therefore they'd be safe. By the time Albert turned up with the Furphy and a gang of volunteers, the entire back paddock was ablaze. Worse still, the fire then jumped a creek and crossed into our neighbour's place.

All looked lost. But under Albert's wise counsel, his thorough knowledge of the area, and his canny back-burning technique, we eventually brought the fire under control. And with not too much damage being done to the neighbour's property. In summary, my lesson – fight fire with fire, and, at all times, be mindful of the direction of the wind, be prepared for the unpredictable, communicate with your neighbours, obey fire restrictions and, most importantly, always take your orders from Albert!

Note 1: This story is adapted from a collection of memories-in-progress by Allan 'Bronco' Brett.

Note 2: The dictionary defines the word 'furphy' as being a rumour or an improbable or untrue story that is claimed to be factual. Its origin came from the Shepparton, Victoria, manufacturer's name of Furphy that was painted on horse-drawn mobile water and sanitary tanks during World War One. The Furphy was a popular place for Australian Diggers – soldiers – to gather for a yarn during a drink or toilet break.

Profile of an Arsonist

In terms of arsonists, look, there's nothing set in stone. But my experience is that the offending is of a pathological nature. I say that for a number of reasons. There's usually a lack of empathy. Like they're not somebody who's going to consider the wildlife that's going to be destroyed by the fires they light or there'll be a loss of people's homes or lives. It also seems to be more of a male thing. More often than not a white male in their mid-twenties with a poor employment history. Quite often they're victims of some sort of childhood trauma, such as neglect and/or mental, physical or sexual abuse, which leads to low self-esteem. As a consequence they can easily be goaded or challenged to do something outlandish, like lighting fires, in an attempt to prove themselves.

More than any other cohort I've met, they're likely to be socially alienated and not well trusted. They can seem aloof. Like, they'll be the person who sits on their own, never has any friends and has fairly acrimonious relationships. They don't get close to others. Another thread is that, quite often in the past, they've been charged for minor crimes such as theft or vandalism. Then there's the addictiveness, in the sense that their fire-lighting behaviour is repetitive, and it seems to be accompanied by an adrenaline rush – kind of a high.

I haven't come across an arsonist who's a volunteer firefighter. But I have heard that those who are usually come from within the brigade's local area. For example, there was a volunteer firefighter from the Hunter Valley region of New South Wales. After he'd started a fire in grassland, he was one of the first of his brigade to arrive at the scene to help put it out. So there's a need to be seen as a hero – someone who helps save the day – and by doing that there's some form of gratification.

The thing is, arson is a premeditated act. It's not a spontaneous action like a man who gets into an argument with someone and, in frustration, lashes out at them. Or a woman who's in an abusive relationship, where she's bailed up in a kitchen and she grabs a knife and sticks it into her abuser's chest.

With arson, first of all the weather conditions have to be right. It's got to be a hot day. They've had to have obtained the fuel or whatever to start the fire. They've sought out a location; somewhere where they won't be seen, usually in tinder-dry dense bush. And then, with all that equipment and knowledge, they get in their car and drive out to light a fire. What's more, they might light a fire in one place, then they'll drive down the road and light another one and so on.

Though women are far less likely to be arsonists, it does happen. For example, there was that woman, Helen White, who lived at Harrogate, up in the Adelaide Hills, in South Australia. She was in her mid-forties, seemingly happily married with two young kids. She'd lived in Harrogate for a number of years. Then over the 2007–2008 fire season she lit a string of fires in the area.

It really put the wind up the locals. So much so that the community had got together and formed a watch group in an attempt to find out who was lighting the fires. And that was something Helen White enthusiastically volunteered to be a part of. She even became a fire spotter, watching over her neighbours' properties.

So you can imagine the community's shock when one amongst them was arrested. And a woman at that. And not even her husband had an inkling that it was his wife who'd been lighting the fires.

It all began in January 2007 when she lit six fires in two hours. On a day in December of that same year, she lit four fires over a two-hour period. Then before Christmas 2007, she lit eleven fires over two days. How she did it was to light mosquito coils and leave them in the undergrowth, on the side of a road. Though nobody was hurt and no houses or farm sheds were destroyed, the largest of the fires burnt near on two hundred hectares of land and fences were lost. As it turned out, her DNA was found on one of the mosquito coils she'd lit at the scene of one of the fires.

After originally being charged with lighting near on fifty fires, she eventually confessed to lighting twenty-one. The thing was, she didn't have the more common traits of an arsonist. She wasn't particularly anti-social. She wasn't someone who sought power and self-esteem through fire lighting. She didn't do it to become the hero-type. She was reasonably intelligent. She had no previous criminal history and, to confuse the issue even further, she seemed to have little to no memory, or explanation, as to committing the crime.

But she did have mental health issues. She'd suffered a number of traumatic events in her youth. That led to post-traumatic stress, a personality disorder which made her feel powerless, frustrated and angry, and she'd become chronically depressed. She was brilliant at hiding her past, including a previous unhappy relationship, and suppressing her emotions – even from her husband who, as I said, had no inkling that his wife was the culprit.

The second example of an arsonist is perhaps more typical and far, far more tragic in that it involved not only loss of property but also of life. The fire was deliberately lit on Black Saturday 2009, in the Gippsland region of Victoria, just out of a place called Churchill. The arsonist was 39-year-old Brendan Sokaluk. Sokaluk had an autism spectrum disorder and an intellectual disability. From an early age he had been bullied. He was a slow learner who, even by Year 11, which was when his parents had taken him out of school, could barely read or write.

Sokaluk was a loner. After leaving school he was employed through a disability scheme as an assistant gardener at a nearby university campus. His workmates found him difficult to work with. They thought he had a disturbed personality. He was always in trouble and had sordid traits like scaring people, just for a laugh. He got a thrill out of teasing animals and he boasted about harming cats, just for the fun of it.

Before compulsory police checking became mandatory for all firefighters, he had a short stint with the Churchill Country Fire Authority – CFA. But after being suspected of deliberately lighting fires, he was asked to leave. On a number of occasions, he'd turn up at a bushfire that he hadn't been told about.

After eighteen years gardening at the uni, due to ongoing disputes, he took stress leave and left. He then delivered newspapers from an old pram, with his dog, Brocky. He also scoured the area looking for scrap metal. And he began lighting numerous fires in his backyard.

Saturday 7 February 2009 was a day of total fire ban. The temperature was in the mid-forties, with a very low relative humidity, and a north-westerly was blowing up to seventy kilometres an hour. On the way back from shopping with his father they'd stopped to watch the local CFA put out a grassfire. Then, after getting home, Sokaluk decided to take his dog, Brocky, for a drive. At the Glendonald Road-Jelliffs Outlet intersection, just out of Churchill, the road cut through scrubland and a blue gum plantation.

Sokaluk told police that his car had been playing up and had stopped and he'd been smoking a cigarette. He said that, after having dropped some lit ash on the floor of his car, he'd wrapped it up in a piece of paper and, thinking it was out, he'd thrown it out the window. And that's the spot where the fire started. He'd then left his car there and had started walking back to town with his dog. Along the way they were given a lift home. He then tried to go back to his car, but by then the fire was out of control. And that's when he called triple zero.

Later that afternoon, Sokaluk and his dog turned up at a property just outside Churchill where a man and his son-in-law were trying to put out a fire that was threatening the house. Sokaluk offered to help – an offer they accepted. But as things started to settle down, they began to think it was very odd for someone to appear out of nowhere, in such dangerous conditions, and offer to lend them a hand. So when the CFA arrived, the owner of the property discreetly asked them to take Sokaluk back to town with them. At another point in time a neighbour said that she'd seen Sokaluk standing up on top of his roof watching the out-of-control fire. She said that he'd told her how you could light a fire with a cigarette butt and get away with it.

Because of Sokaluk's reputation for lighting fires, the police began questioning him. A few days later they took him back out to where the fire had started, near his burnt-out car. He admitted that the fire might've started when he'd thrown the lit ash of his cigarette out of his car window. But he told the police that he thought it was out. He was later charged with deliberately lighting a bushfire and the possession of child pornography.

Note: It's believed that of the 4500 fires that occur in Australia each week, up to forty per cent are lit by people. Whether they are intentionally lit or not isn't known because only one per cent of arsonists are charged and convicted.

In April 2009, after pleading guilty to lighting twenty-one fires, Helen White was sentenced to a thirteen-year jail sentence, with a nine-year non-parole term. The non-parole term was later reduced to six and a half years.

The Churchill fires burnt thirty-nine thousand hectares of property, destroyed over one hundred and fifty houses and were directly related to causing the deaths of eleven people. In April 2012, Brendan Sokaluk was convicted of ten counts of arson causing death. He was sentenced to seventeen years and nine months, with a non-parole period of fourteen years. The verdict made Sokaluk one of Victoria's worst mass killers.

JAFFA

For most of my forty years I've been based just out of Perth. For twenty-three of those years I've been a member of our local Armadale Volunteer Fire and Rescue Service and, previous to that, I served with Roleystone. But as you'd know, with being a volunteer, we still have to pay our bills and so I do paid work as well. At the moment I'm a fly-in fly-out emergency services officer, up in Port Hedland. I'm on a week-on, week-off rotation. Though in saying that, I've recently had surgery for a broken Achilles tendon. So I'm currently sitting at home in a moon boot, in the process of healing. But I'll get back soon.

Previous to Port Hedland, I spent sixteen years working in both offshore and onshore oil and gas operations. I've worked in the north-west of Australia. I've worked in Indonesia and a lot of places in Asia, including Brunei and Japan. I've worked in Spain and America. I've also worked in South America and, for a brief period of time, I worked in a little Caribbean country called Trinidad, and I've worked near Cape Town, South Africa.

Cape Town came about when we took an oil rig from a Spanish island just off the coast of North Africa, called Los Palmas, down to Cape Town, then around Cape Horn to Mauritius and across to Australia. That particular rig had thrusters underneath its pontoons, which meant it could move by itself. Though, to help it along, we also had a rig support vessel towing it.

With regard to the Western Australian Volunteer Fire and Rescue Service, we do get the opportunity to do different sorts of specialised courses. At one time I had the opportunity of taking my Border Collie along to be trained in the Urban Search and Rescue dog-handling unit. They're the dogs that search for people who have been buried under the rubble of collapsed buildings after an earthquake or a landslide, like the one we had a few years back, near the centre of Perth, up in Kings Park.

But seeing how the dogs are rarely used here in WA, thank God, they're trained to be handled by multiple handlers. So if required, they're available to be deployed interstate or internationally. Anyhow, even though my Border Collie didn't end up passing muster, it was great to have some of the best trainers in the state work with her. I thoroughly enjoyed the experience and I ended up with a very well-trained dog out of it.

Something else that may be of interest is that, for the past three years, I've been working in the JAFFA – Juvenile and Family Fire Awareness – program. JAFFA is a program where both career and volunteer fire officers give of their time to work with kids, between the ages of six to sixteen, who have been involved in lighting fires. The aim is to keep them out of the justice system by explaining the dangers of their fire lighting. A referral is generally made by a parent or a school, the police or one of the fire station officers or even a case manager within the juvenile justice department. It then goes to the co-ordinator in our central fire service location who passes it on to the JAFFA support officers. After we receive a referral, we contact the family – say the parents or a caregiver – and we arrange a time to meet with them and the child.

One of the things I've noticed is that there's a belief within the community that these kids are just being naughty and the best way of dealing with them is to give them a good talking to and they won't do it again. But that's not generally the case. More often than not a lot of other factors are involved. So your approach in dealing with these kids varies. Depending on their age, we've been trained to notice the different stages within their growth and understanding. Like, there's a difference between a five-year-old's reason for lighting a fire and a sixteen-year-old's reason for lighting a fire.

The initial meeting may be held in the family home or at a public place like the fire station or a school. For added impact we always wear our full uniform. We start off the interview with both the family and the child there, and we go through some of the possible reasons behind why they're lighting fires. We also alert them to the dangers and consequences that may result from lighting the fires. If it's been in the house, we talk them through things such as the likely property damage, burn injuries and the possibility of loss of life. We discuss a fire escape plan and check whether or not the house has active smoke detectors et cetera. We play videos that show just how fast a fire can progress and how dangerous it can be within a home.

If they've been lighting fires in grasslands, we have a video that shows how rapidly a fire can spread. At certain points along the way we stop the video. Like at ten seconds we'll ask them, 'Do you think you could control this?' Then at twenty seconds, 'Do you think you could control this?' By thirty seconds the fire's probably got a fifty-metre spread. 'Do you think you could control it now?'

And we try to get the message across that, from lighting something small like honky nuts – which are the flammable nuts from jarrah trees – or even just a small pile of dried leaves, they can end up burning down a whole community, including the possible loss of life.

After that we ask to speak to the child separately. That's because, on many occasions, after the adults have been removed, the child will open up more and tell a different variation of the story or provide more information. Being a father myself, you get to the point where you can see that there's more to a family situation than what meets the eye.

Now, I have to be careful what I say here but, to be honest, some of these children come from extremely unfortunate backgrounds where there's a number of external factors at play.

The challenging part is to recognise, firsthand, what this poor child may be going through within the family structure, how they're dealing with it and what we can do to help them cease their fire lighting.

It's a case-by-case situation. Generally, the younger children tend to light fires in and around their homes. They don't usually mean to cause damage and, more often than not, there's no understanding just how dangerous a fire can be. The reasons behind their fire lighting could result from a fascination or a curiosity about fire and/or flame. They may well be seeking attention in response to a change in the family situation. It could stem from the anger or revenge associated with family or friendship problems, or the low self-esteem from the pressures of learning and social difficulties. Or maybe they've never had anybody as a father-figure to help guide them in the direction of what's right and wrong. So the poor child is left to work it all out for themselves and, as a result, they end up going down the wrong path.

As for the older kids going through adolescence, peer pressure is a huge factor. With wanting to be part of a friendship group, to prove themselves to their so-called mates, they'll light a fire in the bush, without understanding that they could be held responsible for an act of arson and go to jail. So accountability is a big part of the JAFFA program, along with the understanding that there may well be lifelong consequences for their actions.

Most times it only takes one or two visits. In the more tricky cases, perhaps three or four visits may be required. Then in the more complex cases, we encourage the parents to seek out further professional support. Though that's very rare because ninety per cent of the kids are good kids at heart, who have simply made a mistake. What generally wakes them up is having a uniformed officer, from an official organisation, telling them straight, 'This may well be your last chance before you end up in front of a policeman or a judge.'

Even though what we do can be quite confronting and challenging, it's also extremely rewarding. JAFFA's been a very successful program with a near on ninety per cent success rate of stopping kids from reoffending, and that's a very good result.

Note: The Juvenile and Family Fire Awareness Program – JAFFA – is a free, confidential education and support program for children between the ages of six and sixteen that have been involved in fire lighting. The program helps them understand the dangers of fire play and fire behaviour, its ramifications and the legal implications of arson.

As family involvement reduces the focus on the child, parents and carers are encouraged to become role models in creating a supportive environment for the children to learn and adopt fire-safe behaviours.

The program in Western Australia was started in 1989 by a small group of firefighters in response to an increasing demand for support from parents, schools and agencies.

All firefighters involved in the program volunteer their own time.

Information about the JAFFA program can be found on the DFES website: https://www.dfes.wa.gov.au/schooleducation/childrenandfamilies/Pages/jaffaprogram.aspx

Other states of Australia run similar programs.

Once Something Starts

The two biggest fires I've been involved in would've definitely been Ash Wednesday in 1983 and Black Saturday 2009.

Ash Wednesday, 16 February 1983, was a terrible day – probably the worst day I can remember. It was an unbelievably hot and windy day and so we knew we were in trouble. We knew the whole state of Victoria was in trouble. Because of that we were up at the fire station early in the morning.

To start with we had a fire near the Daylesford tip. And that's where we were when we heard that another fire had started, about half an hour to our east, at East Trentham. Next thing an urgent call came through for some trucks to get down there ASAP. We were in a four-wheel drive Acco and so we left the other crews at the tip fire and we headed over to East Trentham. From what we could gather, the fire had started in the grass country up near the Pig and Whistle Hotel and it was heading towards Wombat Forest.

We were one of the first groups to get to East Trentham. Even by then the fire was well and truly on its way. It had already got into Wombat Forest and was moving towards Mount Macedon and Gisborne. The Forests Commission was busy building trails around the flanks of the fire and they'd begun to put in a firebreak. So that was sort of the anchor point for everyone to work from.

Though on that day it was impossible for us to actually do much. The thing was, once it got into the forest country, it was extremely difficult to get to, especially on a day like that. And so it ended up burning right up over Mount Macedon. I forget how many homes were lost at Mount Macedon but there were a lot.

That was first time I saw an aircraft used on a fire. An RAAF Hercules had been converted to a firebomber. It was actually heading to the fires further down south en route from Mangalore when they'd diverted it our way. It was a very impressive sight to see as he came out of the smoke and dropped his big load of red fire retardant. But even by then, the fire had advanced too far into the bush for him to hold it.

But that East Trentham fire was just one of many that started on Ash Wednesday. There were hundreds of them all over the state. There were fires at Torquay and Lorne. That fire burnt right into Lorne and it wiped out Anglesea plus some other areas inland. There were some big ones over the back of Warrnambool and Dennington. So it was about as bad as it can get.

At one point it looked as if it might've got into the outskirts of Geelong. But then, with a wind change, it pushed the fire back around and it headed down the coast where it burnt right down to the sea. Something like seven hundred homes were lost along the coast that day, down around Aireys Inlet, Fairhaven and all through that area. Overall quite a few people were killed on Ash Wednesday and, as it went through a lot of property and houses, a lot of livestock were also lost. Not to mention the wildlife.

At that time, the 1983 Ash Wednesday fires were said to be the deadliest series of bushfires in Australia's history. That was until 2009 when we had the Black Saturday fires.

In many ways, Black Saturday was similar to Ash Wednesday. Black Saturday started on 7 February 2009. We were called down to Kinglake West as a regional strike team. We had about five trucks down there from our Region 15 Glenlyon Group. I was a strike team leader and, when I got down there, the sector commander was completely exhausted. He'd worked all through the night and I was asked to take over while he had a sleep. We were based back in Kinglake West. Other groups were staying at Whittlesea, and the Kinglake West crew were sleeping on the floor at their fire station.

Even though Kinglake West only had a very small fire station, there were a lot of structures in the area – all surrounded by the bush. People opposite the fire station had already lost their homes. They were in shock, just sitting there. With all the smoke from the fire, it'd gone so dark during the day that they didn't know if it was day or night.

Other than us, the only other people up there were the police and a couple of people from one of the community ambulances. Then there was also a couple of guys from the shire who were carting bulk fuel for our trucks. The trucks were all diesel. See, with petrol vehicles, when they get hot, the fuel vaporises and so the vehicle comes to a dead stop. But not so with diesel. Diesel doesn't evaporate.

So we looked after Kinglake West and Kinglake, or what was left of them. We put out bits of fire here and there. But it'd already gone right through. Yet amazingly enough, not every house was burnt down. Quite a few houses survived. I remember families were still in their homes, with the fire having been back-burnt right up to their doors. So we spent that night checking on those people who were still in their homes and we were offering them some food.

Now, whether they'd been given the choice to leave or not, I don't know. Or maybe it all happened just too quick. Once the fire came into that sort of area, I don't think anyone would've realised that it'd do the damage that it did. Like there were areas there where houses had virtually been blown away in the firestorm, when the wind change had come through. True. On the western slope I saw the remains of houses as just tin wrapped around trees.

I forget the total numbers of fires there were on Black Saturday. Though, because it was such a horrid day, there was a lot. See, once something starts on a day like that, it's almost impossible to stop it. The humidity was so low and the wind was horrendous. It blew up so much dust and debris that from Daylesford, you couldn't see Mount Franklin. And Mount Franklin's only eight kilometres away. So you can only try to do your best. And that's where I have to hand it to the volunteers in the CFA – Country Fire Authority – and the permanents in the Metropolitan Fire Brigade. They both did a magnificent job, considering there were so many fires.

During Black Saturday we had a lot of aircraft available, including helicopters that could draw water out of the dams and creeks in the bush. The fire from Kilmore, that'd burnt right down towards Kinglake, was caused by a powerline issue. In such high winds sometimes the powerlines clash and fall onto the tinder-dry ground, igniting a fire.

The fire south-east of Bendigo, over towards Eppalock, that burnt south towards Kyneton, had originally been started by lightning. Though that one had begun a few days earlier. There must've been some smouldering on a rocky patch out from there and, in the conditions, it kicked off again and it burnt through to Braford and places like that. Another big fire was around Bendigo. I think that one was deliberately lit and it burnt right into the suburbs of Bendigo, almost to the hospital.

We didn't actually have a fire at Daylesford. We were very lucky. During the January we'd had four days of forty-three degrees Celsius, with no wind. It was as still as, and so you can just imagine how dry the country was. I remember the Victorian Premier at the time, John Brumby, and the CFA Chief Officer, Russell Rees, being on the television virtually every night for a week, warning everyone as to how bad things were going to be on the Saturday. 'This weekend's going to be one of the worst days in history for fires in Victoria.'

Yet, even though all the brigades were getting prepared for it, a lot of the general public hadn't bothered to listen to them. But they were spot on. But look, I don't think anyone would've expected it to be as bad as it was. But it was. A massive amount of homes were destroyed and near on two hundred people were killed.

Then about two weeks after the Black Saturday fires, we had a fire start near Muskvale that burnt around the southern edge of Daylesford, out towards Musk and Glenlyon. In normal circumstances you'd consider it to be quite a major fire because it burnt through about 3500 hectares. But in the scale of things – you know, two weeks after a catastrophic event like Black Saturday – 3500 hectares seemed virtually nothing.

Note 1: 16 February 1983 – Ash Wednesday – was one of south-eastern Australia's worst fire days in a century. Within twelve hours more than one hundred and eighty fires, whipped up by winds of over one hundred kilometres per hour, caused widespread destruction across both Victoria and South Australia. The causes were put down to the heat and high winds, faulty powerlines, arson and negligence, after years of drought and extreme weather conditions.

In Victoria alone, in just one day, the Ash Wednesday fires burnt near on ten thousand square kilometres of urban and rural fringe areas, farmland and forest reserve. Three thousand seven hundred homes and buildings were either destroyed or severely damaged, leaving many homeless. Forty-seven people died in Victoria alone. Non-fatal injuries were around 2700. Livestock losses numbered approximately 340,000 sheep and eighteen thousand cattle. Numerous native animals also died.

Across both states an estimated one hundred and thirty thousand firefighters, defence force personnel, relief workers and support crews, from across Australia, came to help. This was the largest number of volunteers to ever attend an emergency.

In the East Trentham–Mount Macedon area, near on three thousand square kilometres of land was burnt, over six hundred buildings were destroyed and there were seven fatalities.

Note 2: The Black Saturday fires remain one of Australia's all-time worst bushfire disasters. On Saturday 7 February 2009, four hundred bushfires were burning across Victoria. The Black Saturday fires resulted in Australia's highest-ever loss of life from a bushfire with one hundred and seventy-three fatalities. Non-fatalities were numbered at over four hundred, and 3500 buildings were destroyed, leaving many people homeless.

Between 7 February and 14 March, 450,000 hectares – 1,100,000 acres – of urban and rural fringe areas, farmland, forest reserves and national parks were burnt. The causes were put down to drought, extreme weather conditions, falling powerlines, arson, lightning and fires ignited by machinery.

The fires in the Kinglake–Whittlesea area were started by falling powerlines. Driven by near on one hundred and thirty kilometre per hour winds, the fire ripped through plantation areas and rapidly headed south-east through the Wandong area. At Kilmore East the fire plume and pyrocumulus cloud reportedly reached fifteen kilometres high – just over nine miles.

The Kinglake fire complex was named after the Kilmore East and the Murrindindi Mill fires merged following a wind change on the evening of 7 February. It turned out to be the largest of the many fires that burnt across Victoria on Black Saturday. The Kinglake fire complex, alone, destroyed over 330,000 hectares of land – 820,000 acres. Over 1800 houses were destroyed and one hundred and fifty-nine lives were lost.

Chicken Legs

When I first joined the brigade back in the early 2000s, one of the more established guys called me 'Chicken Legs'. And it stuck. But I stuck with it as well. I went on to do my basic training. I've done my BA – breathing apparatus – training. I'm able to be an entry control officer. That's the person who checks and records how much air is available in the BA tanks before a firefighter goes into a structure fire, as in a house. I've learnt a lot about fire behaviour and the various techniques there are of dealing with fire, and on it goes. I mean, to be honest, there's such a lot to learn, and there are always challenges.

I remember going to hot fire training in Forrestfield, just out of Perth. For one exercise we had to put a gas cylinder fire out. That was quite scary because we had to advance towards the gas fire, using a fan of water from our hose as our only protection. That side of training was quite difficult because, even though the instructors were very supportive, they were also there to test us and push us to our limit, to see if we could handle the pressure. And with me being as tiny as I am height-wise, it was, 'You can't do this.' And I'd go, 'You just watch me.' And I did it. I overcame my apprehension and fear. Now I can say, 'Yeah, I can do that now. So how's about you throw me another challenge.'

And by pushing myself I grew, both as a female firefighter and as a person. And so, by the time we had the fire at the Chinese restaurant, I was given the job as entry control officer as well as looking after the traffic control side of things and monitoring the water supply and stuff like that.

But even though most times things are so intense that your mind's in a different space, focusing on putting the fire or whatever out, we do have our lighter moments. I remember when there was a fire at The Rock – Merredin Peak. The Rock's a large granite feature on the edge of town with lots of scrub and bush around it. Though back in the old World War Two days, there used to be an army hospital at the bottom of The Rock. They have culture tours there these days. And if you go on one of those you'll see the concrete platform and the ruins of where the hospital used to be. And laying around the area you'll also see lots of old broken medicine bottles and that. So it might've started there; like from the sunlight being magnified through a piece of the old glass. I was out of town when the fire started, so I'm not sure what the actual cause was.

Anyhow, I got back into Merredin just in time to go out and give some of the guys a break. By that stage most of the fire had been brought under control, but there were still a few little spot fires that had to be cleaned up. I went up there on night shift to check on these spot fires with a guy in our brigade who I got on really well with. We were in the light tanker – a Toyota Land Cruiser cab that carried about a thousand litres of water plus some basic firefighting equipment.

While we were getting bounced around in this light tanker, a song came over the radio. It was called 'Bounce'. From memory it might've been by Iggy Azalea, and there we were being bounced around all over the place in our light tanker singing this stupid song. So that type of humour certainly broke up the intensity of what well could've been a dire situation.

Anyhow, having been a part of the Merredin Brigade for the past sixteen years has been a great experience for me. Like I said, I've been really tested at times but, so far so good, I've managed to somehow win out in the end. And to such an extent that one of the greatest compliments I've ever received was from one of the elders of the brigade. Actually, it was the very same guy who'd jokingly given me the nickname of 'Chicken Legs'. One day, after I'd finished my basic training and we'd been to a few incidents together, he came over to me and said, 'Hey, Chicken Legs, can I tell you something?'

I said, 'Yeah, what's that?'

He said, 'I'll go and fight a fire with you any day.'

Note: During World War Two, an army hospital, complete with nurses' quarters, a surgery and wards was established at the base of Merredin Peak. There were a number of reasons for Merredin being chosen as the site. First: with it being so far inland, the hospital would be an unlikely target for Japanese bombings. Second: with Merredin being at a rail junction, it could receive casualties from a number of different directions. Third: even if the Goldfields water pipeline was to be destroyed, the nearby Merredin railway dam, which was continually being topped up by runoff from The Rock, held a plentiful source of water.

There were a number of disadvantages though. The living conditions at the hospital were quite harsh. To begin with the wards consisted of just twenty-four large tents, each holding twenty patients. The staff lived in much smaller tents, which were crammed with up to six camp stretchers each. Until electricity was eventually connected, all the lighting came from kerosene lamps and, for latrines – toilets – a deep trench was dug along the front of the wards.

Then there was the climate, where summertime temperatures could rise to well over the old hundred degrees Fahrenheit – forty degrees Celsius – and the bitter winters caused one nurse to recall how she had to be super-quick in sponging down her patients or else, if she lingered too long, they'd more than likely freeze.

Another Fire, Another Bruise

I've been living here in Clunes, in central Victoria, for about forty years now. Me and my husband came up here from Melbourne in the late 1970s with our two children, a boy and a girl. They're both adults now of course. Our son still lives here, while our daughter's over in South Australia. Like me, she's had her life's ups and downs. She lost her first husband to cancer. But then she remarried and she's now pregnant with her first child. So all is good.

My husband was a carpenter by trade. But as he got older, I don't know, he just began looking for something. It was like he had the need to be somebody who was seen as important. Yet I don't think he ever realised how important he was to a lot of the people who were close to him. So he started jumping around a fair bit, all the time trying to get his name known. He went from carpentry to becoming a St John's first-aid trainer. Then it was the pelargonium nursery. Then growing strawberries commercially. He was going to do this, he was going to do that, and then he was going to do something else. He was going to write a book. He was going to write poetry.

Finally he got involved in a community radio station over at nearby Daylesford. It was one of those radio stations that you listened to on your computer; streaming I think it's called. Then one day, when he was at the radio studio, he passed away while he was on air. Sixty-six. Three years ago.

He'd joined the Clunes Fire Brigade long before me. That was back in the early 1980s when joining meant you just turned up. There wasn't any induction or too much formal training. When the siren went off, you just rushed down to the fire station, jumped on the back of the fire truck and headed off, hanging on the best way you could – dressed in whatever clothes you'd been wearing, not even necessarily in your overalls. From memory, it was actually quite a while before he was even given a pair of overalls, and I don't think he ever got a helmet. Then, when you got to the fire, you did your best to put it out. After that, you'd come back to the station. There were no debriefs. Nothing. Just a beer and a bit of a chat with everyone before you went home.

I'd always wanted to be involved in some sort of community service group. But like most women, when the kids were young, my life revolved around them. At first I was thinking about the SES – State Emergency Service. They were a separate organisation to the fire brigade. Then in 2003 there was a house fire in town. It was at the place of a person I knew quite well. When the siren kept going and going, I twigged that they were short of people, so I went down to the station and I said, 'Is there anything I can do to help?'

And they said, 'No. You're not a member. There's nothing you can do. Go back home.'

So I turned around and I went back home. But then I started thinking, If not enough people had turned up to go to this fire, the man would've most likely lost his house. 'That's it then,' I said. 'If they're short of volunteers, I'm going to join the fire brigade.'

So I got the forms and filled them out. Basically it was just your contact details. No test or anything. I don't even think there was anything about your medical condition. Then, when I sent the forms off, my husband said, 'Don't be upset if they won't let you on the truck. You'll most likely end up as the tea and sandwiches lady.'

I wasn't their first female member. Helen was in the brigade at that stage and she was an active member. So I said, 'Well, if they want me to be the tea lady, I'll unjoin because that's not what I want to be. Someone else can do that. I'm joining because I want to be a firefighter.'

Anyhow, I got a letter back welcoming me to the fire service.

By that stage there was some formal training. Normally we'd have to go to Ballarat to do that but, because the brigade had a couple of qualified trainers, I did mine in Clunes. It wasn't that extensive. Mainly more about safety than anything else. Like the safe use of the equipment and getting on and off the truck. The safe use of the hoses. I learnt a bit about the things that could affect a fire, like the weather and wind changes.

There was also the use of a rake-hoe. A rake-hoe's a hand implement. At the bottom, on one side, there's metal teeth, similar to a rake, and there's a blade on the other side, just like a hoe – which is why it's called a rake-hoe. You use it to clear vegetation to make a firebreak. They're also handy if a stump or something's burning. You can break it open with the rake-hoe to get water onto it, to put it out. So I had to learn all that before I'd be able to go out on the fire truck to attend a fire.

After my training I went to Ballarat and I got fitted out in my bright-yellow brand-spanking-new overalls, gloves, helmet and leather boots. The boots had a good hard sole and were zip-ups as well as laced. I didn't have to pay for anything. Then, when you'd go out on the truck, you'd get a mask and a pair of goggles. And oh, I can tell you, dressed as I was in all my gear and with my bright-yellow brand-spanking-new overalls, I thought I looked just so smart – so cool. The height of firefighting fashion ... well, that's until someone said, 'Hey, Chris, you look like a tub of margarine.' And that sort of put a bit of a dampener on it.

Before I went to my first live fire, I learnt how to read maps. I did some radio work; you know, how to send and receive messages. On Sundays I'd go out on the truck with the rest of the volunteers and learn how to work the pump and hoses. So it was probably two to three months before I'd ticked all the boxes. And that was it. I was in. I was rip-roaring and ready to go.

There were no certificates or anything. The only time you get a certificate is when you do an extra course, like how to deal with alarms on public buildings. And if you did a first-aid course, you got a certificate for that. I got my first-aid certificate a bit further down the track.

My husband was still involved then. Actually, he was on the truck when I went out to my first fire. That was probably the last time we were ever on the truck together. Helen was also there. Normally there's three on the back and two in the front. But Macca, our driver, stuck me in the passenger seat, and my husband and Helen out on the back. The fire was just outside of Clunes, on the way to Creswick. I'm sitting there in my brand-spanking-new yellow overalls, heart pumping – looking like a tub of margarine – and, with the truck being so high, I almost felt on top of the world.

Then, as we were driving out, I said to Macca, 'Can I get on the back of the truck?'

He said, 'Nup. I want yer to stay in the front with me fer now.' He said it like he didn't want me to do anything, other than just sit in the truck.

When we got out into the fireground, I said to him, 'Can I get on the back of the truck now?'

'Nup,' he said, 'I want yer in the cab with me.'

By now they'd started fighting this fairly big grassfire.

'Can I get out on the back now please?'

Macca said, 'Yer really, really want'a get on the back, don't yer?'

I said, 'Yes I do. I'm prepared, ready 'n raring to go.'

'Okay,' he said. So he stopped the truck and he said to my husband and Helen, 'She's gettin' on the back'a the truck with yer. Take good care of her.'

So I hopped on the back, feeling pretty invincible. There were no fire screens around the back of the truck, only a metal barrier which came up to waist height. Though, with me being quite short, it was slightly higher than my waist. By then there were quite a few fire trucks around us. I don't remember how many because I was more intent on fighting the fire. That was the most important thing. Actually, it's hard to describe how I felt. I guess it was more like a mix of fear and excitement.

Anyhow, we drove to the head of the fire to try and cut it off. There I was in my brand-spanking-new yellow overalls, my helmet and gloves. At that stage I didn't have my goggles or my mask on. When Macca drove us right up against the fire front, I'd never felt anything as hot before, not in my whole life. And because I didn't have my mask on, I was struggling to breathe. I'm like a fish with my mouth wide open, gasping for air. And without goggles, because it was so smoky, I'd had to close my eyes. So there I am, leaning over the edge of the truck, blindly squirting water at the fire. Then Helen tapped me on the shoulder. 'Here, try these,' she said and she handed me a pair of goggles and a mask. 'That should be better.'

When I put them on I went, 'Wow, now I can see. I can even breathe.'

Oh, it was great. But so, so hot. Oven-like. I guess normal people just don't get to experience being that close to a big fire. Then when Macca stopped the truck, to fill the water tank up, Helen gave me one of those plastic bottles of water and said, 'Here, have a drink.'

I'd never been a big drinker of water, so I said, 'No, I'll be fine.'

She snapped, 'Drink the water!'

'Okay.' So I did, and I just sculled it. I'd never drunk a whole bottle of water in one go before, not in my whole life. Because I had all my gear on and I'd been up so close to this hot, hot fire, I was dehydrated. So I just emptied it like that.

'See,' she said, 'I knew you'd need it.'

Anyhow, while the truck was being filled with water, Macca came around and he grabbed me in his arms and he gave me this huge bear hug. 'Welcome to yer baptism of fire,' he said.

He must've felt such a huge responsibility for me and he was just so relieved that I was safe. And these days I'm still in the brigade, yep. But that first fire is still very close to me. I remember it far more clearly than any of the other fires I've been to, and a lot of them have been a lot bigger and more dangerous than that first one. And Macca's still a member. We're still great friends and he's still a sort of father-figure to me. He'd be well into his seventies now. He's tried to retire a couple of times but, because he's got all the right driving licences and so forth, we all want him to stay on as a driver.

See, driving's quite a specialised thing. For starters, you have to have a special heavy-vehicle licence. And if you use lights and sirens, you have to have done an extra course. If you go into the bush, which is where a lot of the fires are, you have to have completed a special off-road driving course. On top of all that, you're responsible for the lives and wellbeing of everyone on the back of the truck, leaning up against a piece of metal, fighting the fire. Which is why I always come back quite bruised. I don't feel it while I'm out there. But I do afterwards. Anyway, these days, when I look down and see all the big purple blotches, I just go, 'Oh yeah, another fire, another bruise.'

Note 1: Women currently make up around twenty per cent of all services' volunteers and, of the younger cadets, near on fifty per cent are female.

Note 2: Clunes became Victoria's first 'gold rush' town after the state's first gold discovery was registered in March 1850.

Permits and Idiots

I've been in the New South Wales CFS – Country Fire Service – for forty years now. During that time I've gone from volunteer to deputy captain to senior deputy captain to captain, and now I'm what's called a group officer. A group officer's basically voted for by the captains in each of the local areas' brigades. Our district here, in the mid-coast, runs from the Karuah River, which is just out of Newcastle, to Kundabung, which is between Port Macquarie and Kempsey. So we've got a decent-sized area to look after and at this present moment we've got five big fires going on, plus a number of smaller fires.

A lot of my work is co-ordinating with fire comms – communications – in Sydney. See, it's very hard when you're on the ground to pinpoint the exact position and movement of a fire. So say I see a plume of smoke here and a plume of smoke somewhere else, I'll get the topographical map out and mark in the co-ordinates. Then I'll take a photo of the map and send it to fire comms in Sydney. And that gives them some idea as to where the fires are. Then they can zoom in via their satellite network and really nail the position and movement of the fires.

If you have a look here on the computer screen, you can see exactly where the current fires in our region are. See, there's the Grafton fires. And if I drag the mouse down a bit, there's the Taree fires. We're still having a lot of trouble with those. They just won't go out. And if you zoom further in you can see where the fire front is moving towards some houses. We've got trucks going out there at the moment.

That other fire, over to the east, is pretty much under control. But being in a big valley, we'll still have to keep an eye on it. Then if I move the mouse around there, nearer to our location, we've got the Tom's Creek fire and another one along Collings Road. Then, if you look more closely, there's a travelling stock reserve burning up there.

Oh and there's the Ponsford Road fire. Kindee's also a bad one. Even though it's a little fire, it's threatening a few houses. That other fire over there, to the right of the screen, has already burnt through something like 1300 hectares of dense scrub and trees. Then there's those two fires, just up north a bit, at Port Macquarie; they're threatening houses and property. So we've got fires going everywhere.

Other than lightning strikes and so forth, most of the others have been started by people. Though they're not necessarily arsonists. What's happened is that the Mid North Coast has turned into a bit of a retirement destination. So it's more of an awareness thing – or lack thereof – where people from the city buy a block of land and they get a fire permit to light a pile of rubbish. And that's okay. But, being from the city, they don't listen to the weather report saying that there's going to be thirty-kilometre winds coming in that afternoon. And once the wind hits, off it goes.

The permit system is basically a legal document. While it gives a person the right to light a fire, a lot of restrictions come with it. If the people are new to the area, even before I issue them a permit, I go out and make sure they're aware of all the rules and regulations. Like they've got to have a decently cleared section of land around where the fire's going to be.

On top of all that, you have to give all your neighbours twenty-four hours' notice before you burn. Fires are not to be lit on high fire restriction days. The wind has to be no more than fifteen kilometres an hour. Someone has to be in attendance at the fire at all times. Plus there must be a readily available water supply, and they've got to make sure the fire is completely extinguished before it's left unattended.

And the vast majority of people do stick to those regulations. But then there's the idiots – the ones with the 'I don't give a stuff' attitude – who leave their fires unattended and just let them go. Our big problem is that under the Bushfires Act we have very little recourse. It's extremely difficult. As the arson laws stand these days, if you take someone to court, you've virtually got to have a photograph of them with a match in their hand, lighting the fire.

To that end, the Rural Fire Service now says that we've got to give people three warnings. So every time a fire goes out of their patch or they do something wrong, they get a letter of warning. Once they've had three warnings it's a $5000 fine. But the thing is, a hell of a lot of damage can be done when either one, two or three fires get away.

While we're talking about idiots; a month or so ago I got called to a fire. It was to attend what we describe as 'a property with assets at risk'. A neighbour to the property owner was worried that this fire might get out of control and spread into his place – which was fair enough. It was ten thirty at night and so I picked up the neighbour and we went over to the place where the fire was.

Now the owner of the property was a repeat offender who's got a large property and – no permit or nothing – he'd just light up and let it burn. And every time we'd go around there and put the fire out, he'd just light it up again. And like I said, with the way the law currently is, he keeps getting away with it.

So when me and the neighbour got there, the fire was already two or three hundred metres behind the house, burning up the hill. Anyhow the bloke's there having a few beers and what have you with his family and a few of his thuggish mates and he greeted us with, 'I've opened all the gates so that the fire trucks can come through.'

I said, 'What trucks, mate? There's no trucks coming.'

He said, 'What about the fire?'

Now I'd already assessed the situation and, with the cool of the night coming in, I knew the fire wouldn't get too far or cause too much damage. In fact, I reckoned it'd soon put itself out.

I said, 'It's not threatening anything. If it gets any worse, I'll get trucks here in the morning. We don't need to bring people out for no reason.'

Anyhow, this bloke's quite a bit under the weather and so he gets aggro and starts hurling around the abuse. You know, 'I pay your f'n wages to put out the fires and you come here and you do f'n nothin' about it.' Plus a few more unsavoury expletives, I might add.

I said, 'Well, for starters, mate, you don't pay my wages.'

He said, 'Yes I f'n do.'

I said, 'No you don't, mate.' I said, 'I'm a volunteer.'

'Well then,' he said, 'you're more of a fuckwit than I thought you were.'

Now I knew a bit about this bloke; enough to know not to push him too far. He was already in trouble with the police for shooting at his daughter and her boyfriend. And he'd also attacked another bloke with an axe. So I'm thinking, I don't like this situation. I've gotta get out of here, and quick.

By now he's saying, 'So we'll have ter go and get our own gear and put it out, will we?'

I said, 'Well, that's a bloody good idea. And when you put it out, go and find the bloke who lit it and get stuck into him, not me.'

Then the whole mob of them starts going, 'Well, we didn't light it! We didn't light it!' Which only gives you some bloody idea as to who actually did light it.

But all this hassle was the last thing I needed. So I said to the bloke I was with – the neighbour – I said, 'There's nothing I can do here, mate. Let's go. I'll drop you home on the way,' and we jumped in my car and we left them standing there.

Another time we were doing a scheduled hazard burn and I needed to get access around a bloke's house. No sooner had we arrived at the place than the bloke walks out with a .22 rifle.

I said, 'Mate, we've gotta do a hazard burn round here. Can you give us access to your property?'

He said, 'No way. Yer not goin' anywhere around my property.'

Now I'd heard rumours about this bloke, how he was a dope – marijuana – grower. I said, 'Look, mate, just tell us where your plants are and we'll burn around them.' I mean, I didn't care. What he grew was up to himself. We were just there to do a hazard burn so that if a fire did come through it'd cause less damage.

He said, 'No yer not. Git out'a here,' and he started to walk towards us in a threatening manner with his rifle.

And that really riled me. I mean, if he would've backed off, it would've been okay. I would've let him be. But he didn't. He kept coming at us. So I said, 'Okay then, we'll get out of here.' Which we did, and as soon as I got around the corner I got on the phone to the police and said, 'Look, fellers, you just might like to pop up and have a look around this idiot's property.'

Note: In November 2020, over one hundred and twenty homes were destroyed by bushfires along the Mid North Coast of New South Wales and another nine hundred and fifty were saved. During just one night, 21,500 hectares of land was burnt in the Taree region alone, with many residents being evacuated to the Taree Showgrounds.

Some of the worst-hit communities in the area were Bobin, Killabakh, Hillville and Johns River.

At Johns River, half an hour north of Taree, the body of a woman was found in a burnt-out house. Twenty minutes south-east of Taree, at Wallabi Point, residents were forced to shelter on the beachfront from the Hillville fire. The Pacific Highway was closed at a number of points. At Bobin, half an hour north-west of Taree, several homes were destroyed, plus the local school which had been built in 1883. Conditions around Port Macquarie, which is seventy kilometres north of Taree, were described as 'apocalyptic' with multiple reports of people being trapped in their homes.

Almost 1200 firefighters and two large air tankers had been deployed to fight the blazes.

Author Bill 'Swampy' Marsh has a sister living in Taree. She remained safe.

Time Gets Forgotten

Ray: Oh gee, we've had some times over here in Tasmania, haven't we, Bob? Remember that feller What's-his-name, the bloke who was burning a little heap of stuff and it got away from him? By the time my crew got there, we couldn't drive in from behind where the fire had started.

Anyhow, we got up onto a flat bit of ground, right on the top of the hill, looking down on it. We couldn't see any flames. Just a lot of smoke. But it was so hot that, next thing, tufts of grass started burning around us. I remember Tony mucking around, trying to put them out with a backpack – knapsack – of water. And every time he'd put one little spot fire out, another one would burst out somewhere else.

I said, 'Tony, you're wasting your time. It's not even worth us pulling the hose out.'

So just imagine how frightening it'd be if there'd been lots of dried scrub, with the fire being whipped up by the wind.

Anyway, I had a truck full of blokes – probably half a dozen or so – so I said, 'Let's have a vote. Do you want to go down over the hill and see if we can edge the fire out as it's coming up at us or do you want to go back down and around the gravel road and try and edge it out from there?'

When no one said anything, I said, 'Well, first off, I reckon we ought to try and get out of here because it's too dangerous, and then we'll try and cut it off before it gets to Friendly Beaches.'

To give you some idea, Swampy, Friendly Beaches is a great little spot. You should go there. It's at the start of Freycinet National Park. That's where we were and, if the fire got into there, it'd be impossible to contain. So we went back out onto the gravel road. And there was that much smoke, I could hardly see where I was driving. No flames at all. Next thing, the fire started burning around the truck. That's how quick things can change.

At that point, I wouldn't say that I was scared. I was more apprehensive than anything else. And that's mainly because I had blokes on the truck with me that I was responsible for. See, if you get scared in pressure situations like that, you can't act with clarity of mind. Over the years, I've been very lucky in that respect. I've been in a couple of life-and-death situations where, for some unknown reason, I became very calm and clear in my head. How it happens I don't know, because other times when I'm not under any great pressure and I've had to make a decision, I end up sitting down and having a good think about it before I act. Anyhow, call it luck or whatever, we got out of there safely and they eventually got the fire under control.

Bob: *I remember that one, and I also remember the time you did go down over the bank and into a fire that was out of control. I mean, if the wind would've changed direction, there wouldn't have been a hope in hell of stopping it. And I was in charge of that one. I was group captain and I'd already been up there for so long that I was sleeping up there. And I remember telling you and the other blokes what not to do, and you didn't listen to a word I'd said. You just went ahead and did it anyway.*

Ray: I don't think that was the case, was it?

Bob: *Yes it was. You and the Mayfield Brigade went down over that bloody bank. That was ridiculous. And you woke me up early the next morning to say you'd put that bloody handline – a handline being a small fire break – in. And I said, 'I told you not to. It's too dangerous,' and you said, 'Well, it's a bit late now, we've done it.'*

Ray: I mean, I guess it could've been dangerous, and there was a southerly forecast. But I remember another fire where we were in a similar situation. We were on top of a hill, looking down this very steep bank, into a deep gully, with the fire burning slowly up the slope towards us.

The wind hadn't hit by then. And, as captain, I would never order anybody to do anything they didn't want to do. But I had a mob of good fellers with me. Among them were two sets of brothers from Mayfield Brigade and, having those big strong farm boys with me, got me thinking, This looks like a piece of cake. So I said, 'It's up to you but, if you want to put a backpack on and grab a rake, I reckon we can get down there and edge it out.'

And we did. We just went down there and we edged it out.

See, most times, you can put out a lot of the fire edge with just a backpack and a rake. And I've done it. Oh, the fire service has got those fancy rake-hoe things these days. But just an ordinary garden rake will do. They're the best thing, especially if you're on the edge of a fire.

To my mind, the fire service rake-hoes are far too wide and far too heavy. That's my thinking of it, anyway. With the ones that we were issued, I went and cut the two outside tines off and that brought them down to about nine inches wide. They're the ones we use now. Though the rake-hoe does have a chipper – the hoe part – which can come in handy. But really and truly, if you just want to bare up some ground, to edge in the fire, a garden rake's the best thing. Absolutely.

So anyway, me and the two sets of brothers, we went down this steep slope with our rakes and full backpacks of water and we did the edges. Then I started making my way back up with a half-full backpack, just in case I needed to clean up any bits and pieces. And by the time I got back to the top, I'd never been so tired in all my life. I mean, to start with, a full backpack holds five gallons of water. So what's that? Twenty litres? So they're pretty bloody heavy when they're full. And I wasn't getting any younger.

But I can tell you, I was so bloody rooted by the time I got back that I just laid down and put my head on a sag – a bit of tufted grass – and I went to sleep. True. That's how knackered I was. Holy hell, next thing, they bloody well near run me over with their fire truck. Then by the time we got back to you, Bob, I think it was about 5 o'clock in the morning.

Bob: *I remember we were still puzzling about how to go about this fire. Like where to put in a handline and build a bit of a firebreak and all of that. Then you and these blokes turned up out of the blue and said, 'Don't worry about it. We've already edged it out.'*

I was just so relieved when you told me that. I'd been up there for all that time, with hardly any sleep. Then after we'd finished, I remember driving home from the fire thinking, Thank Christ that's all over. And I'd actually forgotten just how long I'd been away from the farm. Then it hit me: Oh shit, that fire's taken two days out of me working life.

Then I started thinking about what jobs I had to catch up on when I got back home. That's when it suddenly struck me, Oh shit, I had a wool sale yesterday. And the wool sale was the biggest and most important day of the farm year. And because I'd been so busy at the fire, I'd completely forgotten about it.

Anyhow, as luck would have it, the wool sale company had gone ahead and sold our wool on valuation. But it just goes to show you how you can get so completely sidetracked when you're at a fire that everything else gets forgotten.

Ray: Certainly does, and that's part of the reason why I stepped down as captain. I'd had enough. I was getting older and I was starting to wear out. My son's captain now.

I'm still with the fire service but I don't go out to car accidents or things like that. Though if there's a decent fire I'll go out. Too right I will. Even though I've got a crook hip and I've just had a new metal shoulder put in, I'll still go out to a big fire. There's nothing better than putting on a backpack and grabbing a rake, and I still reckon I can put out an edge as good as anybody.

Note 1: In firefighting terms, 'to put out an edge' or 'to contain an edge' is the act of clearing around the edge of a larger-scale burn. This restricts the fire front from spreading, thus making it easier to contain.

Note 2: Friendly Beaches is an isolated spot on the mid-east coast of Tasmania, almost equidistant between Hobart and Launceston. It's regarded as being the gateway to Freycinet National Park.

Freycinet, along with Mount Field, were declared Tasmania's first national parks back in 1916. Author Bill 'Swampy' Marsh experienced this pristine coastal wilderness firsthand when he visited Friendly Beaches during his Tasmania story-collecting and -performing tour in early 2020.

Did Everything Wrong

I was born up here in the hospital in Clunes. That's when we had one. It's now gone. Clunes being in the Central Goldfields region of Victoria, about forty kilometres north of Ballarat. The history books will tell you that Clunes is where gold was first discovered in Victoria, back in the mid-1850s. I grew up on a small sheep farm between Clunes and Talbot. After I left high school I joined the bank. I did a few months in Sebastopol near Ballarat, then six years both in Clunes and in Melbourne, in Head Office.

When I was a youngster, Dad used to take me to the Talbot Volunteer Fire Brigade meetings. Talbot's got a population of around four hundred. Then, when I was sixteen, I became a member. That's the way it worked. At that stage I was living at home and, even after I joined the bank and went off to other places, I still kept up my membership.

There wasn't too much training. We'd do some fire prevention, like roadside burning and firebreaks. And back then it was quite common for farmers to burn their stubble, so we'd help some of them with their burn-offs. So we got to put the wet stuff on the red stuff and, even though they were only small burns, they could get pretty hot – which made you aware that, if you were going to fight a fifty-times larger fire, on a forty-degree day, with a north wind blowing up your heels, you'd have to be properly prepared and very careful.

We'd also familiarise ourselves with the fire trucks, like how the systems and all that worked, with the hoses and pumps and whatever. Yet even though they were pretty good vehicles, they had little crew protection. If you were standing up on the back, you faced it all full on. And we had no uniforms as such, apart from access to overalls. Though, if we were in a hurry, more often than not, we'd just go out in long work pants, a shirt and our work boots. Mostly our work boots were good-quality leather, with steel-capped toes and zipped sides so they were easy to get in and out of. So no laces. Possibly there were a few helmets floating around, but not everyone wore them.

When I was working in the bank at Clunes, if the fire siren went off I'd drop what I was doing and head out on the truck. After the fire, I'd return to work stinking of soot and smoke and plough on regardless, serving the customers. If it was late in the day, we'd just shut the doors and leave it at that. It was a pretty good life really. But after six years in banking, I'd had enough. I felt like a caged lion. So I bailed out. That was on 19 December 1984. Workwise I had absolutely no idea what I was going to do and, what's more, I couldn't have cared less. I just thought I'd sort it all out after Christmas and New Year. So I went back on the farm.

To that stage we'd had a reasonably cool summer. Actually, 14 January 1985 was our first total-fire-ban day, and that's when we copped it: the Avoca bushfires. Our farm was burnt out. The house survived but not much else. The fire started forty k's from us, at a sawmill just out of Avoca. A few months earlier a clown from over there had been sacked from the sawmill. So to get them back, he decided to burn the place down. Which he did but, in doing so, he burnt out a hell of a lot of houses, property and livestock in the process.

Anyhow, because there's a lot of bush between Avoca and Talbot, once the fire got in there, it started crowning – which is where the fire jumps from treetop to treetop. And that's when Talbot got hit. Then, on a wind change, it came all the way back to Maryborough and Carisbrook.

It was about midday when we received the fire call. By the time my brother and I got to the fire station the truck had gone.

And from that point on, we did everything wrong. We didn't know the full extent of the situation, so we thought we'd be able to stop the fire in its tracks. But that was not to be. Four other blokes were also at the station, so we decided to go out on a private truck. It had a 1000-gallon water tank, which is about four thousand litres, with a hose and pump, but no safety gear whatsoever. So we were standing up on the back of the truck, no shielding or nothing.

We got to a little area called Bung Bong. We knew the old chap there. He was a single man. Up behind his house there was a bit of undulating grassy open country, with some timber on it. But as we were driving towards the oncoming fire, it was spotting ahead of itself. Like, there was a strong north-westerly, blowing the head of the fire in a south-easterly direction. So it was blowing embers ahead of the main front, which would then start another fire.

By then my brother and two others were walking well ahead of the truck, putting out these spot fires. Then suddenly – *whoosh!* – this huge wall of flame descended on us. I remember seeing my brother and the two others bolting towards a creek, a hundred metres or so away. From that point on it was mayhem. Because we were on a private truck, we didn't have CFA – Country Fire Authority – radios, and of course this was prior to mobile phones. We had no chance of saving the blokes, so we made the snap decision to drive blindly through the fire front to get onto the safety of some burnt ground.

All I recall was the burning heat, smoke and the sound of the truck blistering. And I just had this horrible vision of seeing my brother and the other two fellers' scorched bodies lying in the creek. But as luck would have it, just as the front hit, they'd jumped over the creek's embankment and had landed in a couple of feet of water. And then they'd rolled in the water as the fire went over the top of them. Anyway, they survived and they weren't harmed too badly, physically. They'd mostly breathed in too much smoke and we all had plenty of ash and soot and rubbish in our eyes.

So then we drove back to the old chap's house. After we'd got ourselves back together we went around his house, putting out spot fires. The old chap was looking after trotters for the property owner, Fred Miller. Actually, one of Fred's trotters, Richmond Lass, had won the 1969 Inter Dominion Pacing Championship. She'd just had a foal and, I tell you, they were absolutely cooked. If I'd had a gun I would've shot both of them there and then.

As for the old chap who was looking after the trotters, when the fire had come through, he'd got into a horse trough and had kept rolling around in the water. So he survived. But he was burnt raw, as red as a lobster. Then I later heard that they'd put Richmond Lass and her foal down and buried them on the property with a headstone and all.

After that we made our way back to Talbot. By then we were more or less driving on burnt ground and so, by the time we got home, the fire had gone through our property. Yet, funnily enough, our house had survived. For some unknown reason a fire truck had turned up as the fire front had come through. To this very day I don't know whose truck it was or why it'd turned up when it did. So we were lucky in the respect that we actually had a house to go back to.

Mind you, plenty didn't. They'd lost the lot. But our shearing shed had gone, plus three haystacks and most of our machinery. Four hundred head of sheep were scorched. All our fencing had gone. Anyhow, after we'd had a bit of a look around, me and my brother slipped back into what was left of Talbot to give people a hand in there. That's when the wind changed and you could see this great big long narrow thirty-kilometre fire front starting to move back to Maryborough and Carisbrook.

But gee, we heard some stories. One Talbot CFA volunteer said that his wife had to drag their kids through the flames to get them to safety. And, as it turned out, one fellow lost his life. He'd got badly burnt on the day and died a few days later.

Yet, even though it was a big fire, newswise it pretty much slipped through to the keeper. Whereas two years prior, there'd been major fires through a suburb in the hills, just north of Melbourne, called Cockatoo. Quite a few had died in that one and once you have a lot of human fatalities, that's when it hits the news big time.

Anyhow, we survived, and I got to tell the story. The odd thing was, the next day was a perfect summer's day, no wind, nothing. And all our guys got involved with back-burning and clean-up, pulling out smouldering stumps and what have you.

As for us, the first thing we had to deal with was our livestock. And that was terrible. Many of our sheep were still alive, but they'd been burnt so bad that we had to put them down straight away – poor buggers. So it was just a case of having to shoot them where they stood, out in the paddock. A few mates had turned up with tractors and front-end loaders and had dug a huge hole, and that's where we buried them. We left the ones that we didn't think were too badly burnt. But a few days later, we ended up having to shoot most of them as well. Then, because we'd been so badly burnt out, those that were okay, we sent off to agistment on a friend's property down near Ballarat.

So four weeks prior to the fire, I'd left the bank without a clue as to what I was going to do for a job. And now I didn't even have time to think about it. I got into cleaning-up mode. And look, within six to eight weeks, all our fences had been rebuilt with volunteer labour. The VFF – Victorian Farmers Federation – were great. They got people in. When there'd been fires through the western districts of Victoria, back in 1977, a lot of our guys had gone over there to help them out. So a lot of their guys had come over to return the favour. Plus a lot of friends who hadn't been burnt out, they came over to lend a hand as well.

In a way, that was a time of healing. All these volunteers would turn up and so you'd have a barbecue and a few grogs after a day's fencing or whatever. There was little to no counselling back then, and so that became pretty important because we'd sit around and talk about what'd happened and what didn't happen. So we were clearing our heads. Because, when I think back on it, there was an element of fear involved.

But at the time of the fire, there was no point in fearing. It was a case of, if you do nothing you're going to die, so you'd better do something. And our instant reaction was to get our truck out onto some already scorched ground where we'd be safe. Really, for me, the biggest fear was of finding the three scorched bodies of my brother and his mates in the creek. Then, when we found them in a puddle of water, I suppose that fear subsided and became relief.

I suspect they'd suffered more fear than us. But they were three lucky blokes. Three very lucky blokes. Many weren't. And there's people who, long after a fire's gone through and they've rebuilt their farms, the psychological effects still linger. One friend of mine was knocked around big time and he's still having a rough time of it. We had a small fire out here just recently and it all came back to him and he went down in a heap again. And that's thirty-five or so years down the track.

But as they say, fire's a good servant but a bad master. As Australians we love living in the bush. But if you're going to make a career of farming, you need to be aware that fire is one of the risks. So we need to understand more about how it works and how we can prevent it from happening again and again, as it has been of late. In our case, after the fires, a lot of people rebuilt and continued on. For others it proved too much. They took the insurance money and moved to safer areas.

And as for the feller who'd lit the fire in the first place, he got caught on the day and the police got him out of there quick-smart. They were well aware that if they didn't get him away, they'd have problems keeping him alive. He later went through the court process. I've forgotten what he got. But none of us thought it was anywhere near enough.

Note: Close to two hundred trucks and a thousand firefighters were involved in the Avoca bushfires of January 1985. The eastern fringe of Avoca was burnt out as was, by and large, the township of Talbot. In all, the fire burnt through approximately sixty thousand hectares of property. In doing so, it destroyed near on two hundred homes and farm structures and killed 40,500 head of sheep and cattle.

One person died as a result of the fire.

Appreciation

We had a fire up at Cooplacurripa one time. Cooplacurripa's on the Mid North Coast of New South Wales, just north of Gloucester. The fire was where the Cooplacurripa Valley comes over a ridge and goes down into Cells Valley. So the fire was down in the valley and we were up in a saddle on the ridge. A chopper was with us, doing water drops. We had seven forty-four-gallon drums of jet AI chopper fuel with us. Anyhow, it was seven in the morning with the temperature nudging thirty degrees Celsius. The humidity was down to eighteen per cent, as dry as chips, and we get word from fire comms – communications: 'If the fire gets over that ridge, it'll take all before it.'

So okay, then the wind comes in from the west and the fire starts heading our way, up the hill.

I said to one of the brigades, 'Start back-burning.'

We already had a truck down in the valley getting water. A second truck had also gone down to fill up, but it'd got stuck. Then, when the fire started building, one of the other brigades said, 'It's too hot for us. We're getting out.' And that was okay. I always ask around, 'If anyone doesn't feel safe, tell me straight away. Don't stay around if you don't feel safe.' I'm definitely not one of those who says, 'Right, fellers, we're going in and that's it. Just follow me.'

Anyway, that just left my brigade on the ridge. No one else. Just half a dozen of us, a truck with a thousand litres of water and we had about four hundred metres of ridge to protect. The chopper was going around above us, dropping buckets of water on the spot fires as they broke out. Then it was up to us to drive over and mop them up. In situations like that, you've got to use your water sparsely. Because, if you run out of water, the fire will get away from you. And that'll be the end of it.

Anyhow, due to the intense smoke, we couldn't see where the chopper was dropping the water. So the pilot's up above, giving us directions over the radio, 'Three hundred metres right.' So we'd drive to the spot fire and mop up. Then he'd go and get another bucket of water and he'd come back and drop it on another spot fire. 'Two hundred metres to your left,' and we'd head off there.

But I can tell you, it was so hot that when a spark or ember hit a cow pat, it'd ignite right beside you. It was that hot. Just shocking. Anyhow, we continued on like this, water drop, mop up, water drop, mop up. But with just the one truck and only a thousand-litre tank, it wasn't enough. So we called up to the chopper, 'We're just about out of water.'

He said, 'Well, just hang on in there. We've nearly got it under control. I'll go and get another bucket of water. If that doesn't put it out we're in big trouble.'

Okay, so when he dropped his next bucket of water, we went over and mopped it up with the last of our water. And that was it. *Phew!* We had it under control. It was just one of the days. We were very lucky, because other days you could chase a fire, knocking it out, knocking it out, and then, with just ten metres of the fire front remaining, you run out of water and so off she goes again, and you've lost it. So that was a bit of a close one.

But we don't only fight fires. We also do car accidents and rescues and help out in times of natural disasters. Do you remember the big hailstorm that did so much damage in Sydney, back in 1999? We went down there to help with the clean-up. Anyhow, some bright spark came up with the idea that we had to wear our full firefighting uniform. The thing was, so that our fire boots don't burn easily, they've got carbon in the soles. And that's okay in a firefighting situation, but they're extremely slippery when you're walking across a roof, laying tarpaulin over damaged tiles and so forth. Now, I'm not one for smart ideas, but one suddenly struck me. I said to the others, 'Well, next weekend I'm wearing sandshoes.'

Oh and didn't that set a cat amongst the pigeons. 'No,' they said. 'We've been told to wear our full firefighting gear. So we've gotta wear our fire boots.'

I didn't say any more about it, but the next weekend I turned up wearing my sandshoes. There was a bloke working with me called Blue. Blue was a lot bigger than me. As strong as an ox. He was my anchor. By anchor I mean, while I was up on the roof, I had a safety rope tied on to me and he'd be down on the ground hanging on to the other end of it, just in case I slipped and fell. Anyhow, we were at this house. I was up on the roof, laying tarpaulin across the roof. I had my sandshoes on, and this little feller struts up the driveway. Didn't know who he was. He fronts up to Blue and he says, 'What's that bloke doing up there?'

Blue takes a look and says, 'Looks like he's tarping over the roof.'

The feller said, 'He's got sandshoes on.'

Blue takes another look. 'Yep,' he says, 'he's wearing 'em so he doesn't fall off the roof.'

Oh, and didn't that get the feller going. 'I'm from WorkCover,' he says. 'He's gotta have his firefighting boots on. If he hasn't got his firefighting boots on he's not covered by insurance.'

Anyway, like I said, Blue was a big bloke. A lot bigger than me. And tough as they come. So he sees a chance to have a tug on this feller's leg. He said, 'Well, mate, you go and tell him that. I'm not telling him. I'm shit scared of him.'

So then the feller from WorkCover looks Bluey up and down. Then he looks up at me, working away on the roof. After sizing us both up, he turns around and he storms off in a huff. But I mean, the stupidity of it all was that the safest thing to wear, when you're scrambling around on top of a roof, was sandshoes.

But no, that wasn't what the WorkCover rules and regulations book stated: page 240, paragraph b, subsection 3a or whatever it may have been – 'you must wear your firefighting boots'. I just think that's where a little bit of common sense comes in.

But we did a lot of good down there. We helped out a lot of people, and more often than not our efforts were appreciated.

So we do get around a bit. I remember the time we went down to Gosford as a strike team. That's like a backup support unit. There was a big fire out Wisemans Ferry way. We left home at about seven in the morning and three hours later we got to Gosford. Anyhow, they said, 'We've booked you into a hotel. Go there and wait till you get your orders.'

But we were going, 'What? We haven't come all this way to sit in a bloody hotel room all day. Can't we make ourselves useful? How about we go out to the fire for just a few hours and then we'll come back?'

In the end they let us go out. But rather than being there for just a few hours, we didn't get back till about 10 o'clock that night. Anyhow, everyone in Gosford was so appreciative of all us volunteers for being there. McDonald's were giving all the firies free food, and the RSL were providing free drinks and snacks.

Anyhow, when we got back from the fire, we went to the RSL for a drink and something to eat. Then we bought a six-pack each and we went back to our hotel. Later on, about five of us were sitting outside on the verandah of the hotel enjoying a beer when two girls come by.

They said, 'You firefighters?'

We said, 'Yes.'

'Want us to give you a free strip?'

Ah, thank you very much for the offer, but no thanks.

Anyhow, when we went back out to the fire the next day, I said to the boys in the RFS – Rural Fire Service – 'Look, we need to move out of that hotel. We can't get any sleep.'

They said, 'Why's that?'

I said, 'It's a brothel.' I said, 'There's a couple of girls working out of there and we haven't had a wink of sleep all night.'

They said, 'Is there?'

'Yes,' I said. 'And what's more, at three in the morning there were two drunk blokes having a barney outside, fighting over which one of the girls they were going to have sex with.'

Note: The 1999 Sydney hailstorm was the costliest natural disaster in Australian insurance history, causing extensive damage along the east coast of New South Wales. It's believed that the storm, which was classified as a 'supercell' due to its erratic nature and extreme attributes, dropped approximately 500,000 tonnes of hailstones during its duration.

Lightning claimed one life and caused approximately fifty injuries.

Fair Game

The wife and I came to Armadale at the beginning of 1974 and we've been here ever since. Now, don't be mistaken, I'm not talking about the Armidale in New South Wales, that's spelt with an 'i'. This is the Armadale, with an 'a', which is to the south-east of Perth. When we first got here the place had about three thousand people. Then it took off, and now it's a city with a population creeping up towards ninety thousand.

Anyhow, four months after we got here, I was put in as captain of the Armadale Volunteer Fire Brigade. I didn't really want the job, but the bloke who'd been captain since the brigade started wanted out. So then I did twelve years as captain and I followed that up as secretary for eighteen years. As far as fires go, back in the beginning, we were only taking about twenty calls a year. These days we'd be just shy of three hundred, and one year we peaked at three hundred and nineteen call-outs.

My two sons grew up here as volunteer firefighters. As eleven-year-olds they joined our junior brigade. Then, when they were seventeen, they became seniors. And they've since gone on to become perms – permanent – career firefighters. Both are station officers and continue to do great work.

The biggest fire I was involved in was when the Kelmscott Shopping Village went up. And, as a volunteer, I was in charge of the whole bloody shebang. Now what year was that? Maybe around 1976. The funny thing was, we'd already had a couple of false-alarm calls out there that day. Then we got yet another call at around half past seven that night. But when we went out there, yet again, we couldn't find a fire. Anyhow, a couple of the boys went inside to have a look around, and that's when I seen the glow behind the aisles at Woolworths. So I shouted out to them, 'Get out'a there!'

They'd just got out when, next thing, the place basically exploded. What'd happened was, around Armadale we have very strong summer winds called the easterlies. They're a land wind that comes in overnight. Well, these easterlies had picked up and they'd blown the fire right up into the ceiling: And with the place having no fire walls, it went straight through to the roof and – *boom!* – pretty much the whole lot went up.

Now, I'll tell you a little story about what happened while we were out there. And what you've got to understand is that, these days, things in the fire brigade are a lot more serious and far more strict. But see, I'm going back a lot of years when things were a bit more easygoing. So if the opportunity was right, things were pretty much fair game. Anyhow, it was probably 3 o'clock in the morning when one of the other vollies and I saw this television set. It was lying there, in among the fire, but it wasn't damaged or anything. So we said, 'Shit, that'd be great for the brigade to have back at the station.'

Anyhow, just as we're sizing up this television set, imagining where we'd put it in the fire station, this bloody huge six-by-eight-inch H-beam came crashing down from the ceiling and smashed it to smithereens. I mean, we not only lost the chance of getting a free television set at the fire station but we could've well been crushed underneath the beam.

Anyhow, that's just an aside story because, like I said, we got there at around seven or eight that night, and I didn't get home till it was light the next morning. So I had a change of clothes and, just as I'd got to work at the Electoral Commission, I got called back out there because the place had flared up again.

At the time we didn't know how or why the fire had started. But what really got it going was that, in those days, they were putting compressed and sealed straw blocks of board in the

with a box of matches threatening to set the place alight. And when the sergeant asked me what *we* were going to do about it, I replied, 'Well, Sarge, as far as I see it, at the moment *you*, the police, have a domestic situation to deal with. But, if he strikes a match, I guess *we*, being the fire brigade, will have to deal with it.' And I just left it at that.

In those days we didn't have proper rescue equipment and so, if we had to go to a vehicle accident, we had to do the best we could with jemmy bars et cetera. So with the career firefighters – perms, or permanents – having a couple of rescue vehicles, we left most of that side of things to them. Though, with Kelmscott Shopping Village, we did rescue the animals out of the pet shop before that part of it burnt down.

Now, while I'm on animal rescues, there was the saga of the cat. It must've somehow got itself up into the ceiling of the house and it'd fallen down between the brick walls. So then it was stuck. Now I forget the exact procedure, but we somehow eventually coaxed this cat over to one of them ground-floor air ventilators. And, when we lifted that, it must've seen the light because it walked out by itself. Simple as that.

Another time we got called out to rescue a lady's pet cocky that was stuck up a tree. When we got there the woman said, 'It can't fly, so perhaps you can just blow it off the branch with a squirt of water?'

And I'm thinking, Well, how the hell did it get up there in the first place, lady?

Anyway, she persisted, so I said, 'Okay, we'll give it a go.'

So we did. We got out the fire hose and we squirted a beam of water onto this bloody cocky. Next thing – *whoosh* – it took to wing and the last we saw of it, it was two hundred metres away, flapping like buggery and gaining altitude. So it could fly all right.

Another one that amused me was the time we got called up to Bedfordale. Back then Bedfordale was a pretty rural sort of place. Anyhow, a horse had somehow got stuck down a well. So we got there and, while we're wondering what to do, the owner bloke said to me, 'I've got some rope. How about you put it around the horse's neck and drag it out?'

I said, 'Mate, that's a bit radical. We'll probably end up pulling the head off the darn thing.'

'Well,' he said, 'what else can you suggest?'

I said, 'How about we go and get a front-end loader, dig the side of the well out and let the horse walk out.'

He said, 'But that'll ruin the well.'

I said, 'Well, a dead horse in your well won't help it too much neither, will it?' I said, 'You can always fix the well up.'

'Oh yeah,' he said.

Anyhow, in the end, he got a front-end loader and dug the side out of the well and the bloody horse walked out, as easy as that.

Then there was the fire at the poultry place. Look, I shouldn't tell you this because I don't know if the manager bloke's still alive or not. But anyway, this manager bloke was the dead ringer for a bloody chook. True, he had flaming red hair and his nose stuck out like a huge red beak. Now I don't know how the fire started – it could've been electrical – but it was in one of the chook sheds. And when the fire started, the chook-looking manager bloke had opened the doors and let all the chooks out. So there was chooks running everywhere, all around the place.

Anyhow, after we'd put the fire out, we kindly offered to help him round up all these bloody chooks. So there we were, all us volunteer firies, running around all over the place, chasing all these bloody chooks that were scooting off left, right and centre. What a debacle that was. Though somehow, and I didn't know how, but someone, and I don't know who, had inadvertently left the doors of the fire engine open and a few of those rampaging chooks had somehow found their way into the cab. But the manager feller was okay with that. He just said it was a case of finders-keepers and so we could keep them. Though mind you, we'd saved a hell of a lot more of his bloody chooks than what would've died in the fire.

So that's just a small part of my time as a volunteer firefighter. As I said, I was the captain of Armadale for twelve years and secretary for something like eighteen. I also served eighteen years on the WA Volunteer Fire Brigades Association representing the Central Zone Brigades. So, in all, it's been something like over sixty years.

And I'm still involved in the brigade. I now hold the highly esteemed rank of ex-captain – an ex-captain being a captain that used to be a captain once upon a time. And not long ago I got out all the appearance books from over those years and I worked out that I'd attended more than two thousand calls. So that's a hell of a lot of call-outs.

But by the time I'd turned seventy-five, I reckoned I was becoming more of a liability than an asset out on the fireground. So I pulled myself out of that side of things. Now I'm what's called 'support', which gives me more time for golf. I play off eighteen, which isn't too bad for an eighty-two-year-old. But I still do whatever I can to help around the station. You know, just little bits here and there, like cleaning the toilets and sweeping the floors and pruning the roses and digging the gardens. Whatever. It's been my life and I've thoroughly enjoyed it.

So that's about it really. But just before we finish, I'd like to pose you a question: why are fire engines coloured red? Are you ready? Good, here we go. Well, a fire engine has six wheels and six crew. Six and six equals twelve. There are twelve inches in a ruler. Queen Victoria was a ruler. She ruled over the seven seas. In the seas are fishes. Fishes have fins. The Finns fought the Russians. Russians are red. Fire engines are always rushin'. So that is why they're red.

Note: The single biggest loss of houses in a Western Australian bushfire happened in Kelmscott where, in February 2011, seventy-two homes were destroyed and thirty-seven were damaged.

Kelmscott is not only the home of the first Red Rooster restaurant but it's also said to have Australia's busiest drive-through KFC service.

Armadale's Old Jarrah Tree, which is on the corner of Third Road and Church Avenue, is estimated to be between four hundred and eight hundred years old. As it's a tree, it surely must be one of the most unusual entries in the WA Register of Heritage Places.

The Wicket Keeper

I started work at Forthside Vegetable Research Station in January 1969. Forthside – or Forth as it's better known – is on the north-west coast of Tasmania. The facility was set up back in 1962 with the aim of providing research, help and support to develop the state's various vegetable industries. The major focus was on crops such as potatoes, onions, carrots and all the rest of it. Typical research. So that was the vegetable side of things.

Besides that we also began oil poppy research under licence from the United Nations. See, there's a number of derivatives of the poppy. Those include pethidine, morphine, opium and codeine, of which pethidine is perhaps the most interesting. In the southern hemisphere, poppies are best grown on the meridian of forty-three degrees, and that made Tasmania the only suitable state in Australia for the research. The only other place under consideration was Blenheim in New Zealand.

So Glaxo-Allenbury sent a plant development researcher out from Britain armed with all the different types of poppies they'd collected from around the world. He planted one plot here at Forth and another plot at Blenheim, and, luckily, the decision went Tasmania's way. So here's where the poppy industry started, here in Forth, and my position was second officer-in-charge.

When I first arrived to take up my position, my wife stayed on in Sydney working for General Foods of America. General Foods weren't keen on letting her go, so she agreed to remain in Sydney for a couple of extra months. But they weren't too happy about that either. They even offered to fly her down to Tasmania every fortnight for a weekend to be with me. But she didn't come at that either and so, in the end, she quit her Sydney job and she came over here to join me in the May.

After she'd stayed at home for a number of years, my wife being who she is got carried away and did an arts degree at the University of Tasmania. God only knows why. But anyway, she did this arts degree. Then she lectured in philosophy. After that she spent four years dragging – and it was dragging – nurses along the way towards their registered nurses degree.

We lived on the research station for seventeen years. Then, when I was getting close to sixty they said to me ... Oh, the fire brigade. That's right, you're here to hear about the local fire brigade.

I am sorry. I'll just have to go back a bit. Well now, I joined the Forthside Fire Brigade back in 1970. We had a good lot of volunteers, but we didn't have any gear other than a trailer that someone could hook up and tow with their vehicle. Now, I've forgotten the actual size of the water tank it carried, but there was still just enough space in the trailer for our knapsacks and beaters.

During those early years we attended a lot of vehicle accidents, where we had to clean up petrol and oil off the road so it'd be safe to drive on again. We also attended several house fires. Situations such as where Mum had been frying, the fat had caught alight, she'd swung the pan round to stick it in the sink and, in doing so, the kitchen curtains had caught fire and *whoosh*, away it went. A chain reaction.

Because our fire trailer was kept at the research station, where we lived, I was always the first point of contact. Though there was one occasion I didn't get the message straight away and that turned out to be a near disaster. A fire had broken out in a somewhat dilapidated old cottage, just down the road, at Leith. By the time I got there, quite a lot of the brigade had already arrived.

And I couldn't believe it: here's one of them, up on the roof, and they hadn't even cut off the electricity. I nearly had a fit. Dear me, the last place you'd want to be is up on a roof, during a fire, while the electricity's still turned on. And this bloke seemed to be a sensible chap. But he certainly wasn't using his brains that night. He was just lucky that he didn't get fried. Anyhow, we got him down pretty quick-smart, but we lost the house.

There was another time, around '76 or '77 – it must've been a weekend, either a Saturday or a Sunday evening, between half past six and seven. We were out of milk at home and so I said to my wife, 'I'll go down to the shop and buy some milk.'

So I went to Forth. At that stage Forth had three shops. We've only got one now, plus a pub. Anyway, I went to the first shop and I bought the milk. When I came out of the shop, I looked across the river, and there's smoke coming out of the top of the pub – the Bridge Hotel.

So I rush across. By this stage we had a fire station building and we had a truck. I'll tell you about the truck later on. But oh, didn't we have some fun and games because, to start with, we had all the trouble in the world getting our connections onto one of the hydrants. Anyhow, by the time we got the fire out, all the upstairs and the roof area was completely gutted. So after having left home at 7 o'clock at night to get some milk, I didn't get home till 2 o'clock the following morning. And I'm not sure what happened to the milk.

Now, getting back to our truck. It'd been used during the mid-'50s Suez Crisis that had started after the Egyptians had nationalised the Suez Canal and cut off most of Europe's oil supplies. Anyhow, after the crisis was long over, the Tasmanian state government bought half a dozen of these trucks. I've forgotten what the make of ours was, whether it was a Ford or a Chevy or it might've even been an Austin, I don't remember, but it had a water tank that held about three hundred gallons, which was marvellous. It also had a very good pump, with an auxiliary Coventry Climax motor.

Now, just as an aside, the Coventry Climax was one of the best British motors ever built. So outstanding in fact that everybody wanted to nick it and put in their motor cars.

Oh, that truck had everything, including a top speed – provided you were going downhill – of thirty miles an hour. You needed to be going downhill though. It was the most clumsy thing you'd ever come across, but it did a very good job.

Oh, that's right, I missed the best bit. When we got this wonderful truck, the one from the Suez Crisis, we kept it at the research station, where four of us in the fire brigade worked. But only one of us had the correct licence to drive the thing. The other three didn't. So we lined up our truck driver's test with the local policeman.

On the day, the three of us turned up at 10 o'clock in the morning, with the truck. Oh, and this policeman, didn't he put us through hell. It was ridiculous. He asked us just about every question that could possibly be asked in the driving licence manual. Then we had to drive this truck here, there and everywhere else. Up hills with standing starts. Down dales with standing starts. Oh, he put us through the whole works.

Anyway, by late afternoon, the three of us had got our licence. Good, so I drove home. But I didn't come the usual way, through the front gate. Instead, I went down to the side gate where the houses are. Both entries have fences on each side, and there's cattle grids. To cut a long story short, as I drove in through the gate, the side fence got hooked under the wheel guards at the back of the truck. So over goes the fence, and this is just ten minutes after I'd got my truck driver's licence. I was just lucky that the policeman wasn't there or else he would've taken it back.

Now, getting back to the pub. That's right, the fire must've been on the Saturday night because on the following Saturday night, when the publican – who just happened to be treasurer-secretary of the local football club – opened the safe where their footy club's account book was held, a bloke got into the pub and shot him. As it turned out, the bloke who'd started the fire the previous week and the bloke who killed the publican the following week was one and the same person.

What had happened was, when this bloke had been president of the footy club, he'd diddled the books and helped himself to five hundred dollars. So then, after he'd failed to burn the pub down and destroy the account books, the following Saturday, he went back and shot the publican dead and took off with the books. He then hid them down a rabbit hole, up on top of Braddon's Outlook Road. And that's where the police found them: down a rabbit hole up on top of Braddon's Outlook Road. I don't know how they worked all that out, but they did. Anyhow, they'd nicked him before the week was out.

Actually, I used to play cricket with the bloke. He was our wicket keeper. Anyway, after he'd been sentenced and was sent off to the Hobart lockup, we ended up playing cricket against him. He was still wicket keeping, though this time for the Hobart prisoners' team.

But the thing I'm getting around to is that while he was doing his time in prison, he completed his accountancy degree. Can you believe that? He became a fully qualified accountant. But as to where, when and if he ever ended up practising, I have no idea. He may have even changed his name. I don't know. Though the other sad part of the saga was that he had a wife and a young son. And of course, after he'd been sent to prison, they left him. So all in all, it was quite a dramatic turnout and follow-on.

Anyhow, enough of that. So I was captain of the brigade for about ten years. That was from the '70s through to about the mid-'80s. Then, because I'd accrued quite a lot of long service leave and ordinary leave, my wife and I were away travelling for a lot of the '80s. We spent three months in Europe, then a few months in Nepal and India and Thailand.

And also, over a period of eight years, I found that my sight wasn't what it once was. So I pulled out. It was the best thing to do, and nowadays the Forthside-Leith Fire Brigade is tied in with the Turners Beach Fire Brigade. Over the past few years they've put up some new buildings as you head out of Forthside, on the way to Ulverstone, and they've got several top-of-the-range trucks and every little bit of equipment you'd ever likely need. The works.

And that's probably about all. But I just thought you'd like the story about the fire in the pub, the shooting of the publican and the wicket keeper–ex-football club president who became a fully certified accountant. I mean, the dreadful things that some people do, ay, and all over five hundred dollars.

Note: The Bridge Hotel at Forth was established in 1872. In the September of its centenary year, 1972, fire destroyed the upper storey. The proprietor, Ernest Morrison, saved the lives of two guests and the blaze was put out by the local fire brigade. Bar trade resumed within a couple of days. A week after the fire, the Morrisons' golden Labrador – Hey You – was poisoned and Ernest Morrison was shot and killed. Papers from the hotel safe were recovered from a rabbit burrow on a nearby property, but the takings remained missing. A man was later sentenced to prison for the term of his natural life.

Postscript: Stories about the presence of a ghostly female figure appearing at the Bridge Hotel at Forth had become common knowledge by the turn of the twentieth century. Hotel occupants tell of a grief-stricken woman, possibly wearing a white wedding gown, gazing out across the bridge as if she was waiting for her bridegroom to turn up for their wedding. To this day, it's thought that the unexplained footsteps and the shimmering female figure who occasionally appears in the upper section of the hotel's hallway at night may be the intended bride.

Flaming Cow Dung

I was born and bred in Launceston, Tasmania. My mother was also born in Launceston and she lived there all her life. My father was born in Hobart. I'm not too sure how he finished up in Launceston. But he did and he finished up working in my mother's father's business. That was W H Cox and Sons, builders and contractors, who were situated opposite Launceston Fire Station, and Dad eventually took over the business.

My father married my mother sometime before World War Two. He left for the war shortly after I was born in 1940. He was in artillery. New Guinea essentially. He used to come home on leave every now and again, but he was like a stranger. He certainly didn't talk about any of his war experiences. He was a pretty tough disciplinarian, though that didn't do me any harm.

Primary school was at West Launceston. Then I went to Launceston High School and did my matriculation. I wanted to be a pilot in the air force. Trouble was, at high school, my father pushed me into a commercial course, which didn't interest me one little bit. As a consequence, it made it a lot more difficult for me to get into the air force. So I lost interest in flying and I ended up working at a wool-processing company, Patons and Baldwins. They were an English company who had a huge mill in Launceston and a lot of people worked there.

I was in the office for a couple of years before I headed off to Sydney with a couple of my surf-club mates. We worked on the main Pacific Highway, out of Chatswood, doing footpaths and centre strips. I believe that lots of them are still there – the footpaths, I mean. But it was one of the best experiences of my life. We had a Scottish foreman, and in the crew there was a Greek, an Italian, a Yugoslav, a Croatian and a Pole, plus a couple more fellers that'd come from Europe. There were just three Aussies: an Aboriginal bloke, the overseer and me. Most of the crew were older than us. They'd come out to Australia after the war.

The foreman was a brute of a man. He used to pick on us all something terrible. But we were young and fit and, as soon as our hands hardened up, we were given the job of loading the trucks, while the rest of them did the concreting and finishing. And they were good at it. The thing was, even though we didn't speak the same language, we got on real well with all of them, apart from the foreman, that is. And that's what really broadened my life's scope, about how other people lived. I got to understand a lot of things about the world outside of Australia.

So then yeah, after that I came back to Tasmania and I got a job with a company called Dunlop. A friend of the family's was the manager in Launceston. I worked in the floor-covering division and I learnt how to lay rubber and vinyl floor tiles, and in those days there was a fair bit of lino about.

I had nothing to do with the volunteer fire service in those early days. That didn't come till later, after me and some of my mates came up with the idea of finding a place by the sea where we could each have a shack, without being surrounded by other holiday homes. We'd spent some time looking around the north-east of Tasmania, and had made some inquiries. But that didn't work. Anyhow, I'd spent a lot of my past school holidays on the east coast, at a place called Coles Bay. Back then Coles Bay was more of a small holiday destination and so it only had a permanent population of about a hundred. So I said to one of my mates, I said, 'I'll take you to one of the most beautiful spots in Tasmania.'

So I drove him to Coles Bay and we parked up off the top of the main road. A couple of old humpies were dotted about.

Not much else. Then I took him down for a closer look, and I remember us walking along the beach and my mate saying, 'Wow, what've we gotta do to get a piece of this right here!'

Anyhow, my wife's father found out that it was leased land and the old fellow who had the licence had died. As it turned out, the family he'd left it to weren't that interested in hanging on to it, so they agreed to sell it to us. So we started clearing the land in 1978 and that's when I first got involved with the fire service. Back then there was no official brigade or nothing. National Parks had a vehicle and, if a fire got away from them, that's when the locals would get involved. They had an old white International truck. It was quite small, so it only had a small water tank. Other than that they had fire beaters, rake-hoes and backpacks – knapsacks – which held about five gallons. And that was about it.

It wasn't till about 1980 that the Coles Bay Brigade was established. Our first truck was kept in a shed around in Freycinet National Park. Then later on, after we'd built our own shed, the truck was moved there, independent of the national park.

Back then we didn't have too many big fires. We just used to do a bit of burning off. This was before National Parks had a lot of places declared as reserves. So there was a fair bit of Crown land that they were happy for us to burn off. It was the best training. All pretty relaxed and social. We used to go round to the fire shed once a month to have a bit of a get-together, you know, to have a few drinks and a catch-up before we'd go and do a bit of a burn-off. Then, if something was still smouldering the next morning, a couple of us would go back and make sure it was out. And we kept Coles Bay safe for a long time doing it that way.

As for some of those early memories, there was the time a fire came through Swanwick. Someone had been burning a little heap of stuff and it'd got away on them. We had our old truck and, by then, we'd acquired a trailer. The trailer, which I'd hooked up to my vehicle, had a small water tank and a pump and a bit of firefighting gear. It was a hot windy day, with a wild north-easterly and the fire had jumped the road and had got into a privately owned place. I forget the owner's name, but he'd built a concrete yacht that he was going to sail around the world in. Anyhow, even though the ground was pretty worthless, he'd had a few cattle running on it.

I was with a mate and we said, 'We'll do this edge,' which was the eastern edge. And I remember sitting there with the trailer and, fanned by the wind, the flames were just skirting across what little grass there was. But what amazed me was that, with the heat, the dried cow dung was igniting in sparks and flames, even before the fire got to them. That's how hot it was, and that was my first experience of that sort of thing happening. It was an incredible sight. *Pop. Pop. Pop.* Then after we got that edge out, we went around to where the fire was starting to spread through to Swanwick proper.

Anyhow, one particular feller had nominated himself as the brigade's truck driver. But he was absolutely hopeless. To be honest, he didn't have a clue about firefighting. Like, at the drop of a hat, he'd go into a panic. So when things started looking pretty dicey, he told us that he was going back to town to fill up the truck's water tank. So he took off, and we didn't see him for the next three hours. He was a big drinker and so he might've gone to the pub to build up some Dutch courage.

Anyhow, after the fire, I got talking to a few of the others. I said, 'We can't have this. This feller's bloody hopeless.' So, when we had our annual general meeting, it was decided that we'd dismember him – that is, kick him out. And boy, he didn't like it, not one little bit. In fact, he never came back again. But it just had to be.

But them cow pats were amazing. If you didn't put them out properly the first time, they'd just sit there, smouldering away. Then, given another hot, dry windy day – *pop, pop, pop* – they'd start up all over again.

Note: Dry manure is typically defined as having a moisture content of less than thirty per cent. The ignition point of cow dung is regarded as being quite low, though this depends on its degree of dryness and the amount of fodder – dried hay or grass – within the dung, plus its microbial activity.

In some countries, cow dung is used for cooking. In India, for example, cow dung is used for two main reasons: 1) to dispose of their plentiful cow dung and 2) it's an easy and cheap source of fuel for cooking.

Cow dung, though, does have its downsides: it can be highly flammable and explosive in nature, plus the smoke released in the burning process contains hazardous gases.

Spontaneous combustion is also a problem. In 2016, in upstate New York, a barn storing manure spontaneously burst into flames and threatened to destroy a nearby valley. In the end it took three fire departments to put it out. Back in 2009, an escaped manure fire in Southern California burnt through six thousand acres of land and, in 2005, a 2000-ton pile of manure in Nebraska spontaneously ignited and smouldered unchecked for three months.

In Australia, author Bill 'Swampy' Marsh often burns dried cow dung on his campfires in order to keep the rampaging mozzies under control.

That's My Bloody Farm on Fire!

I'm just reading through a letter from my wife's nephew Brian. He lives in the UK these days but, when he heard that you were after fire stories, he penned his recollections of the time he set fire to our farm, in a town called Blighty. Now, I don't know if he got overly excited that the story might end up in print but, just between you and me, some of it's a bit over the fence. Anyhow, I'll read it out and, if you don't mind, I'll make a few alterations along the way so that it's a bit closer to the truth.

Okay, here we go. Brian's titled it, 'That's My Bloody Farm on Fire'. By 'my bloody farm', he means me because it was my bloody farm that the little bugger set on fire.

He begins with how his ancestors emigrated from England in the mid-1850s, to join the gold rush, and that he was born in an outback town. He doesn't mention where, mind you, but that's of no consequence. And when he was three the family moved to Melbourne.

Then he writes, and I quote: 'For many years we visited my mother's sister Marie and her husband, Frank, and my cousins Susan and Karen [that's my daughters] who lived on a farm in the Riverina district in southern New South Wales.

'We were always regarded as city slickers who knew nothing about the country and farm life.'

Which was pretty much right, mind you.

Then he goes, 'Uncle Frank and Aunty Marie were typical hardworking farming folk who lived to the full. Life was tough on a farm that was at the mercy of the natural elements, including drought, flood, locust plagues and fire to name but a few. The farm grew wheat and barley and in the later years, rice, plus there were sheep, cattle, chickens, pigs and several farm dogs.'

So far, so good, so I'll continue. 'This story's about a particular holiday when I was about nine, so it would've been in the mid-1960s.'

In actual fact he would've been more like six. But so be it.

I'll continue. 'We arrived during a very hot summer. Everything was dry and withered. Uncle Frank was a fire marshal and the community was reliant on its volunteers to assist with any fires, as I was to discover.'

In actual fact I was Blighty's fire captain, which makes this story even more embarrassing.

He says, 'I'd found a box of matches. I cannot recall where. Sue, Karen, my younger brother, Martin, and I went for a walk along an isolated dirt track about three hundred metres from the house. As there was little vegetation nearby, I thought it might be fun to light a small fire, something we could easily put out. I found some twigs and dry grass and made a fist-sized clump as fuel. I had feelings of both excitement and trepidation. There were cries of "don't do it" and "go on, it'll be fun". I tried several times to light the twigs on the path, well away from any vegetation, but I couldn't see any flame.'

Now my take on it was that the little bugger had nicked the box of matches out of the house. He was showing off by lighting the matches then blowing them out just before they burnt his fingers. On this occasion he misjudged, his fingers burnt and he dropped the match into the dry grass.

Anyhow, I'll continue. 'Suddenly there was a gust of wind and for the first time I saw flames. The wind blew the lighted twigs and grass in all directions. Some nearby bushes caught fire. We immediately realised we had a problem and we tried to stamp out the flames. But the flames spread and more bushes caught fire and some nearby gum trees started to ignite. Stronger gusts of wind then blew the flames even further. Suddenly the whole area was on fire and we got surrounded. I heard someone shouting, "Let's get the bloody hell out of here!"

'Meanwhile, back at the house, my mother and Aunty Marie saw the smoke and realised that the house was in danger of being engulfed by the flames. So, as a barrier to the oncoming fire, they drenched towels with water and placed them in a ring around the house. It turned out to be a brilliant idea as it prevented the fire spreading to the house.

'I remember the air filled with acrid smoke and the heat of the day made it worse. Gusts of wind sent sparks and flames into trees, bushes and dry grass. We just couldn't stop it. It was out of control and I went into a state of panic, fearful, frightened and afraid of the consequences spawned from a silly act of childishness.

'A few miles away Uncle Frank was with his brother Keith in the family truck, having run some errands. Keith apparently said, "Frank, I think there's a bloody fire over there. Look at the smoke. It's not far from your place."

'When Frank took a look he said, "That's my bloody farm on fire!" And they headed home to help the volunteers from the Blighty Bush Fire Brigade put out the fire.'

If the truth be known, Keith and I were trucking wheat to the storage at the old World War Two aircraft hangars at the Tocumwal Airport. I think I might've even had Brian's father and his older brother with me as well. Then while I was waiting to be unloaded, a couple of cockies – farmers – arrived and said there was a fire out on my place. Now because a form of local amusement was to take the piss out of their fire captain – that is, me – I didn't believe them. But after a few other fellers arrived and said the same thing, the penny dropped. We got out of there pretty quick-smart and, as we got closer to home, I could see smoke in the sky.

Okay, so now back to Brian's version of events. 'From this point on, other than there being a sense of gathering panic, my memory is hazy. This was not helped by the farm animals adding to the chaos with the dogs barking, the chickens squawking and the pig squealing. The pig was kept in a wooden sty not far from the house, which by then was perilously close to the fire. Uncle Frank must've been back by then because I recall him shouting, "Well, Brian, we've got two options for the bloody pig, either we try to save the poor bugger or we give him the bloody chop. We can't just let it roast in the fire. That'd be bloody cruel and a waste of good tucker."

'With that, Uncle Frank grabbed the pig and hauled it out from the sty and, with a swift flick of his knife, slit its throat. Though this happened in a blur, I do have a very clear memory of Frank saying, "Brian, there's nothing worse than hairy pork crackling so, if we ever bloody get out of this in one piece, your penance is to shave that pig so close its skin'll be as smooth as a baby's bum."'

Now I don't know where Brian got all that from other than he wasn't known for telling the truth at the best of times. Because, if the truth were to be known, I had about ten breeding sows and a few porkers that I was fattening for sale, and none of them were harmed. In fact, the fire only burnt one corner post of the sty. And anyway, by the time I got home the fire was pretty much under control and like any well-trained brigade, my Blighty mob were hosing down a few smouldering logs and giving the pigs a bit of a squirt.

Anyhow, back to Brian's version of the story: 'While this was going on, the volunteer firefighters were staunching the flames with the water from a nearby tank. After several hours the fire was under control with no major property damage, other than to sheds, outbuildings and the pig sty. Thankfully, the house was unharmed, and everyone survived. I gave back the box of matches and promised never to play with fire in future, a promise I've kept to this day – apart from the occasional fun I have mucking about with fireworks on Guy Fawkes night, back here in the UK.

'Anyway, for the rest of the holiday I was pretty much in the doghouse, mostly spending my time shaving the pig with a knife and soap.

'In actual fact, after those holidays, I was very much surprised how my family was still invited back to Uncle Frank and Aunty Marie's farm – me included – especially after all the damage I'd caused. But I think deep down, both Uncle Frank and Aunty Marie enjoyed our visits. And so, though I now reside in the UK, I remember with great fondness the times I spent on the farm and deeply regret the fire incident. It will stay etched in my mind forever.'

Now, as to Brian's surprise that he and his family were invited back to our farm after the incident, it's a moot point – one that I'd prefer not to go into other than to say they were just lucky to have been close relations of my dear wife, Marie.

In truth the most disappointing part of the story was that, due to the Blighty Bush Fire Brigade's excellent firefighting skills and Marie's and her sister's efforts, the fire was kept from burning down the house. I had it well insured and, if ever a house needed replacing, our old place did. And so another five years had to pass before we got enough money together to build a new one.

But there's another part to Brian's story that needs airing. Brian's father owned a 1936 Buick sedan which he had parked on the grass near our house. And by the time my Blighty brigade arrived, the fire was burning the grass under the Buick. And when they went to move the car out of the way, they discovered that it was locked and in gear with the handbrake on.

So, with me having drummed into them the firefighter's oath of protecting life first and property next, and with no one's life being in imminent danger, my deputy broke the small quarter-vent window on the driver's door so that they could get into the Buick and shift it. Which they did and, may I add, without further damage. And well, didn't Brian's old man go off when he saw the quarter-vent had been broken on his pride and joy. So much so that he wanted to put in a claim for the Blighty brigade to fork out for the damage.

So that's the story and, of course, with me being the fire captain, I had to put up with all the ribbing as to how the only fire that the Blighty brigade attended that year was at the captain's property to put out a deliberately and carelessly lit fire.

And he was not present to help.

Now if I may, just on deliberately lit fires: my dearly departed mother was a repeat offending fire bug. She lived on my brother's farm, Yaralla, about fourteen mile from Finley and just down the road from me and Marie. And so as not to be caught during high fire restrictions, she'd sneak out in the early hours of the morning and burn the household rubbish and so forth.

Of course, with me being the local fire captain, this was a huge embarrassment. But no matter what I'd say, even threatening her with a fine, she just wouldn't stop. And what infuriated me even more was that she used to tease me about it. Whenever I'd pop in for a visit she'd say, 'And where were you nice and bright this morning, Mister Fire Captain? I had a little fire out the back and you were nowhere to be found.'

Anyhow, I was going past my brother's farm early one stinking-hot summer's morning when I noticed smoke in the backyard of the homestead.

'She's bloody up to it again,' I muttered.

Then I got an idea. A spark of genius, if you will. When I got to the Blighty store, I rung Mum from the public phone. When she answered, I put on my best pretend Irish accent and I said, 'Is dat de the fire captain's home number, Madam?'

'No, no it isn't,' she said. 'This is his brother's number. Why do you want the fire captain?'

Again in my best pretend Irish accent I said, 'I want'a report a fire 'bout fourteen mile out from Finley, on a property called Yaralla.'

'Oh dear,' she said. 'Do you?'

I said, 'Oh dat's all right. I must have de wrong number. I'll ring up the police instead and they can handle it.' And I hung up.

Anyhow, on the way back home, I decided to pop in and see Mum. When I got there, a stack of wet, blackened, half-burnt paper and other rubbish was blowing around all over the place. What'd happened, of course, I'd put the wind up her. She'd panicked at the thought of the police nabbing her and so she'd grabbed the hose and put her fire out.

And that was the last of her fire-bugging.

Note: Blighty lies in the southern Riverina region of New South Wales between the towns of Finley and Deniliquin. The Blighty Rural Fire Service is in the Mid Murray Zone of the state, an area that covers twenty-five thousand square kilometres – 9700 square miles. The current New South Wales Rural Fire Service consists of a number of volunteer bushfire brigades run along council district lines, under the command of a locally appointed fire control officer.

The township of Blighty has a hotel, a school, a football ground and a few houses. In 2011, Blighty and the surrounding area boasted a population of just under four hundred.

The township of Blighty has featured in a couple of Bill 'Swampy' Marsh's books, *Great Australian Outback Towns and Pubs* and *Great Australian Outback Truckies Stories*.

Never Leave You

Swampy: Are you busy, mate, got time for a chat?

Kerry: Look, I'm out on the jetty at the mo doing a spot of fishing with a couple of mates.

Swampy: Where's that?

Kerry: We've got a bit of a holiday place up here on the Queensland coast.

Swampy: What's your time, mate?

Kerry: Hey, Joe, what's the time? Joe reckons it's 12 o'clock on the dot and you said you'd give me a ring at 1.

Swampy: Well, it *is* 1 o'clock.

Kerry: Oh, I know what's gone wrong. You're in South Australia, right? Well, South Australia's usually half an hour behind Queensland. But, because you're on daylight savings and we aren't, you can either add or take away another hour to that. Joe, do we add or subtract an hour from South Australia when they've got daylight savings and we don't? Oh, okay. No, he doesn't know. 'Wouldn't have a clue,' he said.

Swampy: Well, would you like me to ring back in an hour?

Kerry: If you wouldn't mind. It's just that I've had a couple of nibbles, so I need to keep my mind on things here. So yes, make it another hour and that'd be good. By then I reckon I'll be back home scaling the fish I've caught. Yeah, thanks.

Yes, now's a better time. I didn't catch anything, so I've got all the time in the world. Okay, so now for a bit of my background: I was born and bred in Yarraman, which is about an hour and a half north of Toowoomba. My great-grandparents and my ceilings. They used to advertise that it'd stand the heat of a blowtorch. And it would. But the moment the ties that held the straw blocks together broke, it was just like burning bales of hay dropping down out of the ceiling.

But that fire was a real big one. From memory, when I wrote the bloody report up, I wrote that thirty-eight different appliances had attended the fire and seventy-eight different firemen had been through there, on and off, over a week, putting out the smouldering and the smaller fires that'd broken out.

Previous to Kelmscott Village going up, there'd been the Bentley Forum fire. I didn't go to the Bentley Forum fire but that one went up the same way. Then there was another one over on the west coast where exactly the same thing happened. Once that straw-board got burning, it just fell down all alight.

Now I think that the Kelmscott Shopping Village fire happened just before we had BA – breathing apparatus. If we did have it, I certainly didn't wear it. I know that. So we just had to do our best. I mean, to a point you can always protect yourself with water spray. But with that sort of fire being so bloody hot, we were only able to fight it from a distance anyway. Now, just on BA, I don't know if you know or not but Armadale was the first WA volunteer fire brigade trained in it. There was six of us that went through the training. But like I said, I don't think we had it for the Kelmscott Shopping Village fire.

Oddly enough, there was a bit of a twist to the Kelmscott Village fire. Remember me saying that we didn't know how it started? Well, funnily enough, years later some bloke had an argument with his partner and she dobbed him in to the police, saying that he started it. Anyway, I don't think anything ever came of it.

But oh, so many amusing incidents come to mind. I remember the time we were called out to assist the local police at the scene of a domestic argument. So under lights and siren we arrived at the incident to be briefed by the police sergeant. A bloke had poured petrol throughout the house and was sitting in there grandparents were bullockies and they selected out there back in 1898. It wasn't a ballot or anything like that. The government just opened the land up and they came out here and selected a block, felled all the scrub then set it up as a dairy. But I've never dairyed. I had a service station and hardware store in the town and later on we built the supermarket. But I'm retired from all that now, which gives me more time for fishing.

I can tell you, back a bit Yarraman was in the real doldrums. It was more like an old people's town. But in the late '70s, when they decided to put the Tarong Power Station in, a lot of work was created and we were picked up and put back on the map again. It then took them till the mid- to late '80s to finish it. At the end they gave the power station a life of twenty-five years, but it's still going strong and we hope it'll be going strong for a good time yet to come.

Anyhow, although I've done a fair bit of travelling, most of me life's been spent in and around Yarraman. It's where I grew up and did my schooling. As for the fire brigade, seeing how we only lived two doors away from the fire station, I was always interested in it. So then, when a vacancy came up in the early '70s, I applied for the job and I got it.

Back in them days, we had three separate fire stations in the region: Nanango, Yarraman and Blackbutt – Nanango being twenty kilometres from Yarraman and Blackbutt about fifteen. And those three brigades were governed by the Nanango-Yarraman Fire Brigade Board, which was made up of representatives from the insurance companies, local identities and some council members.

Mine was only an honorary position, really. We weren't a rural brigade and, even though we were totally town based, we weren't permanents either. We were what's called auxiliaries, which meant we were pretty much volunteers, with other jobs around the place, and we only got paid for our practices and when we went to fight a fire. You could describe us as being just an ordinary mix of normal people who came from all walks of life. There was forestry workers, mill workers, mechanics and so forth. I used to work at a fuel depot, then later on I ran the service station. So there were no specialities amongst us, and none of us done it for the money. We did it, well, not for the love of it, but just to help the community, really.

With us being a town brigade, our trucks weren't designed to fight grassfires but more so for fighting house fires and that. And anyway, what little water we could carry in our tank wouldn't have lasted five minutes out in the bush. We were totally reliant on town water – anywhere we could connect to a fire hydrant. And the trucks, they were pretty antiquated. To start with we had those real old Inters – Internationals – that were basically museum pieces and as for firefighting gear, all we did was pull on a pair of overalls, slip into a pair of rubber boots and away we'd go.

How the system worked was, if anyone saw a fire, they'd put a phone call through to the telephone exchange and they'd set the siren off from there. Then, when us fellers in the brigade heard the siren, we'd head up to the fire station. Oh and also, that's right, there used to be a few of those fire emergency boxes around town where you could break the front glass and set off the alarm. Remember those little glass-fronted boxes which had something like, 'In an emergency please break the glass and press the button'? Some of them had a little hammer to help you break the glass. Now, in Yarraman I don't think they came with a hammer, so we had to find a rock or something.

Anyhow, the first of us to arrive at the fire station would unlock the door and start up the truck. If nobody else had turned up by then, he'd head off by himself and the others would have to follow out there in their own cars. The thinking was, the sooner you got to the fire, the sooner you could set everything up, ready to get water onto it when everyone else arrived.

Nowadays, of course, because of all this health and safety, no one's allowed to go out by themselves. And while that's okay if you've got a permanent crew who's always there, waiting at the fire station, it wouldn't have worked for us because by the time we all got to the fire station, the fire would've already pretty much taken hold. And that's the big difference between us auxiliaries and the permanents.

As for some of the fires we had, there was one back in the '70s when an old retired bloke went to bed with a cigarette and the bed caught on fire and it spread out from there. He was living in an old millhouse. It was late afternoon when someone spotted the smoke and, like I said, they called the telephone exchange who set off the siren. That was when we had the old Inter. I just can't remember what the numbers on it were, but it was one of them with the swooped back. Like you had the cabin, then the back of it used to be rounded.

So we got to the fire, then we ran lengths of hose from the hydrant to the pump on the truck, then we ran a couple more lengths of hose from the pump to the fire. And even though we lost the house, the old bloke was saved. So that was sort of a good outcome – well, for him it was, and from memory they rebuilt the house at a later stage.

Then the worst fire we ever had was around the mid-1980s. That was when the power station was being built. Two people died in that fire – a father and a baby. It began from an electrical fault. There'd been a party that night and somebody had left something on. The first I knew of it was when the siren went off at around half past one in the morning. When we got there the house was only partly gutted. We did eventually put the fire out. But, try as we might, by then it was too late to save the father and the baby.

Really, it should've never happened. Neither of them should've died. We heard later that when the fire started to get a hold on the place, the wife got out the window and she asked her husband to go and get the baby and pass it out to her. It was such a simple thing to do – to go and grab the baby and hand it out the window. Then he'd get out and they both would've been saved. But that wasn't to be. Because of all the smoke in the house, he couldn't see where he was going and he got disorientated and he walked straight past where the baby was lying in the cot and into the kitchen and he got overcome by smoke.

When we went in, we found the baby first. The baby wasn't burnt or nothing. It'd died from asphyxiation. It was just lying there in the cot. And then we found the bloke. He was lying out over a table, all burnt. It wasn't good, and those are the sorts of things that never leave you as a firefighter. It certainly hasn't left me.

Of course, what made it even harder was that in them days there was no debriefings or counselling. You just had to try and grin and bear it. On top of all that, there was all the news media that come out to Yarraman and wanted an interview. And they weren't very pleasant with the way they went about their questions and accusations. To my mind that only made things worse. So I'm afraid I had no time for them and, in the end, I just told them where to go.

But overall, I'd say we did a fairly good job at containing most of the fires we were called to. Anyhow, I was in the brigade for twenty years or so, and by the end I'd worked my way up to deputy chief officer. Then I finished up in the '90s, around about the time the government took over running the brigade from the boards. I didn't like the change. I could see that things weren't going to run as smooth as they had done. So I decided the best thing to do was to pull the pin and step aside.

Even still, until more recent times, I've had a lot on my plate. I've kept myself busy. But not any more. These days I'm starting to pull out of a lot of things. Like I'd spent two years getting a men's shed up and running, and last month I stood down as president of that. I reckoned it was time for somebody else to take it on and give me more time for fishing. Actually, yesterday I caught a couple of nice cod and a couple of nice bream. But no, things like that with the baby and the father dying in the fire never leave you. They're always in the back of your mind.

Note on house fire safety: Never leave cooking unattended. Keep tea towels, pot holders et cetera well clear of the stove. Grills, fans and cooking surfaces should be kept free from grease and other flammable residue. Ensure heaters are turned off before going to bed or leaving the premises. Keep clothing, curtains and toys well away from heaters. Never overload power boards. Immediately replace faulty appliances. Have a smoke alarm installed outside every sleeping area – test them monthly and change their batteries annually.

Clean chimneys and flues annually. Use a fire screen in front of an open fire. Candles, incense and oil burners et cetera must be kept well away from anything flammable. Keep matches and lighters out of reach of children. Never smoke in bed. Don't leave electric blankets on for any longer than thirty minutes. Never put weight, that is, people, animals or objects on a bed while the electric blanket is on. Allow the clothes dryer to complete its cool-down cycle before stopping it, and clean the lint filter after each load.

Devise a home fire escape plan and practise it. Include two ways of escaping each room in the house and have a designated meeting point outside the house, for example, the letterbox. If you deadlock doors when you're at home, to avoid becoming trapped inside during a fire, always leave the keys in the lock.

Larry the Horse

G'day, Swampy, Lindy here again. Yes, the grey nomads: Lindy the ex-high-school teacher/history buff and my husband, Brian, the old retiree from our local council. Thanks for printing my last story in the outback truckies book. It was a cracker, wasn't it?

Anyhow, just a few weeks ago we had to cut our travels short and come back to Victoria so that Brian could see his specialist. And now, with all these COVID-19 virus restrictions, we can't get out of the place. So we're stuck here. And, with winter coming on, we don't like it one little bit, especially Brian, who, if he's not continually on the move, gets bored and tends to let himself go a bit. So now he's also suffering from gout. But so be it. If I've told him once, I've told him hundreds of times about his drinking. And so, what does he do? No sooner are we back home than he's down in the back shed brewing up yet another batch of beer. Men! I tell you, they never learn.

Now, when we were last talking, I remember you saying how your next book was going to be about the volunteer fire services. Well, while Brian's been down in the back shed brewing his beer, I've been down at the library following up on a few leads. At first I thought about putting a piece together about the Victorian Black Thursday bushfires of early 1851. Has anyone told you about those? Oh dear, they were horrible. Just horrible. They almost burnt out a quarter of the state. Anyhow, while I was thumbing through the history of fires during the 1880s, I stumbled upon a story about Larry the horse. And knowing how much you love horses, I said to Brian, 'Well, perhaps Swampy would prefer this one.' To which he said, 'Yep, go for it.'

So would you like to hear what I've pieced together?

Okay, this all happened in the 1880s before fire engines and all that jazz became so much a part of the scene. Back in those days, firefighting was mostly done by volunteers and local brigades that'd been formed by private citizens or through the local council. In this case it was the Ballarat Council. At that time, the Ballarat City Fire Brigade's main firefighting appliance was a horse named Larry.

Larry the horse was a dapple-grey who stood just over seventeen hands. He was apparently such a character that he was known and loved by every man, woman and child in Ballarat. During that period of time the fire station master was a man named James McKay. James McKay had driven Larry to numerous fires over their many years together where they'd both suffered numerous injuries and burns and so forth. So naturally enough, they'd formed a strong bond.

I've read where Larry had a gentle nature and was quite the ladies' man. James McKay had even taught Larry to lift his hoof and place it in a woman's hand as a form of greeting. And, when he was told that he was going to be kissed by one of the ladies, he'd bow his head in full expectation. But, when called to a fire, there'd be none of those lighthearted shenanigans. It was total focus on the job at hand. At the sound of the alarm bell, Larry would automatically move into position, in readiness for his harness to be fitted and the fire cart to be attached.

Then in the early 1900s, after twenty years of pulling the cart, Larry was retired and sent off to spend the rest of his days in the long paddock, that is, put out to pasture. But then, on 16 January 1902, with the replacement horse having gone lame, Larry was called back into action once more, this time to attend a fire in an outhouse – an outside toilet – in south Ballarat.

Again Larry rose to the occasion. He was placed in his harness and, with James McKay at the reins, they rushed to the scene of the fire. But no sooner had they arrived than Larry dropped dead. Perhaps it was from a heart attack, I don't know. But whatever, down he went, still attached to his harness. A dedicated volunteer firefighter to his very end.

But, Swampy, the story does not end there. Now, I'm still unable to find out what happened to Larry's body but, to honour his memory, the brigade decided to taxidermy and mount Larry's hooves, with his shoes still intact. As far as my research goes, one taxidermied hoof stayed at the Ballarat City Fire Station, where it was apparently used as an ashtray. A second one was presented to the Ballarat Mayor, where it's said to have been used as an inkwell in the Town Hall Chambers, and James McKay was gifted the other two. Anyhow, in due course, James McKay retired and he and his wife moved up to Queensland, horse hooves and all.

Now here's where it becomes very interesting. James McKay's great-grandson, Max Veal, remembered as a child seeing the pair of taxidermied hooves – with their shoes attached – displayed proudly on his great-grandparents' mantelpiece. But he never questioned it. I don't know why, but he didn't. Then after James McKay died, the two hooves were passed down through the generations.

It wasn't until the Ballarat City Fire Brigade's one hundred and fiftieth anniversary celebrations that a relative of Max Veal's was passing through town and he got chatting to a Mr Jones, who'd been a member at the station for forty-odd years. During their chat, the topic of the missing hooves came up. And that's when all the pieces fell together. A year later the great-great-granddaughter of James McKay, Michelle Watson, contacted the Ballarat Fire Brigade Station to arrange a handover of the hooves.

And so, after being separated for a hundred and eighteen years, the four hooves of Larry the horse were reunited, shoes and all. And as Larry had been such an important, much-loved and valued part of the brigade's history, the occasion apparently proved to be quite an emotional one, particularly among some of the older past members.

At the handover, brigade secretary and captain-elect Nicole McGrath told everyone that the reason why Larry the horse was so important to the Ballarat Fire Brigade's past was that – and I quote – 'He [Larry] reminds us of who we are and where we come from.'

Note: The former Ballarat City Fire Station is believed to be the oldest fire station in Victoria to be associated with the volunteer period of the state's firefighting history. At the time of writing this story, Larry's hooves were on display at the fire station, along with other memorabilia, photos and stories from the brigade's past.

The Black Thursday bushfires were a devastating series of fires that began on 6 February 1851 and swept through the state of Victoria. The fires burnt out five million hectares – equivalent to almost a quarter of the entire state. Twelve lives were lost along with a million sheep, thousands of cattle and countless native animals.

The bushfires were a result of heatwave conditions and careless burning off.

One Tree Hill

I've got three service medals. The first is for my service to the South Australian Emergency Fire Service – EFS – which, in 1976, had a name change to the CFS – Country Fire Service. Then my second medal is for my inclusive years of involvement with the SA Emergency Services. That was awarded in 2006. In all, a total of fifty-nine years of service. Then there's the biggest of them all, my AFSM – Australian Fire Service Medal – which is for my distinguished service as a member of an Australian fire service.

I grew up about twelve miles out of Gawler, at a place called Reeves Plains. From Reeves Plains my parents bought a beautiful forty-acre property near the little rural hamlet of One Tree Hill. Of course, it's now a suburb of Adelaide. But back then there were only seven families within a two-mile radius of us.

One Tree Hill was a great place for a kid to grow up. There were plenty of rabbits, foxes, pigeons and wild duck to hunt, along with numerous old mine shafts to explore. To start with, there was no telephone. We had no electricity, so everything was lit by kerosene lamp, and, with the land being far too hilly to ride a pushbike, I had to walk to school. The first school I attended was a small transportable, three kilometres from home, at Tenafeate Creek. Then, when our numbers dropped below six, Tenafeate was closed and I had to walk the extra distance to Uleybury.

Dad was a fire control officer and, when we had a fire, he'd fill milk cans with water and it was my job to soak the jute bags in the cans. These wet bags were then taken to the fire front and handed out. Other firefighting aides at that time were knapsacks, leather beaters and green boughs – tree branches. Later on I remember a great advancement, when a neighbour put a forty-four-gallon drum and a hand pump on the back of his truck.

One of my most vivid memories of a fire was when I was eight or nine, watching in awe as a large bushfire ravaged the hills south of Gawler. I've heard that it was one of the biggest fires on record to that date. Now, whether or not that had any bearing on my future involvement as a volunteer firefighter, I don't know. But I suspect it might have.

That fire was apparently lit by sparks from a steam train that was travelling along the Gawler to Adelaide rail line. The fire then took off, crossing Main North Road, burning uphill through Bentley, Bibaringa and Yattalunga and crossing the One Tree Hill-Gawler Road. With a wind change, it then turned north-east, crossing the South Para River. A lot of volunteers were involved and I can still recall the incredible speed it travelled.

Now, that might've even been one of the first fires that the Yattalunga Pastoral Company's 1944 Lend Lease Ford appliance attended. It was normally used to transport stock to and from Gepps Cross markets plus for general running around. And in this case, even though it was on a well-made road, it failed to travel uphill as fast as the fire, which resulted in the old Ford and its crew experiencing a burnover. A burnover is when a fire front burns right over the top of you. And considering that the truck had no sides, it was some sort of miracle that no one was hurt or killed.

I left school when I was fourteen and started working for neighbours, splitting posts and stripping wattles for bark. We had a dozen or so cows at home so I helped hand-milk them and, as a personal enterprise, I built up a flock of fowls and sold their eggs to Brown Bros in Gawler. Then at fifteen I got into shearing and, over the next thirty years, I sheared all over the state.

During the Black Sunday fires of January 1955, it became obvious that the EFS needed far better communications. To that end, some locals – Eldred Riggs, Lawrence Bills and John Barritt – started work on building one of the first firefighting communication systems in South Australia. It was based on the ex-army FS 6 radios.

Later on I recall meeting with Eldred Riggs and trialling an ex-army field telephone that he hoped could be used for emergency calls. After placing a ladder against a telephone pole, we attached two wires to the phone line and, when we wound the handle on the field phone, we got through to the local manual exchange.

It was a good idea, but it had a few drawbacks: firstly, it was highly illegal to tap into a telephone line; secondly, there weren't too many telephone lines in the district to tap into; thirdly, not many people carried around ladders so that you could climb a telephone pole; and, lastly, telephone exchanges weren't manned on a twenty-four-hour basis. So in the end, radio became the preferred means of communication.

One of the first fires I actually attended would've been around 1958. That was on a property owned by John Poole Snr. It'd started from machinery that was working in scrub. Because the fire was adjoining the pine forest, Wally Barring from Forestry organised for a huge bulldozer to come and push a firebreak through the scrub, in readiness for a back-burn.

The dozer arrived after dark and, due to the large number of disused mine shafts in the area, it was decided that two people should walk in front of the dozer, carrying a light and flag, to safely guide it along. Now, I don't know how it came about but somehow myself and Doug McKenzie landed the job. And I must say it was quite nerve-racking walking in front of the bulldozer, at night, navigating mine shafts, with ten-metre-tall red gum saplings crashing down behind us.

The Snake Gully area was also a particularly bad spot for fires. One of the most devastating fires of Black Sunday began there as a rekindle from a dead tree, and another started from what appeared to be teenagers smoking out rabbits.

I married my wife, Dawn, in April 1961, and we lived in One Tree Hill. Dawn passed away about eighteen months ago and is still greatly missed. After the One Tree Hill Brigade was formed, she did a lot of the base radio work from the fire station, plus she helped out wherever she could, and later on our son also became very involved. Even as a youngster he used to put up a flag to signify when the fire appliance was out.

It's just struck me how Dawn's memories of the 1955 Black Sunday fires were extremely vivid and unpleasant. At that time she lived at Inglewood, where she lost her next-door neighbour to the fire. She also had to help fight spot fires in and around her family home. And one of her starkest memories was of looking out her front window and seeing one end of their pine hedge burst alight, and by the time she turned to look at the other end of the hedge, the whole lot had been engulfed in flames. Such was the speed and ferocity of the fire.

Anyhow, when Yattalunga Pastoral Company was sold, the old 1944 Ford truck went up for sale. And that would've meant the loss of our main firefighting vehicle. So a group of eight of us got together, and on Sunday 2 December 1960 we met in front of the One Tree Hill Post Office and formed the brigade.

As I was secretary, I then registered us with EFS's Adelaide headquarters. As it happened, Yattalunga Pastoral Company then donated the 1944 Ford to council, who then passed it on to us. We had a number of working bees and, with great district support, together with funds from the council, modifications to the old truck were undertaken. These included putting crew protection on the sides of the vehicle and installing a limited-range radio.

Another feature included a hole being cut through the cabin roof, near the driver's seat. A piece of suction pipe was then fitted through the hole, which had a funnel attached to its other end so that someone on the rear of the appliance could speak to the driver. If that failed to gain the driver's attention, a quick squirt of water down the pipe certainly did. The truck's water tank carried four hundred gallons, and Frank McKenzie fitted an anti-spill device to the lid to stop excessive splashing, and baffles which restricted surging.

Tribute for much of this work must be given to Frank. While he wasn't a qualified engineer, he had an amazing understanding of mechanics. He spent hours fitting an Ajax gear pump underneath the four-wheel drive that ran off the transmission. From the pump he ran a length of one and a half inch water pipe along the side of the truck, to the rear of the driver's cabin door. He then fitted a gate valve to the pump.

With the driver having clear vision of the water spray on the fire's edge he was then able to vary his speed, dependent on flame height and intensity of the fire. What's more, the new configuration allowed the driver to put the truck in gear and drive along and single-handedly douse a fire. With Frank being a farm manager on Henry Barritt's property, most of the work was done there. And of course the truck was then painted red, with 'One Tree Hill EFS' sign-written on its side.

Due to population growth, the number of fires in the One Tree Hill district have increased over the years and we started attending more structure fires and vehicle accidents. Some of those you never forget, especially when young children are involved.

Of course, there was no counselling back then. We were only talking about this the other day: about how, rather than letting it build up in our systems, when we got back to the station we'd sit around and have a couple of beers and discuss what'd happened. There was no malice. It was pretty much matter-of-fact. 'Okay, what did we do right? What did we do wrong? And what could we do better next time?' And I found that to be a successful way of helping deal with an extremely tough incident.

But you've always got to remain positive. And over a period of time, hopefully you learn not to repeat the same mistakes, plus you learn how to look after yourself and your brigade mates. Probably one of the scariest times I've had was when I found myself in a situation where I shouldn't have been. It was an innocent-looking fire. I was halfway up a hill, on the end of a hose, with a blackberry patch in a gully below me.

Once the fire hit the blackberries – *whoosh!* – up she came, straight over me. Fortunately, the driver stayed where he was and I doused myself with water until the fire had passed. So that really put the wind up me because back then our protective clothing was little more than khaki overalls and berets and we had minimal water pressure.

Note 1: This story is adapted from Rex Hall's self-published autobiography *Forty Five Flaming Years*.

Note 2: The South Australian Black Sunday fires of January 1955 spread over more than forty thousand hectares. Forty homes were lost plus other buildings including the Governor's summer residence at Norton Summit. Over fifty people were injured and two firefighters lost their lives. After one thousand Emergency Fire Service members, from sixty brigades, were overwhelmed by the fires, requests were made for public assistance and around 2500 citizens volunteered.

The cause of the fire was put down to sparks from clashing powerlines during extreme heat conditions and high winds.

Sacked

Well, I joined the firies because a) they were looking for members and b) a few of me mates was already in it. There was no wages or nothing. It was all volunteer. Oh, I think we might've got ten bob or something for going to a fire. And we didn't have much equipment. Matter of fact, only the driver and one passenger could sit in the cabin and the rest of us either sat or stood up on the back of the fire truck or we took our own vehicles.

We didn't do much of the bushfire type work. Those usually happened further out of town on the properties and the farmers mostly looked after them with their utes, which had water tanks on the back. We mainly did around the town area, where we pumped the water out of fire hydrants which come out of the mains. This would've been back in the late '50s, early '60s I reckon. But they weren't the standing-up hydrants that you sometimes see. These were the hydrants in the road with a metal or concrete plate over them and there was a sign on a post near the gutter telling you where they were. So you just took the plate off and tapped into those. Funny things you take for granted, ay. And we only had canvas hoses too. So if the fire was a bit down the road, we'd have to click all the hoses together so we could reach out to the distance.

Back in the December of 1950, before I was in the brigade, we had a real bad fire. That would've been when Ronny What's-his-name was brigade captain. It was the McHughs' fire. They had a new house, out on the edge of town, and because the water hadn't yet been connected out that far, there was nothing they could do about it.

It happened during the day. It was summer, as hot as Hades, and the children were asleep in one of the rooms. The mother had just popped over to visit her mother-in-law – one hundred and fifty yards away – and when she looked out the mother-in-law's window she saw flames and smoke coming out of her house. Three of the youngest children out of the six kids in the family got burnt up in that one. Terrible it was. Actually, just yesterday, I tried ringing old George to come over and tell you all about it because he would've been one of the blokes who was in the brigade back then. But because he's deaf, he hardly ever gets to answer the phone these days.

Then there was old Dolfy Smith's place – or was it old Billy Wilson's place? See, Dolfy was me mate Andy's grandfather's brother or something. Dolfy was an SP – starting price – bookie and, when Andy was a kid, he used to be a runner for old Dolfy. By 'runner', I mean he'd run around town getting everyone's bets, then he'd run the money back to Dolfy, who'd lay the bet. I think they used to call Dolfy 'one 'n six' or something. The SP was very illegal of course. Well, old Dolfy lived just across the road from where old Billy Wilson lived, right on the corner and – that's right – it was old Billy Wilson's place that was burnt down. And that was also a long time before I was in the brigade.

When I was in the brigade, one fire I remember was when the Galah – Gulargambone – hotel went up. Galah's about thirty mile from here and they called us down because it looked like they was going to lose the pub. So we jumped into the old Bedford and off we went. It was in the middle of winter and it was bloody freezing. I was driving and there was another chap in with me and, because no one wanted to sit on the back all the way to Galah, in the middle of winter, the rest of the blokes went in cars.

So I'm driving along. It's a dirt road. No bitumen back in them days. Anyhow, the old Bedford couldn't go too fast and this other car pulls out and starts coming round us. I said to the chap who was in with me, 'I bet this feller'll break our windscreen.'

And sure enough, as he come around past us – *bang!* – out goes our windscreen. So we had to drive the rest of the way to Galah without a windscreen, in the freezing bloody cold.

Anyhow, we saved a lot of the pub.

With it being in the middle of winter, the rest of the blokes got to warming themselves up by drinking rum. But because I was off the grog, I went over to the café to have a coffee. But drinking rum was standard in them days. They reckoned it was good for you. Now I don't know about that but wherever there was a fire you always took rum. So then I had to drive the old Bedford back home, dripping wet from putting the fire out, with no bloody windscreen, in the freezing bloody cold, while the chap that was in with me kept himself nice and warm knocking off what was left of the rum.

But the worst fire I ever went to was when a cattle truck overturned. It was empty. There was no cattle in it, thank the heavens. As it happened, the brigade captain at the time was a feller who worked for me as a rep at the tyre service I was managing. So I was his boss at work and he was my boss at the fires. Anyhow, a young mate of mine named Doylie and me were in the pub one night when two police came in to get us. From memory they were a feller named Meyers and another feller who I've forgot. They said that a truck had overturned out near Sandhurst. It was still alight and they wanted us to take the fire extinguishers out to put it out.

'Is there anyone in the truck?' we asked.

'No, I don't think so,' they said.

'Okay,' we said, 'we'll follow you out.'

So we got the extinguishers. The police were in their car and young Doylie was driving mine. I think Doylie might've even been on his P plates. But that didn't matter. There was no heed to that because we ended up following the police out there, at about a hundred mile an hour. When we got there we extinguished the fire. That was all okay. But then, when we looked into the cab of the truck, there was a charred body in it. Now for some reason or other that I can't remember, we ended up coming back to town with the charred body in the boot of my car. And, oh my God, it took me weeks and weeks to get the smell out of it.

I stayed on with the brigade till '74. What happened in the finish was, we were at this fire and the brigade captain – the feller who I was the boss of at work and he was my boss out at the fires – he said, 'Come on, let's pack up. We're goin' home.' And like he'd had a few rums. You could drink and drive back in them days.

Anyhow, I didn't think the fire was properly out, so I said to him, 'I don't think we should leave things as they are because I reckon it could easily flare up again.'

And oh, didn't he get all uppity at that. Like I said, he'd been drinking, and so he said to me, 'You're not telling me what I can or what I can't do.' He said, 'You're sacked.'

So bugger it, I didn't even help to clean up or anything. I just got back in me car and I went home. Then at about half past eleven that night the wife wakes me up. She said, 'You'd better get out of bed. The siren's gone off.'

I said, 'Well, I can't help them. I can't go. I've been sacked.'

And it was the same fire again. It'd flared up like I told the brigade captain it would. So I guess they must've eventually put it out. I don't know. I wasn't there. I was still in bed. But anyhow, that brigade captain, the feller who sacked me from the volunteer fire brigade, I ended up sacking him from his job at the tyre service because of his drinking. He loved his rum too much. But he never spoke to me for a long while after that.

Note: Rum has a long history in Australia. After arriving with the First Fleet in 1788 it instantly became a form of currency – administered, in large, by the officers of the New South Wales Corps, who became known as the Rum Corps.

When Governor Bligh arrived in Sydney in 1806 he prohibited the use of rum as payment. In doing so, he made many enemies, including John Macarthur, a former member of the Corps. The conflict came to a head when the Rum Corps stormed Government House and arrested Bligh, who it's rumoured they found hiding under his bed.

Two years of military rule ensued. Two years later the Marine Corps was recalled to England, curbing the trade in rum.

The drinking of rum is believed by some to give you a strong healthy heart in that it may decrease cholesterol levels, be beneficial in the prevention of peripheral artery disease and act as a blood thinner, thus helping clear artery blockages and preventing heart attacks and heart disease.

The negative effects include slurred speech, drowsiness, vomiting, diarrhoea, upset stomach, headaches, breathing difficulties, distorted vision and hearing, liver and heart disease leading to death ... amongst other effects.

Burnt Offerings

My wife and I used to live in a place called Hamlet Grove, which is up in the Kimberley region of Western Australia, just out of Derby. And while Derby had its own Fire and Rescue Brigade, it was only after we'd had a fire in Hamlet Grove village that we started thinking about forming a brigade of our own. So we called a public meeting and everyone was all for it. We then put a proposal to Derby Shire Council, who accepted it. Following that, we contacted DFESWA – Department of Fire and Emergency Services of Western Australia – and got the ball rolling to sort out all the official stuff.

Once that was done we got a fire truck from Fitzroy Crossing. It was an old '64 Dodge four-wheel drive which was set up with some of their old gear. At that stage we didn't have anywhere to house the truck, so it ended up in one of our guys' sheds. DFES then supplied our basic equipment and gave us some bushfire training. And we just worked up from there. The shire paid for our uniforms and they also requisitioned a block of land where we could build a proper shed. The shed was built by us volunteers, which saved on labour costs. Our fire chief was a builder. I did all the electrical work. We had a couple of plumbers in the brigade. A lot of the shed fit-out was donated by the local hardware store, people donated the paint and so forth and we had a bore put down.

By 2000, Hamlet Grove Volunteer Bush Fire Brigade was up and running. While Derby Fire and Rescue had all the proper gear to enter burning buildings and to attend road crashes and chemical spills, we were trained for bushfires so we could only fight house fires from outside the premises. Even so we do help the Derby mob on occasions, as they do us. So that's the set-up. We assist each other. It's kind of a shared thing.

We began with about eighteen members in total, which was almost everyone from around the village. Some were women. We don't discriminate. Then we had a number of associate members who were mainly the wives and partners of our volunteers. These associate members also did a basic firefighting course so that if we were out on a long shift, they could bring food and supplies out onto the fireground.

The brigade's very much a community hub. Our fire station's set up so that, while we're doing our training, the kids can sit in the shed and watch videos or television. We put swings up outside and there's a big lawn area where they can play cricket or kick the crap out of a football. From the word go I was the comms – communications – and equipment officer. Then, after I had the big heart problem and my wife and I started travelling more often, I said, 'It's time for someone else to step up and do it.' So now I just do the electrical work when it's needed and I occasionally mow the lawn.

But over the years we've had quite a few, shall I say, 'different' events – like the night we got a fire call from a nearby town. Now, by the rules, if you have two vollies – volunteers – available, you can go, which we did, me and another guy. And because there was no water out there we took our 3000-litre tanker. So the two of us jumped in the truck and off we went.

When we arrived we couldn't see any smoke. This's strange, we thought. Then while we were doing a drive around, three young teenagers flagged us down. 'The fire were in the house over there,' they said, 'but we put it out with a fire extinguisher 'n we've turned the power off 'n opened up all the windows to let the smoke out.'

'Good. Thanks,' we said and so we pulled up outside the front of the house. I got out and double-checked that the power had been switched off and, sure enough, the teenagers had done the job. The place looked structurally okay so we then decided to go inside and have a look around. I opened the front door and, being night-time plus with the power having been turned off, I couldn't see a bloody thing. So I turned on the torch and shone it towards the back of the house. Everything looked okay, so I took a couple of steps inside and arse-over-tit I go, over this mattress which had a bloke sound asleep on it. Dead to the world. Totally unaware of what'd happened. So I picked myself up and continued on in.

We made our way to the kitchen. I'm leading and my mate's behind me. A stove's over in the corner. Its outsides were all blackened, so that's where we figured the fire had been. Out the front of the oven, there's a baking tray with the remains of a half-cremated bird laying in it. At first we thought it was a chicken but on closer inspection it more resembled a bush turkey. Anyhow, to make sure there were no other fire spots, we continued checking the place.

And that's when a hell of a racket starts up from a room behind us. As we swung around, this huge mountain of a feller came tearing out of the gloom, yelling and screaming about how we've wrecked his bloody dinner. And he's fearsome. He's out to get us good and proper. Like he's gonna do this to us and he's gonna do that to us. The whole bloody works. So while I was trying to calm him down, me and my mate started backing away.

But the feller's not going to have a bar of it. He's got his fists in my face, ready to have a go. So we step back a bit more. Just as we do, he picks up this half-cremated bush turkey and he starts swinging the bloody thing around, threatening us. *Thwack. Crack.* Bits of bird and crap are flying off everywhere, and he's as angry as hell that we've buggered up his dinner.

It was no use trying to calm him down. Nothing would. So while he's flailing this half-cremated bird around at us, we're slowly edging our way out of the place. My mate makes it outside. Then just as I take my last step, arse-over-tit I go, over the bloody mattress again, flat on top of the bloke who's still fast asleep. Dead to the world. Just as I pick myself up from there to make my escape, this big feller goes for me. In doing so, arse-over-tit he goes, flat on top of the bloke who's asleep on the mattress – *thud* – and he's still swearing and cursing with the half-cremated bird in his hand.

Anyway, me and my mate get outside. The three teenagers are still there, amused at what's going on. I said, 'You'd better go in and try and quieten that big bloke down – he's pretty agitated.'

'Yeah,' they said, 'he's not real happy about youse blokes wreckin' 'is dinner.'

I said, 'But you were the ones who put the fire out in the stove with the extinguisher.'

'Doesn't matter,' they said. 'He thinks it were youse.'

'Okay. Fine,' I said. 'But you'd better sort him out or he's gonna kill someone.'

'Okay,' they said, and they go inside only to be confronted by a bout of yelling and screaming.

By now we're heading to the truck, right, to make our escape. Next thing one of the teenagers comes flying out the front door. By flying, I mean flying. He'd been bodily picked up and tossed out. *Splat!* He lands flat on his face into the dirt with the other two teenagers tearing out after him. Right behind them is the big feller, still wielding the half-cremated bush turkey. Bits of charcoal are flying off it, feathers and whatever else, and he's dead-set on cleaning up the teenagers. But being young and agile, they're out of there like greased lightning – *zoom!*

So then the feller looks around and he sees us. By this time we're in the truck, where I thought we'd be safe. But no. He's now up at the front of our big four-by-four cab-over and he's bashing what's left of this poor bloody half-cremated bird on the front of the truck and all over the windscreen. Bits and pieces of mangled carcass and shit all over the place. So I get the truck going and I'm backing out of there. But he's still coming at us. So I blow the horn and put the headlights on him – high beam. That sort of blinded him a bit, so now he's backing off. Beauty, I put the foot down and we take off out of there.

Just as we get to the road out of the town, I said to my mate, 'Gee, I think we're dragging something.'

So when we get a bit further along the track, I stop the truck and we get out to have a look. Lo 'n behold, we're dragging part of a fence. When I'd backed up, I must've hooked the truck's towbar onto the next-door neighbour's fence and when we took off, it came with us.

Anyhow, there's no one around so, 'Bugger it,' we said and we threw the bloody fence into the bush.

When we got home, the front of the truck was a hell of a mess. Blood, guts, feathers, the lot. So I left my mate to do the best he could with it and I went into the shed to write up the incident report, to email down to DFES head office in Perth. On these reports you have to give a brief outline of what the job was and if any injuries were sustained by the firies and all that sort of stuff. Anyhow, I just put down: 'Two vollies assaulted by an extremely large male wielding a cremated bush turkey. No injuries, except to the turkey.' And I just left it at that and emailed it off.

About ten minutes later I get a phone call. It's from the boss-feller in Perth. 'What's this about you fellers being assaulted by someone wielding a cremated bush turkey?'

. So I start telling him the story, right. As I do, I hear all this raucous laughter going on in the background of the Perth office. Next thing there's this huge *crash!* which is followed by a silence.

I said, 'What the hell was that?'

Then a different voice came on the line. 'Don't worry, the boss was pissing himself laughing so much that he fell off his chair.'

Note: The Australian bush turkey or scrub turkey, otherwise known as a brush turkey or gweela, is a common widespread mound-building bird that is protected under the Nature Conservation Act of 1992. Bush turkeys are a nuisance as they remove the vegetation and earth from home gardens to create their incubation mounds – mounds that can get up to four metres wide and two metres long. The female lays up to twenty-four eggs and the young hatch after about seven weeks.

Unlike a lot of other native animals, the bush turkey is not a preferred wildlife food. As one recipe goes, 'After extensive boiling in a pot with a stone, toss the bush turkey and eat the stone.'

Bush turkeys have been known to mate with hens and it's possible for the offspring to resemble half a chicken and half a bush turkey. As author Bill 'Swampy' Marsh advises, 'Even then they're not good eating.'

Always Take a Torch

Nita and me live just out of Bogan Gate, in the central-west of New South Wales, about forty mile west of Parkes. Parkes is where they have that big Elvis Presley Festival each year. Our property is off Coombs Lane East and, with me being a Coombs, you might think that the lane's named after me. But it isn't. It was named after my grandfather.

Grandad first came up here from the Seymour area of Victoria back in 1886 to inspect the property blocks that'd been put up for ballot. And by gee they did it tough, because Grandad and three of his mates rode all the way up here on their pushbikes. True. One story goes that on the way up here, one of the blokes broke the chain on his pushbike so they joined their handkerchiefs together and towed him the rest of the way.

After going through all that, Grandpa missed out in the first ballot. But a bloke who'd drawn a block didn't have the fifty-quid deposit he needed and Grandpa got his block in a redraw. So that's how our family got up here. Then in the 1920s my dad bought the farm alongside Grandad's. I was born in 1934, so I never got around to learning the computer and, because we're in a black spot, I don't even have a mobile phone neither. And now I'm getting phone calls telling me that they're going to cut off our landline because the NBN is supposed to be coming through. But it isn't, at least not from what I have heard. So with all this misleading information going around, I just tell them to drop dead. So we'll see what happens.

I left school at fourteen to go on the farm, working for Dad for thirty bob a week. It was mostly wheat and sheep, and still is. The properties were smaller in them early days so there was a lot more people around. I even started up a cricket club. In fact, Jimmy Taylor, who went on to be our local member of parliament, played cricket with us. Also a neighbour, Ian Walsh, who went on to captain Australia in rugby league, he played cricket with us as well. He's dead now, but he had a good career.

As for the volunteer fire brigade, like a lot of us, I joined when I was fourteen. There was nothing official. We only had a fire drill once a year so we mostly learnt on the job by helping out neighbours and them helping us out. It was just the done thing. And we didn't have any equipment.

My first piece of firefighting gear was either a leafy green branch broke off from a tree or a wet wheat bag. And I can tell you, thrashing a wet wheat bag at a bushfire soon knocked you up quick-smart. Then a bit later on all us farmers started filling up our empty forty-four-gallon drums with water so, when there was a fire, we'd just roll them straight onto the back of a ute or a small truck and drive them out to the fire. We'd then use a small motor-pump to spray the water on the fire or we'd fill up knapsacks from the forty-fours.

We were known as the Bedgerabong Brigade and with the Gunningbland Shire boundary being across the road from my grandfather's place, they had their own brigade. They were a bit more well-off with equipment than we were. One time they gave us a one-horsepower Cooper petrol-driven pump that they were having trouble starting. But one of our blokes said, 'Oh, I'll get it going.'

Anyhow, he pulled out the choke, wobbled it back and forward till the petrol dripped out of the carburettor, then he pulled the starter cord and away she went. 'See,' he said, 'it's easy. Just prime it.'

As for memories, there was the fire in 1952. It'd been a wet year so the plains grass was over a yard tall. Then after it'd dried out, a lightning strike hit and away she went. By the time Clem, my brother, and I arrived, a few older farmers and some young ones were already there. Anyhow, one of the blokes had an old Chevy truck with a few forty-four-gallon drums of water on it so we decided to go out in that to do some back-burning. We stuck three young blokes on the back, along with the one-horsepower Cooper pump that we'd hooked up to an inch hose, and Bill Hodges and me jumped in the front with Neil Scott driving.

Now, if you can imagine it, there was a paddock here and a road going down that way and we headed off to start this back-burn. We were basically chasing the fire across the paddock. But it was an uphill battle. We'd put out a fire here and, when you'd look up, another one would've started over there. Next it'd surrounded us. To try and escape it, Neil cranked the Chevy up to about twenty-five mile an hour and even then the fire was jumping right over the top of us. Frightened all heck out of us.

But once we got out of the plains grass onto ground that'd been grazed, it became more manageable. Then just as we thought we'd got it under control, the wind changed and the fire started heading towards town. They reckon when one feller in the pub went outside to the toilet and he seen the fire coming, the pub got emptied out quick-smart. Anyhow, we eventually got it under control just before it got to town and the pub was soon back to business as usual.

But in the end there were too many little brigades and not enough people to work them. So a lot amalgamated. Bogan Gate Brigade area now goes from the railway line to the shire boundary, and we've been given a lot better equipment. Nice trucks and four-wheel drives. Decent-capacity water tanks and pumps and hoses that throw a good jet of water. We've even got a new fire shed.

And we're a lot more organised. We've now got an area group captain and a fire controller feller has a set-up in Forbes where all the trucks are checked. A couple of years ago the commissioner came and handed out medals to anyone who'd done more than five years' service. With me having near on sixty years' official service, I got a heap of them. Oh, Nita, we should've brought my fifty-year-service medals to show Swampy. I forgot about that. And with a couple of others having joined the same time as me, and seeing how Jimmy Percival was three years ahead of us, the feller said, 'There's over two hundred years of firefighting experience here.'

Another memory I have is when we went to a fire out from Parkes. It was started by a lightning strike in the hills and their local powers-that-be said, 'We'll keep an eye on it overnight and you fellers can take over in the morning.'

There was about half a dozen of us from Bogan Gate and the idea was that, because they had better trucks and equipment, we'd take over their gear in the morning to give them a spell. Anyhow, we got there that evening and stayed overnight in the backyard of the office. Then about six thirty the next morning a Salvation Army bloke turned up with a trailer and a barbecue. After we helped him set up, he got the kettle going and he started cooking us sausages and eggs. This is good, we thought, but then a bloke in a bus turned up. 'All aboard,' he said. 'Don't worry about taking any tucker with you. There'll be plenty out where you're going.'

So he drives us out into the middle of a national park to wait to do this truck changeover with the local brigade. He drops us off, then he takes off. So we sat around for about forty minutes. And nothing. No one turns up. So we sat a while longer. Still nothing. A while later we get the news that the local mob had refused to hand over their trucks. 'No,' they'd said, 'we're not turning our equipment over to them Bogan Gate blokes. We're taking it all home.'

There was still smoke up in the hills, so the fire was still going. But without any transport we were stuck. So we just sat around twiddling our thumbs. Oh, that's right, we did do something: we cleared an area for a helicopter to land. Mind you, by this stage we hadn't had anything to eat since the night before. Then at about 3 o'clock that afternoon the Salvation Army bloke turns up again, this time with a load of curried prawns and rice. I mean, none of us were too keen on that sort of tucker, but it was better than nothing. But a few of us were getting worried how our wives might be worried because they hadn't heard from us. The thing was, there was nowhere to ring from to let them know we were okay.

Then eventually a police paddy wagon turned up. So we conned them into taking us out to the Parkes-Orange road. 'Okay,' they said and, after we'd all crammed ourselves into the back of the paddy wagon and they'd shut us in, off we went. Problem being, one of our fellers went into a panic because he couldn't stand being locked up in confined spaces.

So we started bashing on the back of the police paddy wagon to try and get them to stop, which they did. And after we explained what the problem was, they decided to leave the back door open and they took off again. So I don't know what people would've thought at seeing this police paddy wagon flying by, with its back door flapping in the wind and us blokes sticking our heads out the back, trying to get some fresh air.

Anyhow, when we eventually got to the fire, it was mostly over so we started the clean-up. And you wouldn't believe it, just as we'd finished, someone turned up with some sandwiches. So we wolfed into those. Then it would've been about 11 o'clock that night when a bus came to take us back to Parkes. When we got there, I rang Nita and asked her to let everyone know that we were okay. So I'd say it would've been midnight by the time we got home, and so that was that one.

Another time a brake pad had come loose on one of the bulk carriages of a train that was passing through town and it was hitting the tracks and throwing sparks everywhere. So someone got in touch with someone else to tell the train driver to pull up his train. But by the time it'd come to a stop up near the old army camp, a fire had started running up into the hills. So into the truck and off we went. When we got there, the train driver had pulled up his train carriages right over the bloody railway crossing, hadn't he, and we couldn't get across the track to go up the hill to fight the fire. So then someone had to run all the way down to the locomotive and tell the driver to shunt his train on a bit.

So you live and learn, ay? Simple stuff like raking the burning bark off a tree and then dampening it so you don't waste water. And how you should shovel the burning fuel back onto the fire, which then makes a bare patch of soil around the fire that acts as a firebreak. Another thing is, of a night, always take a torch with you. Because once you've put the fire out you'll end up stuck in the dark tripping over rocks and tree stumps and all that.

But even though I still belong to the brigade, I've had to give up going to fires. Because one thing we stick by is to never put yourself in a situation where someone else might have to come and save you. We had a fire out in the hills a while back. Our captain was in Sydney so the vice-captain and another couple of blokes went out. One of them shouldn't have gone in the first place because he wasn't well. When he started walking up the hill he got chest pains, so the vice-captain had to turn around and take him out to get him attended to. So then they were two men down. And with me now being eighty-five and having had two knee replacements I thought that all made sense. Don't risk someone else's life if you're not up to the job.

Note 1: The township of Bogan Gate featured the first 'unofficial' international horse polo game between Australia and Great Britain. The event came about through a challenge between the noted Anglo-Australian drover, horseman, bush poet and military officer Harry 'Breaker' Morant and the Scottish-Australian poet Will Ogilvie. The game itself was penned by Ogilvie in his poem, 'For The Honour of Old England and The Glory of the Game'.

In 1902, 'Breaker' Morant was convicted and executed for murder during the Second Anglo-Boer War in Pretoria, South Africa. He's been immortalised in both the film and in the stage play *Breaker Morant.*

Note 2: Ian Walsh was born in Bogan Gate in March 1933. He went on to represent the Sydney-based rugby league team St George during their eleven-year consecutive premierships from 1956 to 1966. He also represented the Australian 'Kangaroos' and captained the team in ten test matches from 1963 to 1966. He died in April 2013.

Note 3: Author Bill 'Swampy' Marsh has family buried in the Bogan Gate cemetery.

Scrotum

My surname is Simpfendorfer. For most people, Simpfendorfer is far too long to pronounce and far too hard to spell, so they just call me Simpy. Though mind you, Simpfendorfer consists of thirteen letters, which for some might be unlucky. But not for me. Thirteen is my lucky number. So there you go.

Now, as to the volunteer fire service, the Simpfendorfer-Powel family – Powel being my mother's maiden name – has had a very long association with the service. My uncle, Dad's brother, Uncle Bill – who incidentally was known as Old Bill to avoid any confusion with his son, Young Bill – was captain of the Henty Brigade for many years. Henty being in south-western New South Wales. Then a cousin, Joe Wilson, has just retired from the Henty Brigade after having chalked up fifty years.

My brother was in the Cootamundra Brigade – Coota as the place is better known – and he was captain there for a number of years. My brother-in-law, my sister's husband, Guy McAllister, was in the brigades at Wellington, Young and Dubbo, and my other cousin, Jim Powell, was captain of the brigade at Helensburgh, in the New South Wales South Coast region of Illawarra. He also chalked up fifty years – including many as captain – during which time he was in charge of the first emergency vehicle to arrive at the Waterfall train disaster, keeping in mind that the volunteer fire services are also involved in the rescue side of things.

The Waterfall train disaster occurred back in early 2003 when a train heading south along the Illawarra line derailed and overturned into the rocky walls of a cutting. The Illawarra line runs from Central Station right down to Dapto to which, these days, if you're a senior or a pensioner you can travel return for just $2.50. From memory, something like half a dozen people were killed in the Waterfall train disaster, plus there were numerous injuries and many people were trapped in the overturned carriages. It was a full-on emergency response and, as I said, cousin Jim Powell and his Helensburgh Brigade were the first on the scene.

Anyhow, I joined the Coota Fire Brigade in the early '60s. We didn't do much formal training. A lot of it was common sense in evaluating the risks. I would've been about nineteen and, like I said, my brother was already a member of the brigade, so I knew most of the other dozen or so blokes who were in it. There were no permanents. We were all volunteers, and other than the strong family connections, I guess the other reason I joined was, well, someone's got to help put the fires out.

At that time I was working at Public Works. There would've been about thirty people employed there, so it was quite big. And because we looked after all public buildings, an architectural section was included and water supply was also a big part of it. Public Works oversaw the pipeline system that pumped water from the Murrumbidgee River, at Jugiong, via Harden-Murrumburrah, Cootamundra, right through to West Wyalong.

We were housed in an old weatherboard building and, during the cooler months, the gardener-maintenance man used to light the open fires in an attempt to warm the place up. Morning tea around the open fire used to be a real social occasion. It was a chance for a chinwag and to catch up on the gossip. Anyhow, just after I joined the Coota Fire Brigade, they decided to have a bit of fun at my expense. They got some typing carbon – remember that black typing carbon? – and they put it in the open fire. It not only burnt real well, but it also created stacks of smoke. So then they called me on the intercom: 'We've got a fire. You'd better come and put it out.'

On my way down there I grabbed one of those soda-acid fire extinguishers – the ones you had to turn upside down so the acid would mix with the soda to create the stream. There was only one problem with them: being a pressurised container, once it was inverted and you started spurting out the water mixture through the hose, there was no way of turning them off. So – *squirt* – I quickly put the fire out. Then I handed the still madly squirting extinguisher over to someone. 'There you go,' I said. 'Job done. See yer later,' and I disappeared back into my office, leaving them to clean up a huge mess. So that little lark backfired on them.

Another thing that comes to mind from those early days was when we had a big grassfire, just over the railway line, off Temora Road. It was Christmas Day and, still being new to the brigade, I was yet to be issued with my firefighting gear. When I arrived at the fire station, I didn't have any firefighting boots. So I looked around and I thought, Well, who's away for Christmas? I'll borrow their boots. Then it struck me: Gee, I think Leo's gone off taking a break somewhere.

So I grabbed Leo's boots and off I went to fight this grassfire. Next thing, lo 'n behold, Leo turns up wearing a brand-new pair of slippers he'd just got for Christmas. And I can tell you, he was none too pleased about that because I'd not only nicked his boots but, by the time we'd put the fire out, his slippers were wrecked. For years after that particular fire it was, 'You still owe me a new pair of slippers, Simpy!'

So there's just a couple of memories from my first stint in the brigade at Coota. I then left Coota in June '64 and, over the next few years, I worked in various divisions of Public Works throughout New South Wales. But even after I got married and we'd had kids, whenever we came back to Coota to visit Mum and Dad, it'd also give me the chance to catch up with my old firie mates.

Then as it happened, I got a move back to Coota in '81 and probably the biggest fire I went to during that time was when the showground grandstand went up. And Leo – the feller who turned up at the grassfire in his slippers because I'd inadvertently borrowed his firefighting boots – well, he was tied up with trotters. And when the news of the fire came through, he said, 'No, it can't be.' He said, 'I've only just left the showgrounds and there was no fire. And anyway,' he said, 'I would'a noticed a fire if there was one.'

I was living up on a hill at the time, so I said, 'Hang on a tick,' and I went over and had a look out the window. 'Yep,' I said, 'she's goin' up all right.'

Now, if you were late to a call and you missed the fire engine, you went to the fire in your own vehicle. From memory, we had an International that carried about four hundred gallons of water, which wasn't much in the scheme of things. It only allowed us to get started on the fire while we hooked up to the mains water.

Now the grandstand was quite close to a fence, then there was a road. Anyhow, one of the boys that was late had parked his car on the opposite side of that road. So I guess we'd be looking at something like thirty yards or so from the grandstand. And you mightn't believe this, but the radiated heat from the fire was so intense that it blistered the duco on his car. Fair dinkum. It was incredible. You wouldn't credit it, would you? Thirty yards away and it still blistered the duco. That's how hot it was.

Another time, during that second stint at Coota, I was diagnosed with piles; you know, as in haemorrhoids. So I went in for the operation. Next day I'm lying back, recovering, and I see an old firie mate of mine, John Kennedy. As you do, John and me started talking about our respective operations: me with my haemorrhoids and I just now forget what his operation was. After our chat, unbeknown to me, John rang up radio station 2LF at Young.

Oh, just as a quick aside: not too many would know this but LF stands for 'Lambing Flat' which was the name of the old goldfields at Young.

Anyway, as I was saying, John rung 2LF. In those days there was an announcer over there named Graham McDonald. Around the area Graham was more commonly known as 'Cabbage'. Cabbage was a legend.

So there I am, lying back, recovering from my haemorrhoid operation and next thing, over the radio comes Cabbage. 'We've got a request here for one of the boys in the Cootamundra Fire Brigade who's currently in hospital recovering from quite an invasive sort of operation.' He said, 'Now I'll leave it up to the listeners' imaginations as to just what this invasive procedure might've been, but the request is for the Johnny Cash classic, "Burning Ring of Fire".'

Oh my God! I tell you, that John Kennedy was a right bugger.

Now just a last one from Coota. One of our firie mates passed away. So we had a bit of a get-together down at the fire station. In respect to our past mate, we had the station's flag at half-mast. When the gathering was over, one of the boys said, 'Oh, I'd better get the flag down.'

Now I forget exactly how it happened but this bloke somehow ended up on the roof of the fire station. So he's up on the roof and he calls out, 'Hey, fellers, have a look at this.'

Then he leaps across from the roof and grabs onto the flagpole. And you know how, about a yard and a half from the bottom of the flagpole, there's that metal cleat thing where you tie the rope off? Well, as he slides down the flagpole, gathering in the flag, the cleat goes straight through his pants, then straight through his scrotum, and he comes to a screaming stop.

Holey dooley!

'Fellers,' he called out in a squeaky sort of voice. 'I'm in a bit'a trouble.'

'What do yer mean?' we said.

He said, 'I'm stuck through me balls.'

So we all gathered around. And yep, the cleat had gone clean through his scrotum. It was just the most terrible sight. So then we had to lift him higher, back up the flagpole to unhitch him. By the time we got him down, he wasn't looking too good so we rang the ambulance. 'Please, no sirens, fellers,' we said. 'Keep it nice and quiet because we don't want people asking questions.'

As luck would have it, the ambulance station was only a block or two away and they came around without too much fuss and took him off to hospital. Now, I'm not sure what they did with him up there, like whether they had to stitch his scrotum up or not. But three hours later he was in the pub with us trying to kill the pain.

Note: During the 1993–94 fire season, several major bushfires broke out in New South Wales. Between December 1993 and January 1994, three people were killed, twenty-nine were injured and an estimated seventy thousand hectares of land was destroyed. The Waterfall blaze, in the South Coast region of Illawarra, caused the forced evacuation of Helensburgh – Helensburgh being where Simpy's cousin, Jim Powell, chalked up fifty years as a member of the local volunteer fire brigade, including many years as their captain.

The Greatest Buzz

We've lived in the West Gippsland region of Victoria, here at Bunyip, for almost forty years. So I think that almost makes us locals. As for myself, I've been a volunteer member of the fire brigade for almost the same amount of time and I'm currently a fourth lieutenant as well as a CFA community liaison officer.

To give you some idea as to the current situation, and what we might expect in the next year, we're now in early December 2019. Fire restrictions don't start till next week and we've already had four incidents today. Three in the last twenty minutes: a car accident, a grassfire and a scrub fire where someone who'd been burning off yesterday thought they'd extinguished the fire. But they hadn't.

Our usual call-out average is around a hundred and ten per year, but it's been steadily increasing. That's partly due to the greater, and still growing, population on this eastern side of Melbourne. And with more people comes the higher risks of car accidents or idiots throwing cigarette butts out their car windows or fires starting from clashing powerlines or whatever. So far this year, to date, we've already had a hundred and ninety-two call-outs. And, as I said, it's only early December. So we'll get well over two hundred this fire season, and I'm just hoping it'll be a long time before we have another year with two hundred call-outs.

During the March 2019 Bunyip State Park fires we had about eighty call-outs alone. That fire started up in the Bunyip State Forest, and it went on to cover a fair amount of country. It got to the outskirts of Gembrook and went right through to Nar Nar

Goon North and into Tynong North. Places like Bunyip North, Cornucopia, Garfield North, Labertouche, Tonimbuk, Beenak and Whites Corner were also under threat. Some of those towns lost houses, though there were no fatalities.

I wasn't actually there the Friday night it started. My wife was going overseas, so I'd taken her to the airport on the Thursday night. The plan was for me to then jump on my motorbike on the Friday morning and ride north, up to Wollongong to catch up with some family and celebrate my grandson Hugo's birthday. After that I was going to meet up with the group of guys I ride with and spend a few enjoyable days with them. Then I'd ride back home, grab the car and go and pick up my wife from the airport. A perfect plan. Nothing could go wrong.

But everything did go wrong. The proverbial hit the fan.

By the Friday night, when I arrived at Eden, on the south coast of New South Wales, to see my other daughter, I noticed a heap of missed calls on my phone. But because there was no point in me turning around and riding all the way back home that night, I decided to keep going. Then, by the time I got to Wollongong, on the Saturday afternoon, things were looking very bad.

My son-in-law offered to drive me home. 'You'll be there in eight hours,' he said.

'It's Hugo's birthday tomorrow,' I said, 'and in our brigade it's always family first. So let's have a nice breakfast for his birthday, then I'll make a decision.'

Anyhow, while I was away, I'd organised for a neighbour to come and feed our dog. But when my Melbourne daughter heard about the fire, she got my brother-in-law to drive over to Bunyip and pick up the dog.

My wife and I were on half an acre. We'd planted about three hundred trees and the back half was all bush. When the brother-in-law came for the dog, he set up some of our large garden sprinklers around our house and got them going. He then stayed overnight and, when he left the next morning, he kept the sprinklers running. Just before he headed back to Melbourne, he sent me a photo that he'd taken of the fire from our back fence – and the column of smoke was pretty close. Actually, by the time they eventually stopped the fire, it was only a kilometre and a half from our place.

But as soon as I saw the photo, I said, 'I've gotta get home.' So I booked a flight and I left my bike up in Wollongong and I flew home on the Sunday night.

It was a difficult and distressing time for many. A large number of rural people had evacuated. A high percentage of the population of Bunyip had also evacuated. All the residents from the aged-care facility had been taken for a short holiday, half an hour down the road, to Warragul and Moe. And something like thirty schools throughout the area were closed due to the number of roads having been cut off by the fire.

Because I was a CFA community liaison officer, I immediately started organising community meetings to provide people with updated information from the incident control centre in Dandenong. All that first week I ran meetings in various locations around the area, plus I worked at the Bunyip relief centre.

Just one little story: a lady I know quite well, she and her husband ran a lot of beef cattle. I saw her in the relief centre on the Wednesday and she was in a bit of a state. When I asked how she was managing, she said, 'Well, I went out this morning and I counted my stock and I'm seventeen short.'

I said, 'Did you find any carcasses?'

She said, 'No.'

I said, 'Well, don't fret too much. They'll be somewhere. They've probably just scooted off to another property to escape the fire.' And she eventually got them all back.

Another problem around the area was that we've got a lot of horses that are used for recreational purposes, like for pony clubs and equestrian. I don't know if you know or not, but we've got a large equestrian centre here in town. It wasn't damaged, but it's used a lot. So yeah, people were not only in a panic to get off their properties, there was also the matter of their livestock as well. And while some were able to afford the extra time and expense of trucking their livestock off to other properties, others were forced to leave everything and go.

By the Monday, the fire was basically under control. That's apart from the top corner of the Bunyip State Forest where a section had yet to be contained. By then the fire wasn't affecting any communities and so people were keen to get back to their homes – that is, those who had homes to return to. So from then on we faced the issue of checking houses for their safety. We had to check the roads. We had to check the trees and the powerlines and so forth for fire damage. Plus we were still getting call-outs. One particular day we received seventeen call-outs, mainly to put out smouldering stumps and fence posts.

But a lot of people were just plain nervous. And that's understandable because part of the immediate fire zone had also been burnt out in the 2009 Black Saturday fires. And when you consider that the Black Saturday fires had come through Bunyip Ridge – eight kilometres north of Bunyip – and this 2019 fire came within just two kilometres of the town, you can fully understand the nervousness.

Of course, then there's the aftermath. Some people have rebuilt. Some people are in the process of rebuilding. But because of finance and tougher planning permits, a lot of people haven't yet rebuilt.

Look, insurance companies are insurance companies. They're in the business of making money. But I will say that when it came to a disaster like we had, they weren't too bad. If you'd lost your paperwork in the fire, you'd usually just have to give them your name and details and they'd find it. But there's a couple of other huge hurdles. First of all, the vast majority of people were under-insured. Then, because a lot of those areas are now in what's deemed 'a bushfire-prone zone', they've got to meet stricter criteria when they rebuild, like having safe-tight shutters and special windows to keep the radiant heat out. And all that adds to the overall expense.

In one way the fire didn't start out that quick. But it began in terrain that was very difficult to access and so it was harder to get to. Then, as it got bigger, it travelled a lot wider and it got more erratic. And by erratic, I mean really erratic. And that's when you hit real problems.

See, fires create their own weather patterns, especially in the massive fires we're currently experiencing along the eastern seaboard. What you've got in those situations is that the hot air that's created by the fire rises and it's replaced by colder air. Then, as the hot air rises, it takes the smoke up with it and it creates pyro-cumulus smoke-clouds, which can reach anywhere up to a kilometre high, even more. Then, when it gets to such heights, it breaks the inversion layer, the pyro-cumulus smoke-cloud gets heavy, it condenses and that's when you can get a thunderstorm. Or sometimes it won't rain, you'll just hear thunder.

So anyway, as you might guess, I'm pretty enthusiastic about these things, which is why I love being a CFA community liaison officer and a firefighter, both of which are unpaid positions. But I must say the greatest buzz of all is when people pull me up in the street after I've been out fighting a fire, and say, 'Thank you, and thank you all for all your help and support.'

You can't beat that.

Note: During the Bunyip State Park fire, an estimated thirty-one houses, sixty-five outbuildings, hundreds of kilometres of fencing and much livestock and wildlife were lost. After breaking containment lines the fire burnt through a total of 26,200 hectares of property and forest.

The fires destroyed approximately a dozen houses in Labertouche, Tonimbuk and Drouin West and the townships of

Jindivick, Warragul and Longwarry were under extreme threat. Embers from the fires were starting spot fires up to twenty kilometres away from the fire front.

About two thousand firefighters and ten aircraft were deployed during the fires.

The Bunyip State Park fire was thought to have been deliberately lit.

Spider

It would've been back in 1993 when my wife and I came up here to live in the Adelaide Hills. The idea of joining our local Mylor CFS – Country Fire Service – had been on my mind because we both wanted to become a more active part of the community. Then one Monday evening I was coming home and a CFS appliance – fire truck – was parked opposite the entrance to our property, burning off the undergrowth alongside the road. So I walked over and said, 'Are you looking for volunteers?'

Next thing I knew I was down at the fire station, getting fitted out in my firefighting gear. So that would've been either late '93 or early '94. And apart from the few years when life got busy with the kids and so on, I've been involved ever since.

Mylor's your typical small country brigade. Numbers vary between twenty and thirty, some of which are women. In actual fact, Mylor's got one of the highest percentage of female firefighters of all the brigades in the Adelaide Hills. I don't know why that is. But with us, a couple of women come along and perhaps, because they were there, it drew in some more.

The first fire I went to was in a paddock, up along River Road. The appliance we had back then was built back in the '70s. It was a 'two-four', meaning it carried two thousand litres of water and had four-wheel drive. Being so old, there was hardly any sitting room. So most of us had to stand on the back, along either side of the water tank, hanging onto a safety rail, with all our rake-hoes and brooms et cetera.

So off we go to this, my very first fire. Now, something that'd already been drummed into me was a) to start the pump before you arrive at the fire and b) to double-check that the water tank's full. I mean, the last thing you want is to get to a fire and find out that your pump's not working. The other last thing you want is to get to a fire and there's no water in the tank. Worse still, if you get to a fire and both the pump doesn't work and the water tank's empty, it could spell disaster. You could be incinerated.

So we'd started the pump, which was on the very back of the truck. Our captain was driving and I'm standing on the back with the others and we head out along River Road till we see the fire. It's up the side of a hill. Leading up to the fire was a dirt track. A fence was running between the track and the fire. Then just as our captain turned off River Road onto the track, being the enthusiastic newcomer I was, I thought I'd better double-check the water. To do that, I had to open the lid on top of the tank. And to do that I needed both hands, which meant I had to let go of the safety railing.

Now, if you can imagine, there I am, precariously balanced, unscrewing the lid to have a look inside the tank. And just as I lifted the lid, the truck hit a pothole. Next thing I'm catapulted upwards. But I'm still clinging onto the lid. Then – *splat!* – down I come on top of the pump at the very back of the appliance.

Now, I've got fairly long legs, which is why I'm known as Spider. So when one of our crew turned around, there I was swinging upside down over the back of the truck, with my legs splayed in the air, while I'm still hanging onto the lid for grim life. Anyhow, they managed to grab me by my legs and haul me back up onto the truck.

'You all right?' they asked.

I adjusted my gear. 'Yep, fine,' I said. 'Just double-checking the water.'

So that was my first proper fire and we knocked it down without too much trouble.

But living in the Adelaide Hills, our main focus, especially leading up to and over the summer months, is on bushfires.

Early on 2 January 2015 we got a message on our pagers for us to go on active standby at the fire station. Active standby is when you ready yourself to leave the fire station at an instant's notice. It was about 9 o'clock in the morning and already a wild northerly had hit and the temperature was rocketing up to the mid-forties. On the way to the station, dust and leaves were being blown around everywhere and bits of trees were lying across the road.

And that's when it really struck me: Shit, this could be awful.

When I arrived at the station, there was a community sort of atmosphere around the place. The firefighters were there, ready to go, but they'd brought along their families – kids, dogs, the lot. So we settle in and we're watching the cricket dressed in all our gear, ready to roll. The main part of the station was virtually a tin shed. It didn't have air conditioning so it was like sitting in an oven.

Anyhow, we're whiling away. We had lunch. By mid-afternoon nothing's happened. We're tuned in to ABC Radio, listening for fire warnings. A couple of other volunteers were in the radio room, keeping an eye on the latest information. But still nothing. By 3 o'clock it was like, 'Phew, we're going to get away with this.' So we're keen to go home, have a shower and something to eat, then relax for the night. Anyhow, I just happened to wander into the radio room to see a couple of our guys absolutely glued to the radio.

'There's a shed fire or something at a place called Sampson Flat,' they said.

We looked at each other. 'Sampson Flat? Where's that?'

Someone Googled it. 'It's just up north, around the Gumeracha area.'

A couple of appliances had already responded and we could hear the aerial pilot talking to the guys on the ground. 'How are yer going down there? Do you need any more resources?'

And they radioed back, 'Nah, we're fine. It's only a little shed fire. We'll have it knocked over in ten or twenty minutes.'

Anyhow, there was a silence over the radio. Then five minutes later the pilot came back on: 'Guys, I think you've lost it. I'm calling in more resources.'

And that's when the shit hit the fan. Lots of brigades responded. We were called in as a strike team. By that stage we had a decent one-four appliance with a dual cab that seated five, and it was good in the steep terrain. So we piled into the cab and off we went, trying to find this Sampson Flat place. There was no GPS back then, not in this vehicle anyway, so we were reliant on maps. With the fire being on the city side of Mylor, up beyond Tea Tree Gully, the quickest way to our staging point was through the city.

So we got onto the freeway and even then, just at the sight of the massive plume of rising smoke in the distance, it was, 'Wow, this is big.'

When we got to the staging point, other appliances were already gathered there. And because there wasn't any water out at the fire front, the plan was to send bulk water carriers out to keep us smaller appliances topped up. So off we went. When we got to our designated spot, the bulky – bulk water carrier – was yet to turn up.

It was very hilly, bushy country, so, before deciding on what to do next, we drove up on top of a rise to get an overview of the fire. And it was just horrible. We were probably a kilometre away and we could hear the raging roar of the fire. So then we decided to stay put and defend the nearby houses till the bulky arrived. But it didn't turn up. So there was total confusion.

Anyhow, some of the bigger appliances decided to go in without the bulky. With our appliance, the water we had would've only lasted a few minutes. And with the fear of sending five firefighters into a fire that big, our captain said, 'Nah, we're not going in, not till the bulky gets here.'

So we waited. Still no bulky, and still no instructions as to what we should do. After sitting around for an hour or so of this, it was, 'Okay, let's go in. If it gets too bad we'll turn back.'

Anyhow, we drove down along a road that was on the side of a hill and into a scene of absolute devastation. Everything was gone – trees, the lot. We were surrounded by the acrid smell of smoke and smouldering fire and there was just grey ash for as far as we could see. That's how ferocious the fire was. Further down we came across a broken-down CFS command car. It was parked in the middle of the road, with its bonnet up. So it was, 'Where are the people?'

We tried radioing but the network was jammed. So then we started searching the area for bodies. But nothing, so we just hoped that the occupants had been picked up by another brigade. We then continued on down into the valley until we came to the outskirts of a town. Don't ask me which town it was. I don't think any of us knew. But we started to come across houses; some were alight, with trees and scrub burning all around them. So we set to, going from house to house, putting out spot fires.

When our tank was empty, we found a swimming pool and pulled water out of that. It was just like a war scene. We felt like intruders. People had evacuated in such a hurry, they'd left their doors open. Kids' toys were strewn about. Possessions scattered. Sprinklers had been left on.

And every which way we went we were hampered by fallen trees. Some were still alight, others had just given up and fallen over. Then, as we were working our way through town, lo 'n behold a bulk water carrier appeared. So we flagged it down and we refilled our water tank before continuing on, moving through this town, putting out the fires.

Then it must've been about 8 o'clock. Or maybe the smoke had brought the darkness on quicker. But it was getting dark, when a command vehicle screeched up. It was our group officer. He said, 'Quick. Follow me. We're going into the fire front. There's a lady with her verandah on fire. She's trying to put it out with a hose and her husband's not well.'

That's all the information we got. So we followed the command vehicle into the fire front. Then we saw a house. Fire was all around it. To go into the house we needed BA – breathing apparatus. Luckily, there was another brigade there with BA. So, we pulled up and the guys put on their BA and went inside. They found the wife. She was okay, but she pointed to the shed next to the house. So they went in there. We waited, and they eventually brought out a guy. He'd apparently gone into the shed to fight the fire and had been overcome by the fumes from burning paint cans and so forth. He wasn't unconscious but, because he was so overweight and disorientated, he had difficulty walking.

So then it was, 'Well, we can't expect an ambulance to drive out into the middle of a raging fire zone to pick him up. So what do we do with him?'

It was getting late by then and it was decided that we'd take him to Gumeracha Hospital, where we'd also do a swap-over with a relief crew. So we loaded this guy lengthways on the back seat of our appliance which, of course, left no room for us firefighters. So we hopped up on the back and drove out of the fireground towards Gumeracha and into a refreshing, cool night breeze.

When we arrived at the hospital, they stretchered the guy inside. By then the fire was well behind us, so we just sat around the car park, talking over the day's events, while we waited for the bus to bring in our relief crew so we could do the swap-over.

Anyhow, after about half an hour, I was busting for a pee. We had a female in our crew so, rather than visit a nearby tree like I'd normally do on the fireground, I went over to the hospital. I wandered in and went down the corridor leading to the emergency room.

When I walked in through the double doors, I was met by a formidable-looking female nurse. I said, 'Do you mind if I use the toilet?'

Now, I'd been a touch bothered by something in my eye. It might've been a speck of dust or a cinder or something. It wasn't bad, just a bit irritating. Anyhow, the nurse must've noticed it. 'Are you all right?' she asked.

'Yeah, fine,' I said, 'just something in my eye. It's nothing.'

She said, 'Well, we should have a proper look at it.'

'No need, thanks,' I said. 'I'd just like to go to the loo.'

'Okay,' she said. 'The toilet's just down there on the right.'

So there I was, in all my firefighting gear – my helmet tucked under my arm – standing at the urinal. As I was having a relieving pee, I looked up and there's this huge sign: WEAR YOUR PROTECTIVE GEAR AT ALL TIMES. I mean, it might've been my warped sense of humour after having spent a long day at the fire front but, I thought, What an odd place to have a sign like that, just where you're having a pee.

Then, thinking back to the formidable nurse, it was, Shit, I'd better put my helmet on.

So I came out of the loo, chuckling to myself, and I headed back down the corridor on my way out to have a joke to the guys about having to wear all their protective gear if they went to the loo.

But blocking my way, with her arms outstretched, stood the formidable nurse. 'I think we should have a look at that eye,' she said.

I said, 'No, it's okay. It's nothing really.'

Next thing, I'm being propelled backwards. And then I was laid flat on my back, on a bed. Another nurse appeared and the two of them got to it and started pouring stuff in both my eyes.

Then the doctor arrives. 'Come with me,' he said. 'I'll have a decent look at it.'

So I was taken into a darkened room. As the doctor was checking my eyes, he's discussing with the nurses as to what they should do with their patients if the fire came their way. And just as an aside they asked me, 'So how far away's the fire?'

'Oh,' I said, 'it's a long way off. Nothing to worry about. You shouldn't have any trouble. None at all.'

Anyhow, after the doctor had taken out whatever was in my eye, he told me I was good to go. Mind you, by now both my eyes were stinging like buggery. I was worse than when I came in. I could hardly see. So I staggered back out into the car park. The guys were still there, and through the blur I noticed they were staring up at something. 'Look,' they said, and when I refocused, the surrounding hills of Gumeracha were all aglow. It was frightening. The fire had moved that quickly.

So I went back inside and I said, 'The fire's here.'

The moment they came out to take a look, the doctor was on the phone to his wife. 'Get out now! Don't ask questions, just get out!'

Just then the bus arrived with our relief crew. So we swapped over and off we went. I later found out that at least half of the patients in Gumeracha Hospital had been evacuated. But thankfully, the fire never got to it.

So from what began as a little shed fire, where the firefighters reckoned they'd have it out in ten or so minutes, the Sampson Flat fires weren't fully extinguished till nine days later.

Note: The Sampson Flat fire that started on 2 January 2015 burnt uncontrolled for four days. In doing so, it threatened a number of towns including Kersbrook and Gumeracha. More than 3500 firefighters responded to the emergency, including volunteers from New South Wales and Victoria.

At that stage, the Sampson Flat fire was the most destructive fire in the Adelaide Hills for more than thirty years. It burnt approximately 12,600 hectares of forests, grazing lands, vineyards and properties. Thirty-seven families were evacuated. Twenty-four houses and five businesses were destroyed. Near on a hundred and fifty outer structures were lost, along with numerous livestock and kilometres of fencing. An estimated one hundred and thirty-four people were injured, including sixty-two firefighters. There were no fatalities.

Story Time

When I came up here to the east coast of Tasmania, at Swansea, I pretty much went straight into the volunteer fire service. My mate was group officer of the northern zone that went roughly from Bicheno, through to Triabunna and Mayfield. Then when I became deputy group officer, we worked in well because I was more familiar with the southern part. So we pretty much had the entire zone covered.

I'd say that one of the greatest joys of being a volunteer firefighter would be the camaraderie. Training days were always good fun. After we'd done our training we'd all sit down and have a few beers and a barbecue. And if it was a group training session, you'd learn things from the other groups – stuff that you'd never find in the training manual. Practical stuff like how to handle certain sticky situations. Then, with us being volunteers, say we'd been called out to a house fire or a fire in someone's paddock or whatever, we were never paid for what we did. But it was an unwritten rule that after we'd put out the fire, in appreciation of our efforts, the owner of the property would give us a carton or two of beer. Yes, so that part of it was great as well.

As far as appreciation goes, a while back the local council recognised me as their Emergency Services Volunteer of the Year. That was in thanks for all the volunteering I'd done over the years. Like I'd done nine years with the CFA – Country Fire Authority – in Victoria, followed by my forty-seven years with the Tasmania Fire Service. Another reason for the award was that, because my wife and I are environmentally inclined, I've allocated myself a certain stretch of the highway that I keep clean of rubbish and waste. And there's plenty of that, I can tell you. Ute loads full.

Something else that takes up a fair bit of my time is that I'm a volunteer greenkeeper at the local golf course. I try and keep the course and the greens up to scratch – up to the members' high expectations. And to save unnecessary water wastage through evaporation, I usually do the watering at night or early mornings. As well as that, I look after the game on the golf course. By 'game', I mean the rabbits. At one time I counted over two hundred and fifty rabbits on the course. And just imagine the damage that two hundred and fifty rabbits can do.

So I occasionally run a rabbit eradication program. Though I have to be very careful about that because the course is near a built-up area and you're not allowed to let off a firearm within two hundred and fifty metres of a house. So I have to try and herd them up into a far corner where they'll be a good distance out of sight and more manageable. And I can tell you, herding rabbits is a hell of a lot harder than herding cats. Anyhow, after I've sorted them out, I skin a few and give them to the members of the golf club. So they are pretty happy about that – the members, that is, not the rabbits.

But what I was getting around to telling you about was the time I was out watering the golf course. It was 2 o'clock one morning and there was a big storm about. Next thing I saw was this huge lightning strike go straight to the ground back up yonder. Then about a half an hour later, I saw the glow of a fire. And that turned out to be quite a big one. The fire stretched from Bicheno to Coles Bay, all through that area. Coles Bay borders on the Freycinet National Park and Douglas-Apsley National Park, north of Bicheno. Brigades came to back us up from all over the state, even from Penguin up on the north-west coast and The Tiers over in the Central Highlands.

Now I don't know if I've ever been struck by fear during a fire but my heart rate got up pretty high during that Coles

Bay–Bicheno blaze. The conditions were horrible, with record temperatures over forty degrees and the terrifying winds it brought with it.

I had two of our younger blokes on the back of the truck with me. We were told to line the firebreak up along the highway.

I said to them, 'You, man the pump. You, man the radio, and I'll handle the hose.'

The thing was, all around us it was so thick with dust and smoke that you could hardly see your own hand in front of your face. Like, you couldn't see any flames or anything. Then, next thing, we heard a sound like the roar of thunder. Then – *boom!* – this fireball exploded straight over the top of us. And the force of it was such that we were picked up like leaves and slammed up against the truck's cabin. And that's as true as I stand here. So I turned the hose on the three of us and I started thumping on the top of the cabin, yelling out for the driver to get us the hell out of there.

Anyway, as I said, that really got my heart rate working overtime and I reckon it scared the living Harry out of the two young blokes. I saw it in their eyes.

But the brute force of a fire in situations like that isn't that unusual. Another time we were fighting a fire out in the bush with the forestry people and, when the fire front came through, I saw a bloke literally get picked up and smashed against a tree. And that's true. The fire just went through like a tornado.

That was a bad one too. It burnt all that night and well into the next day, and we were out there throughout the whole lot, fighting the fire. I mean, they won't let you stay out there that long any more. And you can understand why.

Anyhow, I was completely knackered by the time I got home. I just wanted to have a shower to wash off all the fire crap and then curl up in bed and go to sleep. Then I remember getting out of my ute and, as I was walking round to the back verandah, my little granddaughter was there. She was about four or five.

'Oh, Grandpa,' she said, 'you look just so tired.'

I said, 'Yes, darlin', I am. I'm completely exhausted.'

And she took me by the arm and she said, 'Look, Grandpa, you just sit right down there on the step of the verandah and I'll read you a story.'

So I did what I was told to do. Then she picked up one of her favourite books and she proceeded to read me a story. 'Once upon a time ...'

I mean, kids – you can't beat them, can you?

Note: The Australian bushfire season of 2012–13 has been labelled the Angry Summer or the Extreme Summer. In January 2013, the fires throughout Tasmania were particularly devastating, causing huge losses of property and houses, with many evacuations and towns being cut off.

In the state's east, around the Coles Bay-Bicheno area, four thousand hectares were burnt by out-of-control fires. Access to Coles Bay and the Freycinet Peninsula was cut off. Tasmania Fire Service sent out warnings to the local residents that it may well be too late to evacuate and advised them to implement their fire plan and try and protect their property the best they could.

A community refuge for Bicheno residents was set up at the Bicheno Community Hall. Another was set up for Coles Bay and Swanwick residents at the Swansea football ground.

Over Dinner

My husband, Mac, was a member of the North Wakool Bush Fire Brigade for umpteen years, and by this stage had been their fire captain for nigh on twelve years. So he was very experienced. For those that may not know, and I guess there may be many, North Wakool is in the southern Riverina region of New South Wales, about thirty miles north-west of the much larger township of Deniliquin, or simply Deni as it's more commonly known.

I guess, back then, the population of Deni would've been about 6500 – pretty much the same as it is now. So it hasn't grown much. It hasn't changed much either. Then, the North Wakool Brigade was based down Brassi Road, which ran between Wakool and Deniliquin. Actually, three different members of our family owned properties down Brassi Road, totalling around nine thousand acres, though sadly none of our family are there now.

Other than Mac, the other main character in this story was a dear friend of ours, Brian, whom we'd known for umpteen years. Actually, Swampy, Brian featured in your book of funeral stories. If you recall, his parents had never been outside Australia till they'd gone on a much-awaited holiday to the USA. About three days after they'd arrived – I think it was in LA – Brian's father unfortunately suffered a heart attack and died and went to God.

The thing was that when the family came to fly their father's body back to Australia, due to certain rules and regulations, they were told that he had to travel in the baggage compartment of the plane, in a lead casket. And when Qantas said that it'd cost the family six thousand dollars to bring their father home,

Brian's classic quip was, 'Well, we've already paid for his return fare. So why can't you just prop him up in the seat next to Mum, pull his hat down so no one'll know that he's dead, and we won't have to pay the extra six thousand dollars.'

Of course, Qantas didn't go for it.

The other thing was, when they eventually got their father back home, the local gravediggers weren't aware that an American-style lead casket was larger than an Australian one. And, when it came time for the burial, the grave hadn't been dug large enough. So their father had to be left lying on top of the gravesite, in his casket, waiting for the gravediggers to enlarge the hole so that he could be laid in peace.

So yes, that was the story of Brian's father and the coffin.

Anyhow, Brian and his wife, Cynthia, were originally from Melbourne. They were getting quite tired of city life so, every chance they got, they'd come and visit us on our property at North Wakool. While they were there, Brian would do some farm work for a bit of extra money. And he just loved it. He loved the fresh air and he loved being there – as did Cynthia – so much so that they eventually decided to come and live in Deni. Which they did, and they opened a health-food store.

That would've been back in the early '70s, well before things such as health-food stores became popular. And it proved to be hugely successful. Then, later on, Cynthia took over the total running of the store while Brian went into real estate, and he made a very successful business out of that. They became a very popular couple throughout the area. In fact, when Cynthia sadly went to God in her mid-fifties, her funeral service was held in Deni's Catholic Church. The church itself could hold a maximum of five hundred people and on the day it was packed to the hilt. It was amazing; people were even standing out in the road. So, like I said, they were a very popular husband-and-wife team, and Brian remained so right up till he joined Cynthia in the Deniliquin Cemetery.

So now to the fire story. It was during one of Brian and Cynthia's earlier visits. Most probably just after a Christmas because Deni always held a large social function on New Year's Eve – an occasion Brian and Cynthia always tried to be there for. Anyhow, one night Mac and I held a dinner party for about a dozen people, including Brian and Cynthia.

Now I'm not one to boast, but my dinner parties were quite legendary. We'd start off with a mix of hors d'oeuvres: things like devilled eggs, bacon-stuffed mushrooms, salmon mousse canapés and the like. All made by myself of course, and Mac would take pride in organising the accompanying beverages for each course. He was good at that. We were quite a team.

After the hors d'oeuvres there'd be entrées. Both Mac and Brian loved their prawn cocktails, with avocado. Avocado was the big thing back then. It was a bit swish. So that's what we had, along with my special homemade Thousand Island dressing. The following course was chicken-and-vegetable soup. We had our own chooks so I'd made a beautiful chicken stock to which I'd added vegetables, fresh from our garden.

Anyhow, I remember being in the kitchen, just about to serve up the soup when the phone rang in the office. It was for Mac. One of his fire brigade members had phoned to say that a small fire had broken out on a property, just down the road a bit. As I was putting the soup out on the table, we could all hear Mac chatting on the phone, giving a few instructions. You know, 'Do this and do that,' and he told the feller where the extra equipment was that they'd need. 'You'll be okay,' Mac said, 'just keep the water up to it and don't hesitate to call me back if you need to.' Then he returned to the table.

'What's up?' asked Brian.

'Oh, a fire's broken out, about thirty miles out. Nothing too much to worry about. The boys'll have it under control in no time.'

So we settled down to the soup. I noted that Mac had stopped drinking by that stage – I presume it was just in case he was needed out at the fire front. Then it was on to the main course, which was a fillet of beef. I loved cooking a fillet of beef, served with hot potatoes and a garden fresh salad.

I was just putting the finishing touches to that when the phone rang again. Mac again went off into the office. We could hear him. Things sounded more urgent than before. But Mac still seemed pretty calm about it and, being full of local knowledge and authority, he was telling the feller what to do and how to go about it and not to panic.

By the time he returned to the table, the main course was on the table – this beautiful fillet of beef.

'What's the latest on the fire?' asked Brian.

'Oh, the wind's changed direction so I've told the fellers to attack it from another way. They should be right.' Though I did note that, during the main course, Mac's mind seemed to be a little elsewhere.

Anyway, we'd just finished the main course when the phone rang again. We could hear from the office that things seemed to be going from bad to worse. We heard Mac say, 'If you go down by the river and work back up the southern flank of the fire, you should be able to get it under control.'

So that was that. Next came dessert. I had the reputation of being the local 'Dessert Queen'. Dessert was either creme caramel or brandy fruit salad. Mac loved his desserts, though just as he was about to tuck in he was interrupted by another phone call. By this stage we were all thinking that things had got completely out of control and he'd have to leave us to go and help fight the fire. But no, after much discussion, he came back to the dinner table and announced, 'Good news, folks, the fire's out.'

Mac was very happy then. He could now relax and savour his dessert and have a drink. So things became more jovial, with Brian and Mac swapping stories and so forth. After dessert, it was on to the dinner chocolates. I always made my own, so it was homemade chocolates and coffee, with accompanying port and liquor. And it was while we were enjoying those that Brian just couldn't hold his mirth. He said, 'Well, Mac, you're about the smartest fire captain I've ever come across.'

'Why's that?' replied Mac.

'Well,' Brian said, 'I've never known a fire captain to put a fire out over the telephone while hosting a dinner party.'

And that sort of went down in family history as a bit of a joke – the evening Mac put a bushfire out over dinner. Then the next morning Mac took Brian out with him, just to make sure that all the fire spots and what have you had been put out and that all the equipment had been put back in its rightful place in the shed. Oh, he was very attentive, was my Mac. Very attentive.

But in the North Wakool Brigade itself, I suppose there may have been about a dozen members. All property owners of course. It's a bit different now with the political stuff that goes on. But I think that that particular fire burnt out nigh on six hundred acres.

Note: The 2021 Wakool Village Rural Fire Service's Australia Day raffle was drawn at the Wakool pub at 7 p.m. on Monday 25 January. The three $100 barbecue hamper packs each contained a cooler bag, chips and snacks, tongs, Aussie Day picnic gear, Zooper Doopers for the kids, gourmet snags, chicken kebabs and meatballs. Congratulations to the winners Sandra, Gen O and Maney.

Insurance

Now just on insurance issues: if anyone was under the orders of either the brigade captain or his deputy, they were fully insured. At least that's how it was back in the day. Not sure if that's still the case. And while I was captain I had a couple of very interesting claims.

To the first one. See, me and me brother always liked to finish our harvest a week or two before Christmas, and we mostly did. This year we'd almost finished harvesting. It was around midday – stinking hot – when we saw smoke over to the north-west. Not much, but a bit. The thing is, because it's so flat out here, most times a fire looks closer than it is. But you never know. So I got on the two-way to my deputy, Peter What's-his-name, and yes, there was a fire just the other side of town.

'But there's no need for you to rush out,' he said. 'A few of us have already got it pretty much under control. Just turn up when you're ready and you can help us mop up.'

At hearing that, me brother said, 'Good, with a bit of time up our sleeves, how's about we go home, hitch the water cart up to the ute and pop into the pub for a beer on our way out there?' Being the conscientious fire captain I am, I baulked about going to the pub. That's until he added, 'My shout.'

Well, a bloke couldn't get a better offer, could he? So before he could change his mind, I said, 'You're on.'

So we drove the header out of the paddock, then we went back home and hooked the water cart to the ute. Then first stop: the pub. We had a couple – me brother's shout – then we headed out to the fire. It wasn't far out of town, on a property owned by a bloke called Billy Griffin. Griff had been harvesting and one of the bearings on his header had overheated and it'd set off a fire in his wheat crop. It wasn't a big fire. By the time we got there, it'd only burnt about ten acres of crop and a few acres of stubble.

As Peter had said, a few blokes from the brigade had got there before us with their water carts and their knapsacks. Both the carts and knapsacks had been provided by the fire brigade. Though, mind you, with most of us being farmers, the carts were perfect for when we were killing weeds. You know, you'd fill them with poison then go around squirting the weeds. Anyway, as we drove into Griff's place, a few blokes were standing over near a Holden ute that was going up in flames.

I said to me brother, 'Those fellers don't have any firefighting gear, so how's about you take our water cart over and see what you can do?' To be honest, by that stage the car was too far gone. But anyway, that's what I said.

After me brother went off, I saw a Scottish feller, Robbie McTavish. Tav as we'd labelled him. Any rate, Tav was new to the brigade. I think it was his first fire. He'd come out to Australia just a few years previous with his older brother – Big Tav. I thought, Well, being brigade captain, I'll have to write a report about all of this.

So I went over to Tav to get some of the lowdown. Now, because of his thick Scottish accent, I'd always struggled to understand what the bloody hell he was on about. Like he'd describe a baby as being 'a wee bairn' and all that sort of crap. Any rate, with him having arrived late to this, his first fire, plus forgetting his gear in the panic, I couldn't understand a single bloody word of what he was saying. But I eventually settled him down and it turned out that, when everyone had arrived to help fight the fire, they'd parked their cars close together, in a grassy paddock.

Now, one of my main rules as captain was, 'Always start the pump on your water cart before you go out to fight the fire.' That was the rule. Like, the logic of it was, if you arrived at the fire and your pump wouldn't start, you'd be well and truly stuffed. That's how I saw it.

Any rate, I eventually got it out of Tav that a bloke in our brigade – old Smithy – had pulled into where all these cars was parked and he'd proceeded to start the pump on his cart. Now unfortunately, Smithy was very slack with the maintenance of his gear and the spark arrestor on the muffler on his pump had rusted out. Next thing, it's backfired, causing sparks to shoot out which in turn set fire to the grass around all these parked cars.

Luckily there were four or five blokes there at the time who'd just come to look at the fire. That was the blokes me and me brother came across when we arrived. Like they didn't belong to the brigade or nothing which was why they didn't have any firefighting gear with them. But when they saw the grass set alight, they said, 'Holy shit, we'd better shift these cars before they go up in flames.'

Now, back in those days, in the bush you always left the keys in your car. So these fellers jumped into the cars and drove them a safe distance away from the grassfire. All the cars, that is, apart from a brand-spanking-new Holden ute with no keys in it. It'd been locked up with the handbrake on, and so these fellers couldn't even shift it. Next thing the grassfire's got to the ute. Next thing after that it's up in bloody flames, and all they could do was stand there and watch it burn, which was what they were doing when me and me brother had arrived.

It turned out that this brand-new Holden ute belonged to a lad in our brigade, Mick Gaffey – Gaff as we called him. And when Gaff returned from fighting the fire, I don't think I've ever seen a more distressed person. It was like his mother had just died. 'That's me brand-new ute,' he cried. 'Just got it last week. Spent every bloody cent I've got on it. Oh fuck, what am I gonna do now?'

I said to him, 'Gaff, because you're a member of the brigade and you were fighting a fire when it got burnt, maybe we can claim it on our insurance policy.' I said, 'No promises. If they pay, they pay. If they don't, they don't.'

Anyway, I got on well with our shire clerk. A hell of a nice guy. A wily old bugger too, he was. Nifty we called him. Nifty had been around for yonks, so he knew all the ins and outs of things. So Nifty helped me fill out the claim form. After we'd done that, he attached some sort of letter of explanation as to how the ute had caught fire. And you wouldn't believe it, no questions asked, young Gaff got a brand-spanking-new latest-model Holden ute. So that was a good outcome.

Later on, me and the wife moved our operations up to the Northern Territory. And that's where we had another memorable insurance claim – one that really set the cat among the pigeons. See, up here in the Territory we have these Bachelor and Spinster Balls – as in dances. They're particularly popular in areas where the women are few and far between and the men are willing, wanting and able. That's why a lot of these balls are held out on the large station properties and oh, they're big shows. They'll put on a band and young people come from everywhere, even from as far as Darwin, and they get all dressed up to the nines and bring their caravans or tents or swags, or they even sleep in the back of their utes. And being Territorians, they know how to party. Oh Christ, they do. Heaps of grog, heaps of fun and heaps of carry-on.

Any rate, this particular ball was held on a Saturday night, at a station property about ten mile out of town. Then early on the Sunday morning, the place was hit by a dry storm. A dry storm's where there's lots of thunder and lightning, but no rain. Not a drop. With the ball being in the middle of summer, everything was as dry as chips and this lightning set off spot fires all throughout the area.

The nearest town was a sleepy sort of joint with just a few houses, a pub, a store, a primary school, the council chambers, a church and that's about it. But being a central sort of place, it'd been picked out as the area's centre for the volunteer fire brigade. As such, we'd been given three big fire trucks, each carrying 1500 to 2000 litres of water and we'd been donated lots of water carts.

Any rate, the call went out that it was to be all hands on deck to help with these fires. So us older volunteers drove the fire trucks and the water carts out to the property where the ball had been. To give you some idea, it was about eight in the morning when we got there, and the scene was a picture of devastation. There were people sleeping it off in their caravans. People sleeping it off in their tents. People sleeping it off in their swags and in the back of their utes. There were people in ragged and torn dresses and suits spread out all over the ground because they hadn't quite managed to make it to their caravans or their tents or their swags or their utes.

So we pulled up and shouted out for volunteers. Of course, the rule of the bush is, if anyone's in need of help, you drop everything and go and help, regardless. So people started to tumble out of caravans, tents, swags and utes and so forth – still half blotto – and they clambered aboard the trucks and carts and off we went.

Now what you've got to realise here is that not all these people were from the bush. A lot were from larger towns and cities where they'd probably never been on the back of a truck or trailer before. What's more, they didn't have the faintest clue as to how to go about fighting a fire. As an end result, twenty-six of them ended up with some sort of injury or other.

From memory we had a broken leg and three broken arms; a few sprained ankles; and heaps of cuts, scratches, burns, bumps and bruises – all from having either fallen off a truck or a water cart or from tripping over water hoses, rocks, logs or branches. One young buck had even run headlong into a burning tree trunk. Others had come to grief from falling over each other in their hungover enthusiasm to fight the fires. Oh, it was a real shemozzle. But we eventually got all the fires out.

Now, as I said, the law stated that anybody who's fought a fire under the fire captain's instructions is fully insured. So with me being the fire captain, I got together with the shire president and we put in a claim for all these injuries and so forth. Then, when it came to our AGM, the shire president said, 'Any correspondence?'

I said, 'Yes. A letter from our insurance mob.'

'You'd better read it out.'

So I did. And it went along the lines of: Dear Sirs, Given that the fires on such-and-such date were caused by natural causes we are prepared to pay out on your claim. Though mind you, throughout our many years of insuring this state's volunteer fire service, we have never had more than five injuries occur at the one fire. To that end we would like a clearer explanation as to why such a disproportionate number of injuries occurred during the one incident.

Now those meetings were usually pretty boisterous affairs. Plenty of laughter, arguments and toing and froing with general banter. But after I'd read the letter out, there was absolute silence. Of course we all knew what'd happened, but none of us knew what to say in reply.

Anyhow, the old shire president stood up. 'Gentlemen,' he said, 'leave it to me.'

Any rate, I don't know what he wrote in his reply, but it must've been very bloody convincing because we never heard nothing more about it.

Note: Bachelor and Spinsters Balls – B&S Balls – began in the late 1960s–early '70s, becoming a regular annual event throughout most states in rural and outback Australia. They were originally run for over-eighteen-year-olds who dressed in formalwear to attract a partner.

Things have changed since those earlier balls. No longer is there a requirement for formalwear. These days B&S attire is far more casual, even going into 'fancy-dress', such as tutus and hats decorated with sheep dags and the mass spraying of food dye. Other than dancing and huge amounts of alcohol and whatever else is being consumed, many competitions are run over the weekend. For females there's mud and/or jelly wrestling plus wet T-shirt competitions. For males there's arm wrestling and penis 'windmilling'. Beer-sculling competitions and ute-donut competitions involve both males and females. Prizes such as ear tags, stubby holders, hats with built-in bottle openers, flavoured condoms and lubricant, and sex toys are often presented to the winners.

Tickets for the B&S Balls can cost up to $120 for the weekend, with profits going to the Royal Flying Doctor Service, Red Cross, Australian Cancer Council, as well as many local charities.

Over the 2015 Easter long weekend, Daly Waters – six hundred kilometres south of Darwin, with a population of eleven – hosted their B&S Ball. Near on one hundred and fifty people turned up for the occasion including many first-time attendees who were duly marked with the word 'VIRGIN'. The event was written up in the media as being 'the best party ever held in the Northern Territory, and possibly Australia'.

In confirmation of those remarks, one very excited first-timer told author Bill 'Swampy' Marsh, 'You never forget your first one!'

Due to COVID-19 restrictions, many B&S Balls were postponed in 2020.

Awards

Well yeah, as you can see, I've got a bit of décor hanging around the place – as in awards and that. I don't know what will happen to it all when I pass on. I suppose it'll be left for the kids to boast to their mates, 'Look, see what our grandad done.'

Anyhow, I've been a volunteer firie for fifty years and in 2020 they favoured me with an AFSM – Australian Fire Service Medal. As far as that award goes, it's definitely top of the tree as far as firefighting accolades go.

It all started back in October, twelve months ago, when an envelope turned up in the post. It was all very official looking, with my full name printed on the front and the crest of Australia in the corner and all that, and it was marked 'private and confidential'. Anyhow, I brought it home and I said to Jude, my wife, 'Blowed if I know what this's all about, so you'd better open it.'

When she opened it up she said, 'Well, you'll be pleased to hear that it's not from the taxation department.'

I said, 'Thank Christ for that.' I said, 'So what's it all about then?'

She said, 'It's from the Governor-General of Australia saying that you're being considered for the Australian Fire Service Medal in the January Australia Day Awards.'

I said, 'Holy shit!'

Of course, until it was all announced, I couldn't tell anybody or say anything about it. Only Jude and myself knew.

Anyhow, come December I get another letter. Same thing – 'private and confidential', with the Australian crest on the front of it. I open it up. It's not from the tax department – another sigh of relief. It's from the Governor-General saying that it'd all been approved.

Then on Australia Day there was a big announcement with it being in the paper and all over the news. So I was looking forward to going off to Government House and meeting the Governor-General and wolfing into a grand spread of cucumber sandwiches. Then, of course, when COVID-19 hit, they said, 'It's all off. You can't come down to Government House. You're going to have to wait.'

In the end I was presented with my AFSM at Government House in July 2020, and I'm very proud of it. Among other things, it says here 'for your contribution and dedication', et cetera, et cetera.

So that's that one. Another award I got was for being a part of the strike team that went down to the New South Wales South Coast town of Bega to fight the fires out from there. That was back in February 2020. Again it was all about my dedication to the cause and how my efforts were deeply appreciated and how I should be proud of the significant achievement I made. Which I am.

We were down there for ten days and, I tell you what, mate, I've seen fires and I've seen fires, but I'd never seen fires like those ones. Spot-overs were setting off fires three or four kilometres beyond the actual fire front. True. I mean, we were at the fire front and the crazy winds just picked up the burning leaf matter and whatever and it just blew sparks and shit up into the air, right through all the smoke, up and over our heads. Next thing we hear, another fire had started four kilometres behind us.

Mate, I can tell you, attending wildfires like those ones can be an extremely dangerous business. Then there were the burnovers, where they lost a number of firefighters, down in southern New South Wales and into Victoria. And hey, I know it's easy to say that it should never have happened and the firies should never have been there. But, mate, it's easy to say that when you haven't been there yourself and actually witnessed the ferocity of those fires. They were just unbelievable.

So that was that award. Then there's the Emergency Services Medal, which a couple of us got for helping out during the 2010–11 Queensland floods. Those floods were just massive. As simply as I can put it, all over the Somerset region, where I am, in the south-east of Queensland, we just had an unbelievable amount of rain, and the runoff had to go somewhere. Like, we had the Stanley River and the Brisbane River and we had the Cressbrook Creek, and it was just far too much water for the system to hold.

Anyway, armed with the old community spirit that us rural firefighters have, we said, 'Well, there must be something we can do here to help out.'

Esk, which is just fifteen minutes south of us, got hit pretty hard. Redbank Creek had burst its banks for the first time in recorded history and so the place had pretty much gone under. So we thought Esk would be a good place to start. The thing was, we had to wait two days before we could even get a fire appliance through. So a couple of days later we toddled down to Esk. The place was a mess. Even the council premises were flooded. So we slodged our way into the council building and we found our way to the CEO's office. And there he was, sitting up in his flash chair with the water lapping around his desk, and he looked up at us and he said, 'What the bloody hell are you blokes doing here?'

We said, 'We're here to help you out.'

And tell you what, at the end of the day, it was us in the Rural Fire Service that really came through with the goods. A major part of it was that the RFS had a communications network set-up that stretched through all the different brigades in the region – the length and breadth of the shire. So if they wanted an update, or if they wanted something to be done up at the top of the shire, we could sort it out. If they wanted to know what was going on down the bottom of the shire, we could sort that out as well. We were all over the place, everywhere. Great communications.

And that was the start of the Rural Fire Service getting involved with the 2010–11 floods. We gathered our troops together. We filled up all our appliances with water. And, as the floodwaters receded, we began hosing out houses and buildings. We cleaned all the crap off the roads. We cleaned fences. We gave the old pensioners a bit of a lift.

We knew a feller who had a helicopter. A while back we'd helped him out during a bushfire and he was more than willing to reciprocate our efforts. Day after day after day he kicked his chopper into action and we started doing supply drops – dropping food and other provisions. I can remember a chemist – we picked him up in Redcliffe and we brought him over and he opened the chemist shop up so that people could access insulin. And, mate, that was the first time I realised just how many people were insulin-dependent.

Then as the roads and bridges were being reopened and they could finally get transport through, guess what the powers-that-be sent in on their first couple of relief truckloads?

And no, it wasn't beer.

It was bottled water!

Can you believe that? Bottled bloody water! Now that's the city–country divide for you. No awards for the bright spark from Brisbane who came up with that one. I mean, when you stop and think about it, we'd just had record rains. And up here in the bush, every house has a rainwater tank, every farm house has a rainwater tank and every bloody shed's got a rainwater tank hooked onto it. And they were all overflowing. But the powers-that-be in head office thought that people's greatest necessity would be bottled water. Bloody hell, taking bottled water into a flooded area is like taking coals to Newcastle.

Note: During November 2010, thousands of Queenslanders had to be evacuated due to flooding. The floods were caused by a complex weather pattern that was formed when Tropical Cyclone Tasha joined in with a La Niña trough. It caused flooding around Toowoomba, Rockhampton, Bundaberg, Gympie, Emerald, Dalby, Roma and Ipswich. Catchment areas along the Bremer River, the Wivenhoe Dam, the Lockyer Creek – where twenty-three people were drowned – and the Brisbane River overflowed, causing floodwaters to rip through Ipswich and flow into suburbs of Brisbane. Over ninety towns and more than two hundred thousand people were impacted, as was a huge amount of property, wildlife and livestock. Infrastructure was also badly affected, with nineteen thousand kilometres of roads and approximately a third of the state's rail network being damaged.

The estimated total damage bill was between five and six billion dollars.

Near on fifty-five thousand registered volunteers helped during the flooding and the post-flooding clean-up effort.

Thirty-five deaths have been attributed to the disaster.

Communications

I came to Canberra in my early twenties. I'm an IT manager and we've also got a small beef stud, about fifty kilometres out of town, at Yass River. We breed what's called Belted Galloways, and I don't mind saying that we've done all right with them. We've even won a national trophy.

In a kind of way I was pretty much tricked into joining our Yass River–Nanima Volunteer Bush Fire Brigade. Not long after we bought the property, the captain rang to introduce himself, and somewhere along the line he said, 'How about coming down and meeting the mob?'

That sounded like a pretty good idea because it'd give me the chance to meet some of the locals. So I went along and, before I knew it, I was in the brigade and I'd done my training and I was going out to fires. That was seventeen years ago and for twelve of those years I was the brigade's deputy and now I'm senior deputy – though, mind you, that's probably more a case of me having a pulse and being available.

When I joined, there were just ten or so of us and we weren't all that well equipped. Our main truck was a 23-year-old Isuzu SBR. It had no creature comforts whatever, but the good thing about it was that it'd go anywhere and it carried a large 4000-litre tank of water. Unfortunately, with it being an alloy tank, the older it got, the leakier it got. In the end we were just about leaving as much water behind on the ground as was left to fight the fire. Anyway, we had the old Isuzu for about four or five years before it was replaced by a newer truck, which had a lot more creature comforts, though less water-carrying capacity.

These days we're quite an active brigade with near on forty members, and training's a whole lot more organised than the old hit-and-miss method of doing things. We get together monthly with the main objective of building teamwork and camaraderie. My thinking is that, within a brigade, if you don't know each other extremely well, you won't be able to work well together out on the fireground. And that's important. The other thing worth mentioning is that about forty per cent of our members are female. Amongst those we have seven female drivers, and I'm currently training up more. We've made a concerted effort in doing that, because it's a well-known fact that female drivers are a lot easier on the gear than what the male drivers are. And that's also important.

Actually, there's a bit of a process in becoming a driver. After they've got their medium rigid licence, I then take them through a 'rural fire driving course'. That's where they learn what's called 'response driving', which involves the finer points on how to drive in the bush and how to manage their crew's safety out on the fireground.

Now, I've got a bit of a story, and it's one of the most important lessons about firefighting. At the first big fire I went to, we had a certain crew leader. He was quite a large man who obviously loved his food. When we arrived at the staging point, he said to me, 'I'll teach you the first thing you should know about firefighting.'

'Yeah, okay,' I said. 'What's that?'

'Food first,' he said.

Then, to make it look like we'd already been out fighting the fire, he got us to throw dirt and ash dust over each other. After we'd done that, we wandered over to the food area. As soon as the people who were running the barbecue saw the state we were in, they welcomed us with open arms. 'Here, have this. Have that. You look hungry.'

After we'd had a good feed, we headed out to the fireground

where we did a couple of hours' firefighting before we got rolled off back to the staging point.

'Ah,' he said, 'just in time for lunch.'

So I thought, Gee, this firefighting's all right. At least you get a decent feed.

Normally the food's pretty good. It's usually run by one of the local volunteer groups. The mob we really like seeing turn up is the SES – State Emergency Service. More often than not, they've got good catering gear and great food. Also, these days, some of the brigades have their own catering unit. They're run by non-active members who are no longer able to get on the trucks and go out fighting fires. And, let me tell you, they're greatly appreciated. So much so that a few years ago we fundraised and bought a catering truck for our Group 2 and Group 4 brigades. And the same thing – our non-active members are more than happy to be a part of the catering crew. The other advantage of having non-active members on site is that, with them being trained firefighters, if something goes wrong, they're skilled enough to get everyone out of there in one piece.

As for some of the bigger fires, I wasn't available for the 2003 Canberra fires, though some of our brigade were. Now, even though that fire had horrific consequences, some positive changes came out of it, especially with regard to communications. Before those Canberra fires, the ACT brigades were on the HF network while the New South Wales brigades were on the UHF network. So they were on different frequencies. As a result of those fires, these days both the ACT and New South Wales have compatible communication networks. So everything's a whole lot easier and straight-forward and better co-ordinated.

And that was vital, especially during the 2020 Clear Range fires near Michelago. Michelago's on the Monaro Highway, south of Canberra, and it and some nearby villages were under dire threat. But the ACT brigades and our New South Wales brigades worked in together and we managed to turn the fire front before it got to the outskirts of Michelago.

Also, back in late 2019, when the fires ripped through the Southern Tablelands between Tarago and Nowra, down on the coast, the two brigades worked in together to divert it just before it took out the staging area at Nerriga Fire Station. As you may have heard, the 2019–2020 fire season was horrendous. I went up there about six months ago and you could still see just how hard the area got hit.

Now, just on Tarago, about three years ago they had fires go through there. Tarago's on the far side of Lake George – say, between Canberra and the back of Goulburn. See, the other thing is, us firefighters do more than fight fires. We also assist those who have just gone through what's probably the worst experience of their lives.

Anyhow, not long after the fire front had gone through, we went up to a house near Tarago to put out some burning hay bales. The house had survived, but one lady in the house was in such a state that she wanted to jump into her car and drive through the fire into Tarago because she thought it'd be safer there. So I said to her, 'Look, while we're talking about this, can you make me a cuppa?' And so she did. Now I didn't actually want a cuppa, but I thought it'd be something that'd take her mind off things. And that slight distraction calmed her down just enough for me to explain to her that if everything'd already been burnt to black around her, the safest place to be was right where she was.

The way I see it is that if some of these people aren't experiencing some form of post-traumatic stress, then it has to be close to it. So we try to calm them down as much as possible. The trainers call it 'restoring normality', which always gives me a laugh because what's 'normality' after you've gone through a fire like that?

Anyhow, this lady finally settled down and understood what I was on about, and she was pretty good after that. Well, as good as you'd expect her to be. But she stayed put.

We take a similar approach with evacuations. Normally the police are more involved in that side of things, but during the last series of fires we helped with a number of evacuations. That's where we came across people who were so rattled that they'd lost rational thought. The trick is not to order them to do something but to calm them down to a point where they can see the logic of what you're on about and they'll make the right decision for themselves. So you might say something along the lines of, 'Well, okay, I fully understand what you've got invested in this house and/or property. But think about it. Is it really worth risking your own life for?'

Then there's the flipside to all that. During the 2019–2020 fire season in particular, I was absolutely amazed by the amount of people who were in those dire situations, yet they seemed more worried about the welfare of us firefighters than of their own. Like they'd say, 'How are you? Thanks for doing what you do. Have you got the time to sit down and have a piece of cake and a cuppa?'

Note: The Yass River–Nanima Volunteer Bush Fire Brigade's region of operations covers eleven thousand hectares of the highest fire-risk areas in New South Wales. In 2017 the brigade celebrated its sixtieth anniversary.

The Orroral Valley blaze that began in the ACT in January 2020 was accidentally ignited by a military helicopter. That fire burnt through 82,700 hectares of the ACT's Namadgi National Park, 1444 hectares of Tidbinbilla Nature Reserve and 3350 hectares of rural land. It came to within six kilometres of the southern suburbs of Canberra.

The Clear Range fire, in nearby New South Wales, was ignited by spot fires from the Orroral Valley fire. It burnt through more than five thousand hectares, causing the closure of the Monaro

Highway between Bredbo and Michelago. A number of properties were lost and at least seven homes were destroyed. The fires burnt out of control for weeks. Sixteen water-bombing aircraft were used on both blazes.

In December 2019, dozens of buildings and several properties were destroyed by a bushfire in and around the small township of Nerriga. While people took refuge in the historic Nerriga Hotel, firefighters and residents continually hosed water on the pub to protect it from falling embers.

The Canberra bushfires of January 2003 began in the Brindabella Ranges. Multiple fires combined into a larger firestorm that then swept through suburbs on the outskirts of Canberra. It was the first confirmed case of a genuine fire tornado. In all, four people were killed, somewhere near five hundred were injured and about four hundred and fifty homes were either completely destroyed or badly damaged.

Locked Up Inside

I moved up here to Coonamble, in the central-west of New South Wales, back in '79. I'd already been a vollie firie for near on six years at a place down south, so I didn't have to do a refresher course or nothing, because the training is pretty much the same wherever you go. And so by the time I finished up, I'd been a vollie for forty-six years and for thirty-one of those years I was our local fire captain.

I actually got promoted to captain while we were at an incident. There was a street fire up in Walgett and they wanted backup. Our captain didn't want to go, so we left him at home and the rest of us went. When we arrived we got to work. Then when the fire got into a jewellery shop, we broke down the front door and went straight in. Mind you, that was much to the disgust of the owner, who thought we might nick something; either that or he was after the insurance. Anyway, we eventually put the fire out and while we were there, cooling it down, the big area boss from Parkes turned up and he came over to me and said, 'You're the new captain.'

I said, 'Well, I'm not the captain at home.'

He said, 'You will be by the time you get back there.'

It upset the brigade a bit, and the old captain. But that's the way it goes and I reckon that over the following years I kept most of the brigade out of mischief. Up till I chucked it in, I'd attended something like 6200 fire and rescue incidents.

In the early days we had a crew of around fourteen men. Though, of course, not everyone was always available. Plus, if you go to another place as backup, you've got to leave a few of your crew behind, just in case. And seeing how we were further out west from the larger centres where they had full-time staff, we vollies had to do the lot – both fire and rescue. Which means we've got two separate trucks. One's a fire pump unit, for fighting fires, and the other one's a rescue unit. Actually, we were one of the first accredited rescue units to arrive at the landslide site in Thredbo, back in the late '90s, when eighteen people were killed. So we were involved in the rescue of the sole survivor, Stuart Diver.

Our first rescue unit was an Isuzu. Then we got a Mercedes Benz, and the equipment on it was just unbelievable. It had all the hydraulic gear, with the jaws of life and the pressure cutters. It had airbags for lifting heavy gear. It had all the breathing apparatus. It had all the lighting gear. It had cordage gear to get to people who were stuck in holes, up trees or down mountains. It had heart starters – defibrillators – and all the first-aid gear. The works. So everyone then had to get accredited, not only in just your ordinary old first aid but in advanced first aid.

I guess we averaged about a hundred and sixty rescue calls a year. That covered a full range of things including pet galahs up trees, dogs down wells, kids down wells, people locked in domestic disputes, people locked in buildings. We also helped out the ambos and the police. See, around here there's usually only one or two ambulance officers on duty at any given time. So we'd assist them by closing down roads or looking after things while they worked on a patient.

We were also able to handle hazmat incidents, like when the LPG tanker hit a cow and tipped over and liquid petroleum gas started leaking out. And believe you me, if one of those tankers explode, they really explode. So it was an extremely dangerous operation. We were there for almost twelve hours hosing it down with the fog nozzle to arrest the vapour before we could pump the remaining liquid gas across into another truck.

Over time we also had three planes go down. One was a crop duster with all its chemicals. That was out near Gilgandra and the pilot was badly injured. But see, people don't realise just how dangerous those chemicals can be. So the ambulance went out and picked up the pilot and brought him back to the hospital with all the crop-dusting chemicals still all over him.

Anyhow, I had words with the duty doctor. I said, 'I've gotta shut down both the ambulance and the hospital.'

She said, 'You can't do that.'

I said, 'I can,' and so she rang my boss and he said, 'If it's got anything to do with dangerous chemicals, he can shut anything down.'

By then they'd rung the air ambulance. When they arrived they said there was no way they'd transport the feller while he still had chemicals on him. At that time the hospital didn't have a decontamination bay. So we got our hazmat unit in and, with all our protective gear on, we brought him out and we had to thoroughly hose him down before the ambos would even think about flying him out. In the end it took about two days to decontaminate both the ambulance and the hospital from the chemicals.

Another feller committed suicide by drinking rabbit poison and the ambulance picked him up and took him to the hospital. Same thing: they should've got our hazmat unit in. But they didn't. So again they had to completely decontaminate everything. See, it's incidents like that where people think, If you can't see it and you can't smell it, it won't hurt you. But it does. It'll hurt you all right. It'll catch up with you. And even though that particular feller didn't survive, even if they're dead, they're still dangerous. They're still contaminated.

So they're just some of the smaller things we had to attend to. Because, when it came to the rescue unit, I ended up attending three hundred and forty-seven incidents where thirty-four people lost their lives. Mostly vehicle accidents. And while I could go into the full details of every single one of those thirty-four deaths, I won't. I don't want to go there. They're too hard to take.

Well, for example there was the two buses head-on. Then at 2 o'clock one morning, a young bloke who's in the brigade now was a passenger in a bad prang at one of the main crossroads where his brother and two of his mates got killed. Then there's the lifelong injuries that are caused by the accidents. One of the worst was when a truck got rolled over by a big dust storm. The driver was strapped in the cab, suffering head injuries. And nobody knew he was there until the dust storm had passed and someone came along and found him. And while he's still with us, he's brain damaged.

There was the intentional head-on where a feller drove straight into a truck. Then there was the feller Bond, just out on the road here, who rolled his car. Young Richard What's-his-name was in the car with him. We eventually got Richard out but he's got brain damage. And even though we got Bondie out, the cut he received on his knee wouldn't heal. And that's when they found out he had bone cancer, which he's since died of.

Do you want me to go on? No, I didn't think so. But perhaps that might give you some idea why I keep a lot of that sort of stuff locked up inside. It's better that way. Better for everyone.

Then as far as fires go, because the brigade has all the proper equipment to go into a burning house, we've got the power of entry, whereas the police and the ambos don't. We've even got power of entry onto an Indigenous site, which no other service has.

But the fire that stirred this town up the most was back in the early 2000s when Belinda and Anthony Conn and one of their twin boys died in a house fire. They were all locals. Luckily, their three other children got out alive. The Conns lived on a property, Wilga Downs, about sixty k's out of town. They had four children. Samantha was around twelve at the time. Then there was their eldest son, Matthew, who was about ten; and the twin boys, Joseph – Joey – and William, who were about four.

Their house was your basic timber and fibro place, with

concrete and wooden floors and a corrugated-iron roof. They think the fire might've been started by an electrical fault in the laundry. Anyhow, Samantha later said that her mother had come into the lounge room where she'd been sleeping and had told her to get outside because the house was on fire. So Samantha went outside along with her father, Matthew and young Joey, while her mother went to get William. When the mum didn't return, the father decided to go back inside and help them out. Then, when he didn't return, Samantha went over to the car in the hopes of finding a mobile phone. But by then the car was also on fire, so she decided to walk for help.

Their nearest neighbours were Glen and Dianne Elliott. The Elliotts lived about four miles away. So Samantha set off barefoot, carrying Joey and holding on to Matthew, and with their family dog in tow. When they got there, Glen and Dianne were woken up by their own barking dogs and Samantha's screams for help. The Elliotts then got in touch with their neighbours, Tom and Carolyn Lyons, and while Glen and Tom went to Wilga Downs, the women called triple zero. So that would've been around 5.30 a.m.

By the time we arrived it was too late to save the house. But as I said, being firies, we were the only ones with right of entry into a burning building. So when you walk into a room of a burnt-out house and find the charred remains of two parents and a little four-year-old, you might be able to understand why I keep a lot of that bad stuff locked up inside. In fact, this is the first time I've ever really talked about it.

So that was back in the early 2000s. But it wasn't all the dramas that caused me to finish up with the volunteer fire service, it was mainly due to the bureaucratic side of things. The bureaucracy was just getting too much. I had a wife and kids and it was taking away too much of my family time. But I don't regret a day of it. Not one day. Not even the traumatic times. Anyhow, so that I'd clock up my fifty years' service, they even tried to talk me into staying on the extra four years. But like

Kenny Rogers sung, you've got to know when to walk away. And I knew when to walk away.

Note: Following the Conn family tragedy, the Coonamble community rallied in support of the three orphaned children. Service clubs, sporting organisations, local businesses and residents offered cash, clothing, furnishings and household electrical goods. Following a segment on the *Sunrise* program, a car was donated. Coonamble Shire launched a Lord Mayor's appeal, with the Premier's office of New South Wales donating. *Women's Day* contributed. Coonamble Rotary made a donation. Coonamble Lions Club also ran a statewide appeal. In all, over fifty thousand dollars was raised.

Elvis

Well, there's my name on top of the honour board. See? 'Treasurer 2002–2007'. But actually I was treasurer a long time before that when I had the joint jobs of secretary–treasurer. Then the brigade split them in two and so from 2002 onwards we had a treasurer and we had a secretary, and I was the treasurer.

But anyhow, what some of the readers might not fully realise is that the Victorian CFA – Country Fire Authority – don't just fight fires; we help out in a lot of emergency situations including attending road accidents. Some of those are pretty terrible. Not for the faint-hearted. So let's leave that one. Someone else may be prepared to tell you a story or two there, but not me. But we also do search and rescue.

As far as search goes, I remember the time back in the '70s when a young kid went missing. We got the call and so this big search gets underway. I'm not exactly sure now, but it might've gone on for a couple of days. Anyhow, we eventually found the little feller hiding under someone's house. Apparently, he'd got into some sort of strife at home and he just took off.

Then there's the rescue side of it. Another time we rescued a cow who'd got stuck in a dam. That was on a property just a couple of miles down the road from town. We'd had a pretty dry summer, so there wasn't a lot of water in the dam. Just a little puddle out in the middle. Anyhow, this cow must've got thirsty, so it decided to take a walk out through the mud to get itself a drink. Then when it turned around to walk back out again, it couldn't. It found itself stuck in the mud – well and truly.

So we got the call to go and help get this stuck cow out. Actually, that was a bit of a dicey incident because there was quite a stretch of mud between us and the cow. Like, it wasn't just a case of getting in there and leading it out. In the end, we had to tie a rope onto one of our younger volunteers and we sort of dragged-swum him out across the mud to put a harness on the cow. It was then a case of towing the poor cow out, inch by inch. So they're the sorts of other things we do.

But, just while I'm on dry summers, with the dry start to this current 2019–2020 fire season, we've already had well above our average number of call-outs. Now I'm no expert on all this, but how it works is that it starts off with a triple-zero call to Telstra. Once the incident has been reported, it gets relayed on to what's called a CAD – computer-aided dispatch – system. The call's then processed and they advise whatever emergency services it concerns – like either the fire brigade, the police or the ambulance. Or all of them.

In the case of a fire, the CAD centre gets straight in touch with the respective fire brigade who's closest to the incident. When the fire alarm's triggered, everyone in the brigade gets notified via their pager – a pager being a small cigarette-packet-sized monitor that each of the volunteers carries. When the signal comes through on the pager, the person's first alerted by a tone, which is then followed up by a notification.

These days they also use what's called a BART system. BART meaning 'Broadcast. Alert. Respond. Turn-out.' And that runs off a volunteer's mobile phone, like off some sort of an app. When the BART alert comes through, the volunteer can respond by pressing a green button or a red button to signify if they're available or not available to attend the incident. Now don't ask me how all that works, because I haven't got it on my mobile phone. It's all a bit over my head, which is why I still use the old pager system.

Then, when everyone gathers at the fire station, a television monitor displays the location of the fire or incident plus any further information that's required. So it's all pretty high-tech. Like I said, well above my head.

So then all the volunteers get into their gear and off they go. Of course, during the daytime, the number of available volunteers has become a bit of an issue because, these days, a lot of people work away from the town. And that's not only with our brigade; a lot of the other volunteer brigades are in the same boat. A few years ago it wasn't so bad. You'd have eight or ten people turn up. So that's the basics of how it all works. But, like I said, I'm no expert.

The biggest fire I've ever been involved in would've been Ash Wednesday, back in 1983. I think Ash Wednesday was the first time they seriously started using helicopters with water tanks in them. In many situations they're more mobile than the aircraft because they can get into places where an aircraft can't. And also, because there's usually so many dams around the area, they can fill up with water and be back at the fire instead of having to return to an airport and fill up there. Mind you, when they drop a load of water you have to be well out of the way. That's why they give everyone a siren warning before they drop a load of water. So you'd better watch out.

The next biggest set of fires would've been Black Saturday, 2009. I wasn't directly involved in Black Saturday because I was working in communications out at the airfields with the air cranes. There's a bit of history there. The original air crane came out to Victoria from America back in the late 1990s. Now, my memory's not what it used to be but, from memory, the first one that came out got the nickname of Eric the Water Bomber or something like that. And it was used to fight fires in the Frankston area and also up in the Alpine National Park. And it did such a great job that it was brought out for every fire season up till 2000–2001.

And that's when Elvis the air crane first came upon the scene. Why it got called Elvis was that it'd been working for the American government, out of Memphis, Tennessee, which was Elvis Presley's old stomping ground. I believe that it was dismantled to a degree in America before being shipped out here and, on its arrival, it was reassembled, ready to go for our fire season.

Anyhow, no sooner had Elvis been reassembled in Melbourne than it was sent up to New South Wales to fight the big fires they were having around the Sydney area. And that's when it really captured everyone's imagination. Because Elvis not only helped save a hell of a lot of homes in those fires, but it ended up being involved in saving the lives of a dozen or so firefighters who'd got trapped by another fire up in the Blue Mountains.

But it was in those Victorian Black Saturday fires of 2009 that I got to know Elvis. Oh, and what a magic machine it was. Elvis was a Sikorsky helicopter that had originally been built for the Russian Army. But, for some reason or other, it didn't end up suited for the Russians' needs. It might've been something to do with its design, maybe. I don't know. But as a firefighting vehicle, Elvis was worth its weight in gold. So much so that another couple of Sikorsky helicopter air cranes were sent over to Australia to join Elvis.

To give you some idea, when you actually see one of them in the sky, they look like a great big flying mantis. Then as far as their more technical aspects go, they've got a cruising speed of a bit over one hundred and fifty kilometres per hour and they can carry something like nine or ten thousand litres of water or retardant. And believe it or not, the tank's only bolted down with four main bolts. They've got two pilots and an observer, who keeps an eye on things. But, mate, I wouldn't like to sit in the cabin all day. It's that tight in there.

And, when they want to fill up the water tank, the pilot just hovers the air crane over a dam or some other available water source, and he drops down a snorkel from the guts of it. And, in less than a minute, they can suck the water straight up into the tank, and away it goes again. Oh, Jesus, it's just incredible. And of course, then there's the choppers with the huge buckets under them that they fill with water.

Actually, I was talking to one of the pilots one day. He was Canadian, and I said to him, I said, 'Well, when you're not using Elvis for firefighting, what do you use it for?'

And he said, 'If you take the tank out, you can do almost anything with it.' He said, 'We can even put a crane underneath it and go out into the backwoods of Canada to lift the timber out.'

So there you go. But that Elvis, I'd reckon it'd be near on forty years old now. From memory, it last came out here in 2016 to help fight some fires over near Sydney. But by gee it did Australia a great service. So much so that, these days, a number of air cranes are brought out for each bushfire season to be stationed, ready to go, in the more fire-prone states.

Note: The Victorian government leases a large number of firefighting aircraft to assist the regional fire brigades during the fire season. These not only include air cranes, but there's also a variety of fixed-wing aircraft, ranging from small single-engine planes up to extremely large aerial tankers, similar to commercial passenger jets.

Elvis was last seen in Santiago, Chile, in 2017.

Sirens

Over here in Western Australia, even though things have improved with regard to our current communications set-up, our fire brigade still has a town siren. It's one of those old air raid ones from way back. I'm not sure of its exact history other than when our station was built, back in 1959, the siren somehow came with it. Of course, nowadays people think it's redundant, so there's a push to get rid of it – which is something I disagree with.

Take what happened just recently out in Kalgoorlie. When a fire broke out they lost the power station and they lost the Telstra tower, so they lost all comms – communications. Not even the comms centre in Perth could contact the fire station. The only way the brigade members were alerted was when someone actually drove down to the fire station and physically pushed the button to manually activate the siren. Then it was, 'Hang on, what's that? That's the town siren. Better get down to the station.' And so they turned out.

So that's why I'm keen to keep our town siren – just in case. Like an insurance. And like many brigades do, at a certain specified time, on a certain day of the week, we activate the siren just to check that everything's in working order. In our case it's at 12 o'clock midday, every Saturday. That's been a tradition of ours now for the past sixty-one years and one I hope continues for another sixty years.

Now, talking about sirens and so forth, at one time I was brigade captain out at Laverton. Do you know where Laverton is? Well, if you draw a line from Perth to Ayers Rock – Uluru – Laverton's just about in the middle. It's the most remote

Volunteer Fire and Rescue Brigade within the biggest fire district, if not in Australia, then most definitely in Western Australia.

I went up to Laverton as a teacher in 1997 and, when I became brigade captain, they didn't have a siren. So, when the old mine site out at Mount Morgan was going into care and rehabilitation, I said to the guy, 'Can I have your old evacuation siren?' That's the siren they use to let everyone know within cooee that they were going to set off an explosion on the mine site.

He goes, 'Gee, you'd better be careful.' He said, 'This siren's four times more powerful than your usual one. It'll wake the dead.' He said, 'While most town sirens have a five-kilometre radius, this one's got a twenty-kilometre radius.'

Anyway, we got it. They gave it to us. But because of the extra power that was needed to run it, we had to put in an extra powerline. Then, because it was so loud, there were the usual expected complaints. But there was a bit of a twist to that because, when we'd set it off at 7 o'clock of a Wednesday evening, it became the signal to all the young kids that it was bedtime.

When I first arrived in Laverton to teach in the district school, Western Mining was still operating and the town had a population of around 2500. Then, when Western Mining pulled out the following year, a thousand people left. That's almost half the population and, of course, we lost half our Fire and Rescue volunteers as well.

As far as our gear went, we had a GPA – a general-purpose appliance – which was a four-wheel drive Isuzu fire engine. For our light tanker, we had a Land Rover. Then we had a rescue trailer. All the rescue gear was stored in the trailer and, if we needed to cut anyone out of a vehicle, we'd tow the trailer out to the scene of the accident. But with our original fire station being virtually non-existent, we began lobbying the government for a new one.

When I talk about a 'new station', in the end all we got was a tin shed. But that was okay. We liked it. It housed the vehicles and all our gear and there was a nice space at the back where we could all get together. Oh, and regarding our remoteness, I remember when the commissioner came up in '99 to open the new station – the shed. When we were showing him around the place, he asked me, 'Ken, what are all those jerry cans lined up with the 100 markings on the side of them?'

I said, 'Well, Commissioner, because we cover such a vast area, if we get a call that's say out at Blackstone Ranges, we know it's going to be an 800-kilometre return trip. And seeing how there's no petrol station between here and there, and with eight times a hundred equalling eight hundred, we take eight jerry cans with us.'

'Well,' he said, 'I've never heard of that before.'

Of course, back in the '90s, there were none of the helicopters that they now have in places like Kalgoorlie, Geraldton, Albany and Broome, where a chopper picks up a container with all the cutting gear in it and drops it off with a couple of firefighters, right at the scene of an accident.

Other than attending road accidents, we've also had a couple of big bushfires. Though more often than not, because of the vast pastoral leases out around Laverton, we tended to just let them go.

Look, I'll tell you a story. Print it if you like. It's now public knowledge. One time we were asked to do a burn-off within the boundary of the federal government's Jindalee over-the-horizon radar complex, which is out from Laverton. It was going to be quite a big burn-off of a few hundred acres.

When we got there in the morning, the weather was excellent. Even when the wind started to pick up a bit, I thought it'd still be okay. So I said, 'Yep, right, okay, let's do it.'

We were well-enough equipped. We had four light tankers, which were four-wheel-drive utes; there was ours and the three others were from the shire. But as we were to find out, the shire vehicles weren't particularly well maintained. Anyhow, we arrived at around eight in the morning and we got set for the back-burn with rake-hoes and putting containment lines in and all that. So then we did the burn. All went well. Perfect.

Anyhow, at about midday, after we'd finished the burn-off, I asked one of the shire guys to start mopping up the fire with what little water we had remaining. So he was just putting out the bits and pieces. Anyhow, with the shire unit not being well maintained, the end of the hose fell off. And being high pressure, he couldn't just simply put his thumb over it and spray the water all about. So all the water just poured out on the ground, till we had nothing left. We were empty.

And that's when the shit hit the fan. At that very moment the wind picked up, and off the fire went like a rocket, over the grass and scrub. We're all going, 'Christ, this's going to be big.'

Anyhow, with Jindalee being a high-surveillance government complex, the whole area was enclosed by a security fence. And by now the fire had taken off through the security fence and was heading out into the pastoral leases. And so we had to go right to the end of the security fence to turn around and come back the other side to get to this out-of-control fire.

Now, to give you some idea as to how fast that fire was travelling, I was trying to race ahead of this fire in one of the vehicles, right. And we were doing forty-eight kilometres per hour in that vehicle and that fire was keeping up with us. True. Anyhow, we eventually got ahead of it and we got around the fence and we started a back-burn to contain it. By then we'd already lost it for four hours. So by now it would've been about four thirty in the afternoon.

Then, just as we had it contained, the wind spun around a complete ninety degrees and it took off again, across the road and further into the pastoral leases.

Anyhow, in the end, one of the shire rangers said, 'Oh, fuck it,' and he grabbed a VB – beer – out and he sat down beside the road and downed it. He said, 'That's it. Stuff it. We've done all we can do.'

And he was right. We couldn't do anything more. We'd lost it and that was it. It took off again into some of the pastoral properties. And to this day that's the third biggest scrub fire in Western Australia's state history. That was in '99. And I was sort of famous after that. Because, when some of the cockies – farmers – put up a case for us having burnt all the sheathing on their fences, I had to go to court and explain what'd happened.

See, on the fencing out there, they've got this green rubber that goes around the fence wire, like an outer sheath, to stop it corroding so quickly. And the fire got that hot, it melted the outer sheathing. So instead of their fences lasting ten years, they were now only going to get a couple of years out of them.

So part of the cockies' claim was to be compensated by the government for having to replace their fencing. But our argument, and DFES – Department of Fire and Emergency Services – backed me up, was that, if the cockies would've maintained their required three-metre firebreaks, there wouldn't have been enough heat to have melted the sheathing on the fences. And we won. Though, mind you, we didn't get too many requests to do those type of big burn-offs again.

So that's just one little story.

Note 1: Jindalee Operational Radar Network is an over-the-horizon radar network that is used to monitor air and sea movements across an area of thirty-seven thousand square kilometres. The network's main ground stations consist of a control centre at the RAAF Base Edinburgh in South Australia and three transmission stations near Longreach, Queensland, Alice Springs in the Northern Territory and Laverton in Western Australia.

Note 2: There are two basic types of sirens: pneumatic and electronic. Pneumatic sirens are the older type, which consist of a rotating disk with holes that interrupt a flow of air from fixed holes on the outside of the unit. When the holes that are in the rotating disk break up the free flow of air, sound is produced.

Electronic sirens incorporate circuits such as oscillators and modulators which, when played through external speakers, create a selected siren tone depending on how quick and fast the siren's pitch moves up and down, that is, either a wail or a yelp or a hi-lo et cetera.

Both types of sirens have their disadvantages in that a) they don't work if there is a power outage or the siren has been removed for servicing and b) they use a lot of power.

In terms of coverage versus cost, both types of sirens are considered uneconomical. Though in areas where residents can't be contacted by mobile phones, sirens can be clearly heard even in the worst black spots.

A Hard-Headed Bastard and a Hero

My name's Vince Balanzategui. I'm currently chief officer of the Stone River Rural Fire Brigade – Stone River being north of Townsville, in the Hinchinbrook Shire in Queensland. Ingham's at the centre of it and we're a hundred kilometres south-west of there. Even these days, while there are some cattle, our main income still comes from sugar cane.

Okay, so I'll give you a bit of background as to the sorts of fires we get up here. For most parts, the burning of cane before harvest is no longer carried out. That given, what we now do, which is green cane cutting, has a fire risk of its own. Now, a good stick of cane could be anywhere up to fourteen foot long. The machine goes through and cuts it up into billets – pieces – of six to eight inches. That's what gets loaded onto the cane trains and taken off to the sugar mill. But during the harvesting process, all the extraneous matter, which can be up to fifteen tonnes per hectare, gets thrown out onto the ground. Over the course of the next couple of weeks that dries out. So you end up with a heap of flammable residue and, given the conditions, if a spark gets into that – *whoosh!* – it takes off and it can do a hell of a lot of damage.

So with 99.9 per cent of cane farmers being very savvy of that, the fires we get up here either start through machinery breakdowns or lightning strikes or from powerlines going down because a bird's hit them or there's some sort of electrical fault. As far as deliberately lit fires go, they're extremely rare.

Anyhow, I took over this cane block back in the early to mid-1970s. That's when I realised the dangers. So I got together a few of my primary producer mates and we formed a volunteer fire service. To start with we used my Nissan ute, with a slip-on on the back. By slip-on, I mean a small water tank, a firefighting pump, a bit of gear and some hose. Me and the wife paid for all that.

Now, a rural fire truck's good for twenty years before it's considered obsolete and it has to leave the fireground. So Rollingstone, which is on the way to Townsville, had five years left on their appliance and, being financial, they decided they'd get a new one. And this's how we got a step in the door. With the part-help of a government grant through the Rural Fire Service, we raised the balance and we bought Rollingstone's old appliance. It was a Mitsubishi Canter – a proper fire truck for real fires. At that stage, fuel and maintenance also had to be paid for by the brigade. So for the first couple of years, my wife and I also covered that, at our own expense.

The problem I was then faced with was: how long could the wife and I keep forking out the money to keep the truck maintained? That's when I came up with the idea of placing a levy on our local rate payers. We've got about a hundred and fifty rate payers in the area and I worked out that if we tacked thirty dollars per year onto everyone's rate notice, it'd cover the ongoing expenses of the fire truck.

Anyhow, before we could go down that track, we had to have a public meeting to get the nod. Now you'd think that everybody would be for it, wouldn't you? But you'd be surprised. Let me put it this way: if I knew what I was getting into when I instigated the levy, I would've thought a lot harder about doing it. Mate, you've got no idea. As soon as you mention the word 'levy', even though you've got all the best intentions in the world, you wouldn't credit the amount of knockers who were trying to shoot us down. All I'll say is that someone had to pay for its upkeep and it definitely wasn't going to be my wife and me – not any longer. And so, being the hard-headed bastard I am, I eventually railroaded the levy through and so I managed to snag this truck – the Mitsubishi Canter – and with the levy, we were now able to cover its ongoing expenses.

So there, and these days, for what it's worth, all my knockers now agree that they were wrong. But that's not the point. Mate, it wasn't like I was trying to rob anyone. No way. Every cent the brigade collects has to be audited by a proper auditor. Then when a new government came in, it flicked the switch and all of a sudden they were supplying new vehicles for the obsolete ones. So after a couple of years, our Mitsubishi Canter went to Abbot Point and we got a new truck. So see how the progression goes? So now, as far as equipment goes, we've got a four-wheel drive Isuzu dual-cab fire truck which seats five people comfortably, with a tank that holds around 1500 litres of water. It does all it's required to do, and that's good enough for me.

Our next battle was to get a decent shed where we could keep our appliance and our equipment. So me and a mate, along with a bit of support from our Hinchinbrook MP, became the driving force behind the brigade acquiring a block of land and putting a new fire shed on it. And while we've got rivers, which have plenty of water in them, they're too difficult to access. So now we're putting in a grant for a 27,000-litre bulk water tank at our new fire station where, in case of an emergency, we'll be able to fill up with ease.

Of course, once again there's been the knockers. Mate, I hate knockers. Look, I'll tell you straight, occasionally there are times when I just don't want to help some people. I've been in situations, say at night, when you've worked your guts out at a fire, you're dead tired and some of these ungrateful bastards are still abusing you like crazy. True, but you wear it, because if you drove away and there's a wind change or whatever, who knows what damage the unchecked fire can go on and do throughout the community.

Which brings me to some of the fires we've had. As far as big ones go, back in November 1990 we had a very bad fire. People came from all over to help us. In those days we had very little firefighting gear, so we were lucky no one got hurt. Then two years ago we had another very bad fire season. But the thing was, by then we were a lot more organised. Like I said, our gear was better, communications were better, we had a decent fire truck et cetera, et cetera.

Even so, from October through to the end of November, I never got to do an ounce of farm work. True. Every morning the second-in-charge of parks would rock up at my place in his dual cab and off we'd go consulting everybody. See, the thing is, you've got to get everybody onboard. You just can't wander onto someone else's property and start back-burning. It's got to be a co-ordinated effort. Everybody has to be on the same page. But that doesn't happen in five minutes, so every day we just went out and did what needed to be done.

As for my farm work, what else could I do? If you've got these severe fire conditions, you just have to deal with them. And with me being first officer of the brigade, as far as I was concerned, that was just part and parcel of my job. What's more, if I wasn't prepared to do those extra yards, how could I expect anyone else to?

And so, you do have to put everything into it – well, I do anyway – and being the hard-headed bastard I am, I always have. Which was probably why I got awarded the 2010 Volunteer of the Year for the northern region of Queensland. Then in 2015 I got the AFSM – Australian Fire Service Medal – in the Queen's Birthday Honours List.

For us firefighters, the AFSM is like getting a VC in the military service. The wording of it goes along the lines of how it recognises the distinguished service by a member of the Australian Fire Service who is seen to have demonstrated a high degree of commitment and devotion to duty in a particular situation, or in special duties above and beyond normal work responsibilities. And that was the pinnacle of my success – well, it's the pinnacle of success for any volunteer firefighter. I mean, you don't nominate yourself for these awards. So when they rang me up and told me what was happening, and where I had to be on a certain day, it just blew me away.

The award was presented in Cairns by the Governor His Excellency the Honourable Paul de Jersey. And oh, there's a story to all that as well. Previous to the award, I'd broken my wrist and so the Governor couldn't even shake my hand. What's more, it took me eighteen bloody months and I couldn't tell you how many operations, to get over it.

What happened was, we'd been out fighting this fire since daylight. By about 11 o'clock at night we'd nearly finished the back-burn. Just a spot-over or two needed seeing to. No big deal. So I stepped out of the truck to go and start the water pump up. But being volcanic country, there was all this loose rock lying around, from softball size, to soccer ball size, to bigger. Anyway, when I stepped out of the truck, I tripped over on these rocks and – *snap!* – I broke my wrist. Simple as that. No one was mucking around. There was no rush. We were tired and it just happened.

And hey, they tell us we're only supposed to be out there for eight hours. But when there's no one to replace you, you just can't pack up and go home, can you? You have to stay. There's no time clock out on a fire front, so you just put your head down and do what has to be done. And so I ended up driving the truck two hours home, broken wrist and all.

Anyhow, when I rocked up to this event in Cairns to get my AFSM there was a young woman in her thirties standing there with her two little kids. I heard that she was up for some sort of bravery award. And on the day of the reception, when they went through the spiel of what she'd done and how she did it, I just thought, Well, bloody hell, there's a real fair dinkum hero.

A couple of years previous, she'd been leading a group of Australian walkers and all their porters out along the Kokoda

Trail. Then one night this mob of rascals attacked their camp and killed a couple of the porters and hacked into a few of the Aussies. And during the attack this woman stepped in and she talked the rascals out of killing any more people. Then she led the walking group back out to safety. Anyway, mate, on the day of the awards, if you would've seen the size of this young woman, at the most she would've only been seven stone wringing wet. True. So for me to receive my AFSM at the same ceremony she received her bravery medal, well, it was the most humbling experience of my life. It really was.

Note: In 2015, Christiana Jane King received the Star of Courage at a ceremony held in Cairns. The Star of Courage recognises conspicuous acts of bravery in extremely dangerous situations, in this case for having placed others' lives ahead of her own.

In September 2013, Ms King was leading her first trekking party along the Black Cat Track in the northern Morobe Province of Papua New Guinea. On their first night out they were attacked by a group of 'bandits' who were armed with a shotgun, machetes and knives. Two of the nineteen porters were killed and a number of the others were rendered unable to walk due to the severe leg injuries they received. Four of the eight Australian trekkers were also injured, two with serious head injuries and two with leg and arm injuries.

During the attack, Ms King confronted the bandits and negotiated a stop to the violence and for them to leave the camp. She then led the trekkers on a five-hour hike to safety, mostly in darkness.

Shearing

Prior to the Black Tuesday fires of early 1967, other than a roughly shod Rural Fires Board and a few fire wardens, there was no real officially organised fire service here in Tasmania. If a fire got out of control, all us farmers would get together with beaters, knapsacks and whatever else we could find around the place to help each other out. The best we got was to put a couple of forty-four-gallon drums up on top of a trailer to cart water, which was a similar outfit that we used for dipping our sheep.

The big turning point came with the Black Tuesday fires. We'd had a wet spring which was followed by a summer drought. I remember Tuesday 7 February as being one of those days you could just about burn water. It was hot and dry with a north-westerly and, before you knew it, everything was alight. It went through the southern part of Tasmania – the south-east in particular – like a firestorm, similar to the 2019–2020 fires they've just experienced on the mainland.

Most of the Tasman Peninsula was burnt out. I really don't know where or how it started but it ripped through thousands of square kilometres of native vegetation, forest plantations, townships and farming areas. And, even though no one here on the Tasman Peninsula lost their lives, by the fire's end, somewhere over sixty people had died throughout the state and thousands had been left homeless. On top of that, I shudder to imagine what the loss of livestock and wildlife was.

As a result, the Rural Fires Board broke Tasmania up into segments – districts and zones – with the idea of each area forming its own brigade and having its own fire permit officer. In our case I was the fire permit officer. Then, in conjunction with our local council, me and a friend formed the first firefighting committee on the Tasman Peninsula. If you can imagine, our area went from Dunalley down to the bottom of the peninsula.

With me being their secretary, I wrote to pivotal people such as councillors in the various towns to see if they'd like to get a brigade up and running in their community. In the end, Eaglehawk Neck, Taranna, Port Arthur and Nubeena all formed brigades, as we did in Koonya, a brigade that I'm still a part of, and am proud of.

Our Koonya Brigade is a bit of an unusual brigade. With Koonya being the more central point of our particular fire zone, that's where the main fire station is. But, because I live about twenty kilometres away, on an outer end of the area, we've basically split the zone up into two sections. So I keep a second part of the brigade and some of the equipment here on the Saltwater River side of Norfolk Bay. Like, I've got a Land Cruiser housed here with a pump and a tanker and all the basic gear on it.

So after the Black Tuesday fires, things started to get more organised. As I said, I'd taken on the role of our local fire permit officer. With regard to the permits, people would just get in touch and say, 'Look, I want to do a burn in this spot on this particular day,' and if that was okay I'd say, 'Yes,' and issue them a permit.

The beauty of that was I knew everyone within my area. I could trust them, and take their word for it, which meant that I didn't actually have to go out and check each individual application. So since Tasmania Fire Service started running the show back in 1979, things have become far more professional and the process of getting a permit has become more formalised – which it probably needed to be.

Nowadays, any fire bigger than a cubic metre requires a permit. And on your permit you've got to put all the fire's details, no matter if you're burning garden rubbish or a large log fire which, because it has to be permanently stoked, could burn for weeks. Another of the conditions is that for the larger burn-offs, you have to plough a certain distance around the area, as a firebreak. The owner also has to remain in attendance of the fire and, of course, there's strict rules about the weather conditions, like not lighting a fire during a forty mile an hour nor-wester, when it's stinking hot.

Initially, there was a bit of resistance to this stricter system. And perhaps there still is to some degree. Occasionally you'll see a fire where you know they haven't gone to the trouble of getting a permit. But there's been a big upside to it in that Tasmania Fire Service have given us more and better equipment.

When I first started with my permit book, I had a couple of knapsacks that I'd loan to whoever I issued a permit to and, when they'd finished their burn, they were supposed to bring them back. And I can tell you, you had a devil of a job lifting those big old knapsacks. Too right you did and, once you got them on, you had a devil of a job to stand up. From memory, they held about forty litres and they had a little hand pump attached and your back was permanently wet. And even after they reduced the size of them, they were still a pretty hefty load.

The first bit of proper equipment we got was a trailer-unit with a pump on it and a tank that held about a hundred and fifty gallons of water, which we'd hook onto one of our farm vehicles or a tractor or whatever. So we started out with that. Then later on we got an early model Land Cruiser with a slip-on tanker unit.

Eventually the old trailer-unit got farmed out to the next smaller brigade down the line. But though it was all a hand-me-down sort of system, at least they had something. Then, because the council workers were such an integral part of the brigade's operations, in about '75, our committee got the council to install two-way radios into their vehicles.

The thing with the council workers being such an important part of the brigade was that, no matter where they were working, if they got a call, they were able to drop everything and go and help fight a fire. And, with being involved with roadworks, they had a bigger truck with a larger-capacity water tank on it and, in most cases, a grader. Even though their trucks were more cumbersome, their great advantage was that they were handy for servicing the smaller units. Like you could pump water from them into the smaller units. And a grader, of course, was ideal for making firebreaks.

So that all came out of the '67 Black Tuesday bushfires.

The biggest fire we've had since '67 would be the Dunalley fires of 2013. By then I was getting a bit long in the tooth to actually go out and fight those type of larger fires, so I helped out elsewhere. Seeing how all the power had gone down during the Dunalley fire, I helped service the gen-sets – generator sets – for all the essential services like radio communications and all that. And so, other than fighting a smaller outbreak on a neighbour's property, that's what tied me up for the week or so of the Dunalley fires: maintaining the gen-sets.

I mean, when it comes to fighting a fire, you really do have to take into consideration your health and your age. The last thing you want is to be the weak link in the team and let everyone down. And seeing how I suffer a bit from asthma, I have to be aware of the possibility of having an asthma attack. And that's even though we're supplied with good-quality face masks.

So there's been a hell of a lot of changes, mainly as far as equipment goes. And with all the modern gear Tasmania Fire Service has given us, we've had to do courses in how to properly use the stuff. Like there's chainsaw courses and we're instructed in how to deal with structural fires. There's also a course in the use of the breathing apparatus – BA – so that we can now enter a burning building to fight the fire from within the structure and to check that no one's trapped inside.

Then there's the training for wildfires. Because most of our brigade started out as property owners, we already had a bit of an idea as to what to do there. Whereas many of the new volunteers may come from an office environment, so they begin with the mindset that you just race in and fight a wildfire head-on. But that's wrong. There's far more to it than that. There's a whole strategy to it all. So they've got to be taught about the vagaries and unpredictability of a wildfire, as well as how to read maps and how to use the correct equipment. And, with a lot of the younger ones, all this training takes time out of their lives, and they're reluctant to commit to that. They lose sight of the fact that we're basically a volunteer organisation.

In my time, when the chips were down you dropped everything and off you went. It's just what you did. I remember one time being halfway through shearing a sheep when the fire emergency call came through. So I just shoved the sheep back in the pen and headed off to the fire, and I mightn't have come back till the next day or even the day after. So there's the poor old sheep, half undressed, back in the pen, wondering what the heck's going on.

Note 1: In terms of the loss of life and property, the Tasmanian Black Tuesday bushfires of February 1967 are considered to be one of Australia's worst disasters. Indeed, they're the most deadly and damaging bushfires that Tasmania has ever experienced. In all, sixty-three people died, nine hundred people were injured and seven thousand people were left homeless. Near on 1300 homes and over 1700 other buildings were destroyed. Also destroyed in the fires were eighty bridges, 4800 sections of powerlines, 1500 motor vehicles and over a hundred other structures. It's believed that somewhere around sixty-two thousand farm animals were killed and the loss of wildlife is uncountable.

During the period of the fires, eleven separate fire fronts burnt through 2643 square kilometres of land – 652,000 acres. The fires even entered the outskirts of Hobart.

The cause was put down to a heatwave within extreme drought conditions, back-burning that got out of control and arson.

The Black Tuesday bushfires of Tasmania and the 2009 Victorian Black Saturday bushfires, where one hundred and seventy-three people died, share the same commencement date of 7 February.

Note 2: During record-breaking heatwave conditions through late 2012 and into early 2013, high fuel loads, coupled with a record-breaking heatwave, caused a number of large bushfires to break out in south-eastern Tasmania. Over the course of several days the fires killed one person and destroyed four hundred and thirteen buildings – two hundred of them residential. In all, the fires burnt approximately twenty thousand hectares – forty-nine thousand acres – of mixed residential and native forest.

In the worst-hit town of Dunalley, sixty-three homes, a primary school, the police station and a bakery went up in flames. With the fires having cut off access to and from the township, a seaborne rescue operation was launched to save the thousands of people sheltering on beaches and in boats and at the nearby Port Arthur Historic Site. More than two thousand people were ferried to safety by police, commercial vessel operators and private volunteers, and another two thousand took refuge at a community centre at Nubeena.

The 2012–2013 fire season lasted for an unprecedented six months. Firefighting crews came to assist from many states of Australia as well as from New Zealand.

No Politics in the Bush

My name's Brad. My wife and I came out to the central west of New South Wales, to Cobar, in October 2004. Previous to that we'd been living in the Shoalhaven area, south of Wollongong. But seeing how my wife was virtually born and bred in nearby Dubbo, she was keen to move back a bit closer to home.

Then one time when we were on a visit to Dubbo, she saw an advertisement for a management position with Children's Services, here in Cobar. So she applied for the job and got it. Basically, she oversees Children's Services throughout the western area, from the Queensland border down to Wellington, which is south of Dubbo, then across to the South Australian border. Children's Services looks after things like employing governesses to look after the kids while their parents are out working the property. She also covers family home day care, before- and after-school care and vacation care. So she's a busy woman.

Before the move, I'd worked with the Shoalhaven Council as a relief supervisor cum leading hand. Then lo 'n behold, when we came out to Cobar for my wife's interview I saw the local council was looking for a mechanic. And the rest is history. Up till a year ago I was a depot co-ordinator and fleet and maintenance supervisor. In a larger place all those roles would be singular positions but, with Cobar being a smaller town, I got the lot. And that was fine. It kept the blood pumping. But now I've had a career change and stepped into the role of buying, selling and sourcing the council's and their contractors' materials.

I'm Peter. My family originally came from Shepparton, Victoria. Then, with Dad being a builder, we went to Western Australia for a while. He had a job over there. That would've been in early '72. By then my grandmother had moved up to Cobar from Bendigo. Anyhow, when we popped in to visit her, Mum and Dad liked Cobar so much they decided that we'd move up here. I was about twelve by then so I was in Grade 6.

But then Mum got homesick for Victoria so, in early '73, we went back to Shepparton. We were there till winter hit. Now I don't know if you know or not, but Shepparton winters are bitterly cold. And that got to Mum. So we turned around and came back to Cobar where the weather's warmer.

At first Dad got a building job in town. Then he joined the mines, renovating and maintaining their houses. So I did a couple of years' high school back here before I went to boarding school in Forbes. Then at the end of Year 11, I got an apprenticeship with an electrician in Cobar. When I'd finished that I went out to the CSA mine. That's Cornish, Scottish and Australian, which were the nationalities of the people who found the ore body in Cobar. Back in those days it was copper, lead and zinc. Now it's all copper.

I actually remember the day I got employed at the mines. It was 16 August 1982. The reason I know the date so well is that it was five years to the day after Elvis Presley died. Both the wife and I were and still are great fans of 'The King'. Anyhow, back in those days, all the mine managers dressed up in suits and ties and when the underground manager asked me, 'What would you like to do?', being a bit of a smart-arse, I looked him up and down and said, 'Your job looks all right.'

'Oh,' he said, 'then you'll have to go to university and become an engineer.'

I said, 'Blow that. I want to be a worker.'

'Okay,' he said, 'I'll give you a job, but I reckon you won't last long.'

That was thirty-seven years ago and I'm still there. So I proved him wrong, ay?

And I'm Barry. I've been in Cobar for thirty-four years. Previous to that I worked at an asbestos mine, just north of Tamworth and eight k's out of the town of Barraba. And before you ask, Wittenoom, in Western Australia, and Barraba were two entirely different asbestos ore bodies. Whereas Wittenoom had the deadly blue asbestos, with the hooks in it, the benign chrysotile asbestos from Barraba was a white and furry asbestos. So it was okay. I mean, it must've been. We pretty well lived with it for ten years, so to speak.

When the mine shut at Barraba, I went over to Western Australia to work with Western Mining at the Windarra nickel mine, which is north of Kal, out from Laverton. Very remote. Anyhow, when that also shut down, I came back east. Actually, a few years back I said to the wife, 'Let's go to WA. I'll show you where I worked.' And when we got there it was, 'Hang on, where's it all gone?'

Anyhow, one day after I'd come back to Cobar from the Windarra mine, I ran into a young bloke in a pub who'd been one of my apprentices at the Barraba mine and I said, 'Where are you working?'

He said, 'Out at the mines in Cobar,' and he gave me the contact. So I got in touch and they gave me a job. I was a fitter and turner by trade, but I worked at Elura mine more as a fitter. I mean, once you get into the mining game you rarely get on a lathe anyway.

Brad here again. As far as the fire service goes, it was something I was always interested in. Before I came to Cobar I'd been with the Rural Fire Service – RFS – just north of Nowra, at a place called Berry. Then lo 'n behold, when we came out here there was an opening as a volunteer in what was then called New

South Wales Fire Brigades. I started there more as a dogsbody and over time, with people leaving town or retiring and so forth, I worked my way up.

Then about seven years ago, when our captain had to step down due to ill health, I went through the application process and ended up top dog – the captain. We're talking January 2005 now and, even though it's a volunteer position, I get a small retainer for being captain.

Fire and Rescue New South Wales, as we're now known, is a government organisation that employs permanent firefighters in most of the state's major towns, out as far as Dubbo. And with Cobar being smaller and a bit west of Dubbo, other than my small retainer, we're volunteers. Though I'm definitely not in it for the money. Between the three of us here, Peter, Barry and myself, I'd be confident in saying that we're all in it to serve our community. Absolutely.

Peter here now. As to how I joined the RFS, that came about after I joined the volunteer mines rescue team. That gave me the skills of mine rescue, first aid, firefighting, vertical rescue, breathing apparatus use and so forth. Then in 2001, one of the mine rescue guys invited me along to see what the RFS was all about. And well, I wanted to give something back to Cobar. This town's been very good to me. I've raised my kids here. My daughter's now away at uni, my youngest one's in his second year of a local apprenticeship and the eldest bloke's also in the mines. He's met a schoolteacher here in town and I've now got two grandbabies.

Anyway, I went along to the RFS meeting and I joined up. And while a lot of my mines and rescue training swapped straight over, I had to get some extra skills through the RFS trainers that come to Cobar. You know, like familiarisation with the trucks and some of the equipment. We've got two units: a Category 1 and a Category 7. Cat 1 and 7 relate to the different truck sizes and the capacity of their water tanks. We've also got the use of a bulk water carrier as well.

Barry again, mate. Well, my pathway was very similar to Peter's. I started mine-rescue training at Barraba after a good mate was run over by a mine's haul truck that had a sixty-tonne load on board. We've never been able to find out why, but for some unknown reason he parked his Valiant station wagon right behind the haul truck and it reversed straight over his vehicle, with him still in it.

This happened back in the mid-'80s and, in those days, we didn't have a mine-rescue team. All we had was some old first-aiders – retirees basically – who'd picked up a bit of spare work out at the mine. There was no kind of rescue unit in Barraba either. They only had an ambulance. So we called them out, and when they arrived nobody knew what to do. It was a case of, 'So how do we get him out of the car?', and we eventually had to cut him out via means that you wouldn't use today, like with gas axes and so forth.

Anyhow, that's what got me thinking about mine-rescue training. And when I moved over to the Windarra mine, in WA, the trainers there put us through the rigmarole of firefighting and fire safety and the use of a breathing apparatus and all that sort of stuff. I continued with that when I came here to Cobar to work in the mines and from there I joined the SES – State Emergency Service. SES is also a volunteer organisation where we have to do all our own fundraising, which makes it very difficult in a small town like Cobar. Like, to raise a hundred thousand dollars for a rescue truck, with all its gear, is nigh on impossible.

Actually, just the other day my wife and I were trying to work out when I joined the SES. And I vividly recalled the director general coming up to Cobar to have a look at our facilities. When he walked into what was basically a lean-to shed, there was a horse lying up against the side of the rescue truck, fast asleep. The moment the director general saw that, he said, 'What the hell? The New South Wales State Emergency Service has gotta do better than this!'

Yes, and so while I'm not a volunteer firie, the RFS, Fire and Rescue and the SES all work hand in glove. Basically our core role is to deal with storms and tempests. But we don't get too many storms or tempests out here so unfortunately our main role is to attend road accidents. With those we also all work in together, along with the ambos and the police. I always say, 'A road accident is potentially the worst day of a person's life. So they don't give a damn what uniform someone's wearing, just as long as they get 'em out and get them help.'

And mind you, some of these road crashes can be pretty horrific. At times I've come home shaking like a leaf and the wife's said, 'Are you all right?' and I've just burst into tears. I'm just thankful that these days, all the services now have counselling available – things like critical incident and stress debriefers, peer support groups and all of that.

But basically I'm pretty well medically grounded at the moment because of a mishap I had at the last accident I attended. A vehicle had gone off the highway and run into a tree. There was one fatality. Anyhow, we had to drive off the highway, go over some pretty chewed-up and boggy ground, through a barbed-wire fence and on about two hundred yards down to the accident scene.

The thing was, we didn't want to cut the barbed wire on the fence, so we pulled three star pickets out and we pushed the fence over. To help keep the fence on the ground, I was standing on a star picket at one end and a young RFS firie from Wilcannia was standing on another one a bit further down. But when the big SES rescue truck came through, the spare-wheel carrier, underneath the vehicle, snagged the top strand of the barbed-wire fence. Next thing the fence was ripped from under both me and the young firie and we got thrown up in the air.

The thing was, the driver of the truck didn't see us. He kept going. And so then our overalls got tangled up in the barbed wire and me and the young firie got skull-dragged across the ground behind the truck. And when you're my age – near on eighty – and you're back-slammed and dragged over the ground, the body doesn't take it too well. So I was screaming out, 'Stop! Stop! Stop!'

Worse still, when they eventually heard me, they decided to reverse the truck and all I could see was the wheels coming straight back at me. Oh Jesus. But as luck would have it, just before I was run over, they stopped the truck and then they managed to untangle us. But by then both of us were severely bruised on our backsides and down the back of our legs where the barbed wire had caught us. Though, with the young firie being eighteen and fit, he bounced back onto his feet. He was okay. But not so me. Age proved to be my enemy, so my doctor said, 'No, no more for you, Barry. You've got to rest for a while.' And that's what I'm currently doing.

Peter here again. See, we've all got our core responsibilities. While the RFS is basically here to attend bushfires, Brad's Fire and Rescue brigade's main area of responsibility is the town area. But if any of the other emergency services needs a hand, our RFS system goes into overdrive and we man up a truck and turn up to help them out. So without too many bushfires breaking out around Cobar, the majority of our work is helping Barry's SES with road crashes.

What I'm trying to get at is, we don't strictly have 'That's your area of responsibility and so I won't intervene, and this is my area of responsibility and so you're not allowed to intervene.' We're all in it together. Like I've always said, 'Out here, there's no politics in the bush.'

Barry again. Of course one of the things we really struggle with in a small place like Cobar is membership. Because of the downturn in the mines, a lot of people have moved on. Just recently three families left. Up till then we had about fifteen on our SES books. Though only half a dozen of those are active, and they're aged forty plus. Then there's me who's just on eighty. And of course, with the mines bringing in the fly-in fly-out workers, as they do these days, and then with the twelve-hour shifts, that also affects the availability of people. And also, when half your crew's fifty k's out at the mine site, they just can't drop everything and come in.

Peter here. We've got twenty-five on our Rural Fire Service books of which fifteen are active. Though, because a lot of our volunteers work at the mines, and the mine works 24/7, not all our members are available at the one time. And with people like me, on the mine's rescue crew, I can't just up and leave the site because, if there's trouble on the mine site, I'm needed there, right on the spot. So if there's a fire or an emergency, usually only three or four of us mine workers can go out.

But as for future memberships, we're currently trialling a cadet firie system. They're kids between twelve and fifteen. They can't yet attend emergencies, of course. We just show them the ropes till they become full members at sixteen and then they can come out with us on the trucks.

Brad here, mate. At the moment with Fire and Rescue we're running on a strength of sixteen. Though more often than not we hover around ten active members. But you were asking about the lows and highs. Well, Cobar's had some pretty tough times. Back in 2014 we had – and I don't like to dwell on it – a real tough time. All of us were involved.

We had a pub fire where unfortunately, when the building collapsed, it injured two of our firefighters, one fatally. It's been through a coroner's inquest and everything, which was also tough in itself. So yeah, when it's one of your own, that's when it really hits home. And that's not only within all the emergency services, but it also deeply affected a number of townspeople. There's still some, even now, who are going through a tough time over it.

As you come into Cobar from the east, it was the pub on the edge of town, on the opposite corner to the RSL. It's a vacant block now. The alarm was raised at around 6 o'clock in the morning and it didn't take long for it to develop into a full-blown blaze. Fire and Rescue were the primary responder, but all the other various emergency services were there in support roles, on the front line. Our first priority was to evacuate the residents who were still in the premises. So everyone was cleared and evacuated. Thankfully, the pub wasn't close to any other buildings, so the chance of the fire spreading was minimal. The major task was to try and keep it contained, and then get it out.

On the day a whole raft of dynamics were going on. Other than my mob, Fire and Rescue, the RFS had enough men available to supply an appliance. SES was there, as well as the ambos and police. Due to the pub being on a highway, council put up road closures. They were also supplying bulk water tankers. Oh, and both the Bourke and Nyngan fire brigades came across to help.

As it happened, me and a couple of other firefighters were away in Sydney at a test match between the Wallabies and the All Blacks. I was coming up Lapstone Hill, into the Blue Mountains, when I first found out. So I was co-ordinating the best I could from afar, on the phone. But with the pub being of the older style of brickwork, with the false façade and the awning coming off that, the internal structure supports burnt out and let go. Basically, the laws of physics came into play and down it all came.

Unfortunately, some of our firefighters were in there, trying to extinguish the fire, and one of them didn't come out alive. So yeah, you wanted a low, there's a low for you. And that's about all we need to say about it.

Then on the high side, we attend all the community events, and to just see the kids' faces light up is a real high. 'Here comes the big red truck with the lights flashing and the siren flicking on.' And we have community awareness days where both my Fire and Rescue and the RFS open our doors to the general public. We put on a sausage sizzle and hand out sample bags and stickers and the kids get transfers and plastic fire hats. Then we've got the dress-ups where Mum and Dad can take photos of their kids. There's the social aspect too. We've got an emergency services social club that we all contribute to, out of our own pockets. And about every six months we all have a get-together, where we just let our hair down and relax.

Note: The New South Wales Rural Fire Service has over 2100 brigades and a volunteer membership of around seventy-two thousand. In addition, just under a thousand staff members are employed to manage the day-to-day operations of the service in such places as district fire control centres, regional offices, customer service centres, operational and mitigations support service bases and at the RFS headquarters at Lidcombe.

Characters

After the wife and I came back from our honeymoon in 1968, we moved over to Dubbo. Dubbo's a big regional centre, about four hundred k's north-west of Sydney. Anyway, I just rocked up to a meeting of the local fire brigade and said, 'I've been a volunteer before and I'd like to join whenever you have a vacancy.'

They said, 'You're in.'

Dubbo Brigade had about fifteen volunteers and a permanent fire officer. So it was a bit more structured and formal than other places I'd been. Like you'd fall in and number off and a deputy captain would report how many men were on parade and all that sort of thing. And that was fine. I didn't mind that side of it.

The biggest fire I attended in Dubbo was at the flour mill, about a block from the railway station. I believe it was caused by internal combustion. When we got there, the fire was only on the bottom level of the silo-tower where all the wheat was stored. But the thing was, the tower had been built of pine, then clad with corrugated iron. And that made our job extremely difficult, in as much as we had to pull off the corrugated iron sheeting before we could get to the seat of the fire. Anyway, by that night we'd managed to save the mill. And that was a great relief.

The following morning they started to auger what remained of the wheat out from the tower. Everything was going fine until the auger broke down, and that created a funnelling effect inside the tower. And once the oxygen got in, it set the fire off again. And it was a biggie. Brigades from Narromine, Wellington and Gilgandra came over to help us. Though this time we lost the mill, buildings and all. The odd thing was, we'd poured so much water onto the tower that about three days later the remaining wheat started to germinate.

While I was at Dubbo we also went to a lot of firefighting competitions. And we always did pretty well. On one occasion we even came second in the state. The demonstrations were held biannually, in different places across the state, over a week. About eighty brigades would turn up. And I tell you, some of those little brigades like Canowindra and Finley were almost unbeatable in some of the events. We'd do things like running out fire hoses and hitting a disc that'd been suspended three metres off the ground, with a stream of water. There was Alarm and Rescue. That's where you'd start off lying down, as if you were asleep. Then when the alarm went off, you'd have to jump up, put your uniform on, run a certain distance to pick up a dummy, then carry it back over the finish line.

I remember the time we went to a comp over in Queanbeyan and the Cootamundra Brigade were a couple short. To help them out, we formed a composite team called Dubbumundra. We were staying at the same motel and one night we all went off to the pub. Lo 'n behold, we won a huge snapper and a whole stack of prawns and oysters. Now the fridge in our motel room must've been on the blink or something because we said to the Coota blokes, 'How about you put everything in your fridge for safekeeping and we'll divvy it up tomorrow before we leave?'

'Yeah, okay,' they said and the next morning when we went to share up the booty, the buggers had eaten all the prawns and oysters! All that was left was the snapper. So we took the snapper back home to Dubbo and, to give you some idea as to the size of it, we had a family barbecue at the station and it fed all of us, including all the wives and kids.

But oh, we had a great social club, we really did. Our preferred watering hole, or home pub, was the Garden Hotel. The Garden was only a couple of blocks from the fire station which made it very convenient. The pub's where we did the bulk of our fundraising, running meat raffles and so forth. If you ever go to Dubbo, the Garden Hotel's in Fitzroy Street, east of the railway station. The Railway Hotel was on the other side of the track. And that was an extremely interesting watering hole. In those days it was a real blood-house, which was why it was known as The Bunch'a, in as much as it was the most likely place in town where you'd end up getting smacked by a bunch'a fives, as in a closed fist.

What also made our Dubbo Brigade interesting was how everyone had a nickname. Doug, our volunteer fire captain, was a milko – milkman – and because we reckoned he used to water down the milk, he got called Watery. Vinny, our next senior officer, was a football referee. Vinny was a little bloke with lots of flair so he was called Show Pony. At one game at Robertson Oval, just as someone dived in for a try, Vinny got knocked over. So there he is, sitting on his rump, and in real Show Pony fashion, blowing his whistle and pointing for a try.

Bob who lived upstairs on top of the fire station was known as Storky, 'cause of his long legs. Then Laurie was nicknamed Septic. Laurie was a greenkeeper and the story goes that, when they built the West Dubbo Bowling Club, they put in a septic tank. After it'd been covered over, a heated discussion ensued as to whether the lid on the septic tank had any reo – reinforcing – in the cement. Laurie was adamant that it did. 'Hundred per cent guaranteed,' he said and, to prove his point, he started jumping up and down on top of it. Then – *zoop!* – down he went into the deep dark depths of the septic tank, right in the shit, so to speak. So that was Septic.

Another feller, Kevin, got labelled Scratchy because he was always scratching around for something or other. PC got his nickname from his initials. PC's brother, who was an extremely small bloke, was called Tiny. If ever we were at a fire and we had to get up into a ceiling through a manhole, Tiny was our man.

A bloke with a German surname got called Fritz. An inspector who used to come to check the brigade over had the surname of Partridge. So naturally enough we called him Mr Feathers – though only behind his back of course.

So yes, we had some really interesting characters, and some very interesting times. Remember how I was telling you about Watery, our volunteer fire captain? One day he strolled over to the fire station and the fire engine had gone missing. We might've had the old Thames Trader by then. But being the captain he should've known about any call-outs. So he goes, 'Perhaps I'm goin' deaf and I didn't hear the fire alarm go off.' But no, that couldn't be right. So he has a think about it and comes to the conclusion that the fire truck's been nicked. So he's straight onto the police: 'The fire truck's been stolen!'

So a big search gets underway and the police eventually found it up at the Garden Hotel where a few of us were helping get someone's pet cockatoo out of a tree. But Watery wasn't only our highly esteemed fire captain, he was also our social club president. Oh, and I still have a laugh about the night he stood up in front of us and announced, 'Welcome, everyone, to our quarterly annual meeting.'

Oh, and there was the day Show Pony called in to the fire station. By this stage he'd given up refereeing. Anyhow, there was a couple of large plane trees out front of the station. Come autumn/winter they dropped their green-orangey-brown leaves and made a hell of a mess. Now, as his wife always did, she'd given him a two-dollar note so that he could get into the footy and have a drink. Remember how the notes were green-looking? So there were a few of us standing about outside the station and I said, 'Anybody got a two-dollar note?'

Of course Show Pony says, 'Yeah, I got one.'

I said, 'I'll show you something very interesting about the two-dollar note.'

'All right,' he said and he hands it over.

After I showed it around I said, 'If you look real close at a two-dollar note, you'll find one well-known television show and two classic films.'

Show Pony goes, 'Oh yeah?' and he looked at it, thought for a while. Nothing came to mind, so he said, 'Well, I don't know. So what's the answer?'

I said, 'The two-dollar note's got four corners. So there's the television show.' I said, 'As for the two films,' and I ripped the note in half, 'one's *Jack the Ripper*,' and, as I threw the two parts of the note in the air, I said, 'and the other one's *Gone with the Wind*.'

And up into the air went the two halves of this two-dollar note and they landed in amongst the orangey-brown leaves of the plane tree. And didn't we have a hell of a job, scrounging around amongst the pile of leaves trying to find the two halves of this darn two-dollar note so that Show Pony could get into the footy and have his drink.

Now to Storky. As I said, he lived upstairs above the fire station. One night he'd had a few more beers than his normal quota – which would've been a hell of a lot to start with. Then about 3 o'clock in the morning the fire alarm goes off. Storky's first thought is, Well, I'd better have a pee before I go 'n fight this fire.

But being as disorientated as he was in his current condition, he inadvertently walked over to the wardrobe, opened the door, stepped in and relieved himself. And didn't he receive a hefty sort of a dry cleaning bill for doing that.

Oh, and there was the time the welding works in West Dubbo caught fire. The alarm goes off, we get to the station, clamber into the fire truck – Storky included – and we rush over to the welding works and we ended up putting the fire out without too much damage.

So we're packing up our gear and someone says, 'Where's Storky? I thought he'd come with us.' So we're all looking around the place. 'Storky! Storky!' Anyhow we couldn't find him anywhere. He'd disappeared. God knows where.

'Blow him,' someone said. 'It's getting late. Let's just go back ter the station so I can get back home to bed.'

And as we were about to pile into the fire truck, there's Storky, sound asleep on the back seat, contentedly snoring away.

Note: The name of Dubbo comes from the Wiradjuri word meaning 'red earth'. The town's noted for winning the 'Australia's best meat pie' competition in 2003, 2005 and 2007, and also for having a historic gaol in the main street where eight men were hanged between 1859 and 1966.

The revamped Garden Hotel – or 'The Garden' as it's more commonly known – is within a ten-minute walk from the Dubbo Regional Theatre and Convention Centre and is just a ten-minute drive from the Taronga Western Plains Zoo.

As storyteller Peter Simpfendorfer described to author Bill 'Swampy' Marsh, 'What I like about The Garden is that it not only serves the coldest beer in the central west and that the tasty grub comes from the region but, more importantly, there's not only a salt-and-pepper set on each table – there's also chicken salt!' (Peter Simpfendorfer is not a shareholder of the Garden Hotel, just a keen patron from his firefighting days.)

Memories are Something Special

My name's Rex Hall. In late 1960 I became a member of what was then known as the South Australian Emergency Fire Service. So that was a long time ago, and along the way since then I've received an Australian Fire Service Medal, which is the pinnacle of recognition that a firefighter can receive for their distinguished service.

Down here at Naracoorte, in the south-east of South Australia, we've got a strong brigade with around twenty-five to thirty members, plus we have a decent number of firefighting appliances. These days I'm not so much an active member. Age has made me give up going out on the truck to fight fires, and that's something you've got to be mindful of. You need to be reasonably fit.

But I was fortunate enough to have been a deputy group officer of our state's south-eastern region for a number of years. In more recent times I've done a lot of the base radio work. Actually, I've still got a sub-base there in the house, where I can track the fire traffic. Then more recently I became a member of the State Incident Management team, working as a staging area manager.

As a member of the State Incident Management team, you can get called to go anywhere in the state where there's a fire or a major incident and be part of the team that helps look after things. The site's normally at an oval or some other secure central location, away from the fire front. Because it's usually very hot, air conditioning is essential. So we could be sited in a hall or a container – a 'hub' as we call it – where the fire can be tracked and the volunteers briefed before and after they go out to the fireground. There's also areas set up for catering and accommodation. There's a first-aid station. There'd be forklifts for moving equipment and so forth around.

The main section I was involved with was looking after the maintenance and the refuelling of all the fire vehicles and the recording of who comes in and who goes out. Plus we made sure there was always plenty of ice and water available for the volunteers. So yes, there was always something challenging, and I found that extremely rewarding.

But for a number of years now, my main focus has been on getting the South Australian Volunteer Fire Fighters Museum up and running. I've always believed that memories are something special and, because they give us such a great reward and satisfaction later in life, we should safely store them. So I guess, in a way, that's where the germ of the idea for the museum came from.

The reality of it started about eighteen years ago, after a number of us CFS – Country Fire Service – volunteers went to New South Wales, then across to New Zealand to attend a volunteers' conference. In New Zealand, we travelled to a little fire station not far out of Christchurch, at Ashburton, where they housed some appliances from the old steam-engine days, plus other firefighting memorabilia.

Something else we also noted was that the New Zealand Fire Service acknowledged the years that their volunteers gave. We didn't have anything like that in South Australia. So when we got back, we put the suggestion to the then chief officer, Ewan Fergusson, who agreed to set up a Volunteer Medal. So now we've got a lapel badge that records every ten years that a volunteer gives to the fire service.

To that point in time, South Australia was the only state in Australia without some sort of a firefighters museum. So, along with a number of other CFS volunteers, we resolved to record and preserve our firefighting history. And with a huge amount of support from the CFS, the project got underway. Since then much of my, and a team of dedicated others', time has been working on developing the South Australian Volunteer Fire Fighters Museum.

First off, the committee had to find a suitable location to establish the museum. Of the many options considered, Naracoorte was chosen. The main reason for that was the area's proud history in community fire safety, the high visitation rate to the district, the willingness of local volunteers to sustain the proposed museum and the general ambience of the town.

After many years of planning and negotiation we secured a block of land from the state government which, being at the entrance to the town, was ideally suited. That decided, one of our working parties who had visited the Fire Services Museum of Victoria was extremely impressed with their Memorial for Fallen Fire Fighters. And our block of land was ideally shaped to also accommodate such a memorial, which would be devoted to those volunteers who'd lost their lives while fighting fires in country South Australia. That was our first goal and, through the dedicated service of our museum's members, local community volunteers and the kind donation of materials and labour, the memorial was officially commemorated and opened on 4 May 2016 – International Firefighters' Day.

But that particular memorial is only stage one of a much larger museum development to be undertaken. Eventually you'll see a complex that'll house an extensive collection of statewide CFS memorabilia. We've already collected, and in many cases restored, an impressive number and variety of decommissioned firefighting equipment. And if the initial donations of memorabilia are any indication, that collection will also continue to grow exponentially.

So, as I said, the museum's been my main focus over the last eighteen years or so and, through our many ups and downs, we've already had some great outcomes.

Note: The South Australian Volunteer Fire Fighters Museum was opened on 50 Kingston Avenue, Naracoorte on 16 February 2020 – the anniversary of Ash Wednesday 1983.

Dinga the Ringer

Yep, Dinga the Ringer, that's me. Well, I don't know how many's in the brigade these days; not now, not since the dispute. That's when I got out of it. Then after I left they got a beautiful new fire shed. I'm not exactly sure how long our old one had been there for. Twenty-something years, maybe. I get lost with time. These days I even forget my own birthday. But everybody was invited to the opening – bar me. Anyhow, later on I got talking to the fire captain and I said, 'Well, are yer gonna get the new place really up 'n going?' and he said, 'Nah, I don't think so. I'll just keep it going as it was – ticking along.'

I don't even know if they train much these days. Oh, they might have a session every now and then and start up the fire unit – the truck – just to check that everything's running okay. But that'd be about it. And they leave the truck in the shed. You never see it outside. When I was captain, if it was going to be a hot day, I'd have the truck parked outside, ready to go. But that never happens any more. And if I stayed out at a big fire, I used to sleep in the cab of the truck. These days, if there's a fire, everyone gets contacted by the pager. In my day I'd do a ring-around. Like of a Sunday morning I'd ring everyone, just to give them a bit of a weather report and see if they'd be available if there was a fire. But really just basically to stir them up a bit, because we used to meet on a Sunday.

I remember one time ringing one of our volunteers. He was a farmer from down the road. When I rang him up, he said, 'Dinga, how come you always ring me up at 8 o'clock every Sunday morning?'

I said, 'Just to see who's available to come to the meeting and to see who's home in case there's a fire.'

He said, 'But, Dinga, why ring us so early?'

I said, 'Because if I left it any later, I might be pissed 'n forget.'

So yeah, I'd ring them up early on the Sunday. But to be honest it was more of a reminder call because, with us being such a small brigade, everyone knew what everyone else was doing and where they were anyway. And back in them earlier days we only had a trailer with a tank on it. Our captain used to keep it down at his place, and when I was captain, that's what I did.

See, I was in it for something like fifteen years, maybe. I get lost with time. These days I even forget my own birthday. But it was just an ordinary old trailer, with a tank on it that you hitched up to your vehicle. The tank would've only held about a thousand litres of water, maybe. But it's amazing what you can do with a thousand litres. If you get to a fire early enough you can slow things down and if there's not too much heat in the fire you might be able to get on top of it.

We had a couple of house fires when we had that trailer. One was up the end of the road. We fixed that one up. Saved the house, pretty much. Then there was another feller's place down at Swanport, his whole house burnt down. Another day we had all these fires. We had the trailer on the back of a ute. I went down to Orford and picked up one of our volunteers. I can remember him being up on the trailer with the hose, filling the tank. I was on the water tap and you can get a hell of a lot of water pressure coming out of those taps. Anyhow, I had it going full bore and, when he took the hose out of the filling hole, it threw him about like a buck-jumper. Oh, he was swinging around all over the place. Gee I laughed. And when I turned the water off he come back down to earth with a thud.

But mostly we done scrub fires. You know, hot summer days with high winds. Then sometime after that the Tasmania

Fire Service gave us a bigger unit with a really big tank. I forget how much water the tank held, but it was a lot. So we'd often get called to fires to top up all the other brigades' smaller water tanks.

Then there was the fire up the army range way. I was taking water up to them, to top up their smaller tanks. And see, with some of these fellers, as soon as they see a fire they want to put it out. But that's not necessarily the best thing because sometimes it's best to let them burn so that, when the next fire comes through, it's already been cleaned up a bit. Anyway, they wanted more water. Then they wanted even more water, really for no other reason than to squirt it about. But like I said, my feeling was for them to let it burn, to clean the area up good and proper.

Anyhow, the next time after I went down and filled our big tank up with water, on my way back up I went past a place where an old bloke called Coates used to live. He was a hermit sort of feller. He had a bit of a house up there, and for some reason I pulled up at his place with all this water on. Next thing old Coates comes out of the chook house.

'Would yer like a drink?' he said.

It was a hot day, so I said, 'May as well. They're only wasting water up there anyway.'

He said, 'I got some homemade beer here.'

I said, 'What's it taste like?' You know, because I'd drunk some pretty rugged homebrews in my time.

He said, 'It's wet.'

I said, 'Well, that'll do me,' and so we sat down and had a few of his beers. And it wasn't too bad either.

So by the time I got back up to the army range, the fire had cleared out a fair area. So that was good.

But we used to do a lot of back-burns on the weekends, to clean up around the place. I done a lot of grass slashing and so I got to see what needed doing around the place. And if I seen anything that needed a bit of a clean-out, I'd just go to the council and say, 'Listen, this block needs burning.' And they'd say, 'Well, get the brigade onto it then.' And so I would.

But they don't do that no more. See, back then the brigade was very close-knit. We'd have regular meetings. Planning. And it was a very social sort of thing. Like we'd get together and have cricket matches. Everybody in the district would come along – all the different brigades – and with all the wives and kids you'd have up to fifty people turning up. I used to put on a big camp oven with a roast of lamb and baked potatoes and everything and we'd form ourselves into a couple of teams – south versus the north.

Oh, they were big days. Even some of the hierarchy from Hobart would come up. And that really helped us, you know, knowing that they were interested and willing enough to come along to those sorts of events. So they became like friends. There was a district officer. I forget his name now but he looked after the whole east coast of Tasmania, from the top to the bottom. And if there was anything we wanted, he didn't mind getting stuck into his bosses about it. And gee, he could tell some stories. He had pigs and we'd sometimes meet up at the Bridgewater sale. Then I think he had a few problems later on after he'd gone down to help out with the Port Arthur massacre, where all those people got shot. He was a really good bloke, but I haven't seen him in a long time since then.

And the Christmas parties, along with all the other brigades, were amazing. They weren't just a men's thing. Whole families came along, and we'd buy presents for all the kids, and Christmas hats, and the kids would get a bit of a ride-around on the back of the fire truck. It was a good day. We'd have a barbecue and there'd be all sorts of races and competitions. And that social side of it was what really held all the brigades together. Most definitely. But that's all gone. No one around here's doing it now.

And when the year 2000 was coming, that was a real big occasion. We had a massive New Year's Eve function. Everyone was camped down on the oval having a real good time. Then, when we were doing the parade, we seen all this smoke going up over at Dolphin Sands. Next thing we get the call and so we had to pull the fire unit out of the parade and get around to the fire. I think we spent all night down there. We didn't lose any houses, but I didn't get back till the next morning.

Anyhow, I reckon that's about it. I can't think of much else really. These days I get lost with time. A lot of what we did in the fire brigade was a lot of fun but, the older you get, you start to forget a lot of it too. These days I even forget my own birthday.

Note: The Tasmanian New Year celebrations of 2000 were beamed throughout the world. During the year, Queen Elizabeth visited Hobart. The state's first 'Sorry Day' happened at Risdon Cove.

Pet Interests

May I talk about three of my volunteer fire services pet interests? One's about road crash rescue in country areas, the other's about succession within the fire brigade and the final one is about women in firefighting, of which I am one.

First to road crash rescue and some of the things that drivers need to be made aware of. Before the international COVID restrictions came in, we were called to a number of accidents where overseas visitors had forgotten which side of the road they were supposed to be driving on ... thus getting disorientated on the long straight roads. Another major cause of road accidents is tiredness. A lot of these people come from countries where you can cross a continent in a day and so, while Perth to Broome may look like a short distance on a map or a printed A4 sheet of paper, it isn't. It's a bloody long drive.

It's the same with some of our Australian drivers. Now that we're currently not allowed to go overseas, people from down south are going stir-crazy, so they want to get away from the cold of the city and head north, up to the warmth. Now, I don't know where some of these people got their licences from but, to be honest, their driving is bloody atrocious. Again, tiredness is a major factor and also, with an increased number of caravans sharing the same strip of highway as road trains, that's another recipe for disaster.

What a lot of people also don't realise is that, in these more remote areas, it can take hours from when Fire and Rescue receive a road crash call-out till they're able to get to the scene of an accident. Still, we do what we can and all the brigades back each other up. We're lucky here on the Coral Coast in that Geraldton's only sixty kilometres to our north, so backup's within the hour. Jurien Bay's a little over an hour to our south and Moora's a couple of hours inland.

Now I know they might sound significant distances, especially if you're trapped and injured in an overturned vehicle. Though we're nowhere near as isolated as places like Carnarvon and Kalbarri where their brigades cover far greater road distances and you may have to wait for hours before a brigade can reach you.

Another thing I'd like to mention is that, in small communities like ours, when you get a call to a road accident, the first thing that goes through your mind is, Could it be someone I know, like a local or a friend or one of our brigade member's family? And that has happened. So just be very careful on the roads please. Because our crews have experienced some extremely confronting situations with having to cut people out of cars, especially if they've been killed. And that's an everyday reality that we, in Fire and Rescue, face. It does affect us deeply.

Though thankfully we've moved on from the old days' attitude of 'suck it up, princess', which led to so much PTSD – post-traumatic stress disorder. I mean PTSD can still happen, but these days we've got a really solid support system from both within each of our brigades as well as from DFES – Department of Fire and Emergency Services. After a traumatic event, our first line of looking after each other is to gather in our training room for a chat, drinks and nibbles. After that the initial hot debrief may be led by the incident controller, the officer-in-charge or our captain. Otherwise it's the more experienced people and peer support officers checking in with everyone to see if they are okay.

The thing is, because of privacy issues, we can't talk about a lot of this stuff with the general public, and the last thing you want to do is to spill the gruesome details to your immediate family. And, believe you me, the after-effects of a particularly difficult incident can hang around for a long time before it surfaces. So we all keep an eye on each other and, if we or the family notices a behaviour change, we're there to follow it up. We're all there for each other.

Within the organisation of DFES, there's also several layers of peer support. Some of the DFES peer support team have previously been regional station officers, who have experienced horrible incidents, and they're on hand to talk with anybody who's stressed. Professional psychologists are also available. So we're well looked after, and that's a big organisational and cultural change that's only happened in fairly recent years.

Now to keeping our brigades strong and active. Because everybody reaches a use-by date, our great challenge is to make sure we pay attention to planned succession. In the smaller remote places like Meekatharra, it's extremely difficult to get volunteers. And those few that are volunteers often have to double up with ambulance and fire brigade. When they go out to an incident, they have to decide what hat to put on. So somehow, and I don't know how, we've got to make sure to get the younger people coming on – both male and female – especially if they've got local knowledge. Because local knowledge is vitally important, particularly in country areas. We know it and DFES recognises it. We've got a lot of local farmers and fishermen in our brigade who have grown up understanding the local weather patterns.

As an example, over here on the West Australian coast, in the hot weather, there's a total change of wind direction in the afternoon. If you're unaware of that, just when you think you've got the fire under control, the sea breeze will blast in and the fire will take off in a completely different direction. So suddenly, the long fire flank will now become a huge fire front, which can turn into a very dangerous situation. But if you've got that local knowledge, you're able to pre-plan your method of containment and/or attack. And so that's why we need some of the younger locals to step up and join our brigade.

The other pet interest of mine is women in firefighting. Now, I don't want to tread on any toes here because it may sound like sexism. But men and women have a different way of doing and looking at things. While men are generally stronger than women, to my mind they tend to be quite tunnel-visioned. Men see a job that needs to be done, so their total focus is on trying to get that job done. And that singular focus may well lessen their ability to consider the peripheral options. And that's one area where women come to the fore. Simple things like taking a little time to assess a situation instead of rushing in like a bull at a gate.

In our brigade we have a mix of both men and women. Our Fire and Rescue lieutenant is a young female. When our captain was away, she stepped up as acting captain and she did a great job. There she was, this young woman, telling men who'd been in the brigade since it'd started thirty-three years ago what to do. And while it might've been a bit of a challenge at the start, she proved herself. In doing so, she's earnt the respect of the entire brigade and we're all very proud of her. And that was bloody good. So we need more women.

Anyhow, we've got what we've got and I love working with what we've got. Our volunteers are all altruistic. They all contribute – both male and female – and we value them all. Mind you, some are rough diamonds, with some being rougher than others. But they've all got hearts of gold and it's a real privilege to be part of the team like I have for the past twenty-one years.

Note: In 2019 there were 152,798 volunteer firefighters in Australia. DFES WA alone supports over twenty-six thousand volunteers. Though the total numbers are increasing, females still only make up around twenty-five per cent. Yet, amongst cadet firefighters, the female ratio is nearing fifty per cent.

The self-governing Aboriginal community of Lake Tyers in East Gippsland, Victoria, has Australia's only all-Indigenous all-female fire brigade. These Gunaikurnai women protect four thousand acres of bushland, including sacred sites and community homes. Most are mothers and grandmothers and, while they say men are welcome – in fact they'd love the fellas to join – as 52-year-old fire captain Charmaine says, 'They don't seem to last too long. Maybe it's because they don't like taking orders from me!'

Rusty Kraut and Drip Torch Jack

My name's Rusty Kraut. Kraut as in German. No offence meant there. I'm chief officer of the Toogoolawah Rural Fire Brigade, just north of Brisbane. As to how that came about – well, to be honest, at the time, nobody else was willing to take on the job. So they roped me in, and I'm still there. Anyhow, they must want me to continue because they sent me a letter a while back saying how much they appreciated all the time and effort I've put in.

The thing was that on the envelope they sent me, they'd addressed it to Patrick Ross Kraut and when I first saw it I wondered, Who the bloody hell's this Patrick Ross Kraut feller? Have I got a brother or something that I don't know about?

Then I realised that it was me and, because I'd been called Rusty for so long, I'd completely forgotten what my real name was.

Like it's always been, 'G'day, Rusty. How's it goin'?'

'Good, mate, and how's yourself?'

I got labelled Rusty from right back when I first started school at the convent in Gatton. As the story goes, I used to keep forgetting to bring my thruppence along to school to buy a writing pad and the nuns used to point their fingers at me and say, 'You've got nothing but a rusty brain.'

Of course, with kids being kids, they soon started saying, 'You're rusty. You're rusty.' And so all through my school days it was Rusty.

Now I was a pretty good rugby league footballer. Without boasting, at the age of eighteen, I was captain of the Under 20s in Gatton. That was in the Lockyer League. Anyhow, when my boss at the time wanted to transfer me to Toogoolawah to open up a tyre shop, I thought, Gee that'd be pretty good. I'd love to go up there. There's mountains where I can go hunting and deer shooting. And it's close enough for me to come back and go to training and play footy. It's ideal.

Then, when I moved to Toogoolawah, I started to introduce myself to everyone as Ross Kraut. Ross being my middle name and what my parents had always called me. Anyway, I'd say, 'G'day, I'm Ross Kraut.'

But because rugby league football was a big thing back in them days – like in the Lockyer League there was Gatton, Laidley, Esk, Kilcoy and all those places – they'd go, 'Hey, you look a bit like that Rusty feller who plays footy for Gatton.' And I'd say, 'Yes, that's me, the one and the same, Rusty Kraut.'

And it just got that way that I thought, Oh bugger it. I may as well stick with Rusty and be done with it. So from then on I'd say, 'Oh yeah, Rusty Kraut, that's me.'

So now everyone calls me Rusty, and Rusty's the handle that's sort of stuck. It rolls off the tongue pretty easily, 'Yeah, Rusty Kraut. We know him from way back when he used to turn up at the fires in an old Morris LC 3 with a couple of forty-four-gallon drums of water on the back to fill up the knapsacks.'

Now that would've been way back in the early 1960s because that's when the brigade first started. So whatever happened to the old days, ay? But that's the way it is and now with all the government help and that, we've gone from the old Morris LC 3 and knapsacks to these days where we've got a brand-spanking-new shed with a million dollars of assets in it.

Another feller we've had in the brigade from right back when we first started is a certain identity we all know as Drip Torch Jack. Drip Torch Jack's a real identity. He's a lovely bloke who'd probably be in his early seventies now and, for the life of me, I've completely forgotten what his real name is. And just like me, he probably has as well.

Now there's just some people that you don't go ordering around. They rile against any form of authority, and Drip Torch Jack's one of them. Like these days the Rural Fire Service is very regimented in its approach to occupational health and safety and all that sort of caper. And with me being first officer, the obligation is on me to make sure that everyone's up to speed wearing the right PPE – personal protection equipment – and all that.

And fair enough too. I'm currently training a dozen new blokes and last night we were talking about what'd happen if they were fighting a fire and they got some sort of shit in their eye – like a cinder or dust or something. Was there any workers' comp available? And I was telling them how workers' comp would say, 'How come you've been issued with, or should've been issued with, goggles and masks and all the proper protective gear, and you still got shit in your eye? Didn't you have glasses on?'

And it may well be, 'Well, no, I didn't have my glasses on.'

'Well then, you have no claim under workers' comp.'

End of story. That's the system.

Look, at the end of the day it's probably the right way, but in the real world that we live in, with people being what they are, a lot of it is bullshit – which brings me right back to Drip Torch Jack. Like I said, he's been with the brigade since year dot. He's a farmer-grazier and, if nothing else, he plays by his own rules. If there's a fire and you ring him up, the answer might well be along the lines of, 'No worries. I'll be there as soon as I can. I'm just shifting the irrigation. So give me about an hour.'

'Oh, okay. Righto, Jack.'

So he's not one who jumps to the word of authority. He's more of the loose cannon type. In actual fact, to give you a clearer picture, Drip Torch Jack reminds me very much of that Kerrigan feller in that movie called *The Castle*, where he's always saying, 'Tell 'em they're dreamin'.'

Well, Jack's a little bit different to that because, if you said, 'Jack, the powers-that-be say we've gotta do it this way,' his answer would be, 'Tell 'em to go 'n get fucked!'

If you're out at a fire front and you said, 'Jack, the powers-that-be say that you've got to wear the right bloody trousers,' his answer would be, 'Tell 'em to go 'n get fucked.'

So he's a real character, and at times quite a difficult one. And with the 'f' word being common to Jack's vocabulary, we certainly don't let him get anywhere near the radio. It'd sound a bit offensive to some.

But, in saying all that, he's the most efficient drip torch operator you'll find anywhere – which is why he got the moniker Drip Torch Jack. In fact, we'd back him to be number one in Australia out on the fire front. He's got his own drip torch, which no one else is allowed to go anywhere near. He does his own fuel mix, which is probably a little bit more – I won't use the term 'explosive' – so let's just describe it as being a little bit more 'potent' than your usual diesel-fuel mix.

So that's Drip Torch Jack, and if we haven't got those sorts of characters in life, let alone in our fire brigades, well, I reckon we'd be the lesser for it.

Note: A drip torch is a handheld canister of varying sizes that can hold up to five litres of a fifty-fifty or a sixty-forty mix of diesel and fuel. A breather valve allows air into the canister, displacing the fuel as it exits through the spout. At the end of the spout there's a wick which, when lit, drops flaming fuel onto the ground where it's needed. To prevent the fire from re-entering the fuel canister, the spout has a loop in it.

A drip torch is used along a control line in back-burning operations, ahead of the main fire.

Role Models

For my husband and me, volunteering was just the thing to do. We grew up with it. Both our families have done, and still do, a lot of volunteering. They've been our role models. Ever since I was a kid my parents have been involved with Apex, Lions, Canteen plus lots of other organisations. At one time Mum was involved with Girl Guides. She's also volunteered with St John Ambulance. And, even though they're now in their seventies and have slowed down a bit, Mum and Dad are still volunteering at the local hospital.

It's the same with my husband. His parents have always been volunteers in various groups and organisations, and his mother still volunteers at the local hospital, along with my parents. Before we met, my husband's father was also a volunteer with St John, as was my husband. In actual fact, we met through St John. With Mum being in St John, I also decided to join. After my initial training, I started out in the nursing division. Then I transferred over to the division that my husband-to-be was in. Anyhow, I just wandered in and there he was. We started courting, then I moved in with him.

As it turned out, he was also a volunteer with our local fire brigade and so, when his pager would go off at night, he'd head off out on the truck and I'd be left at home. So I decided that, instead of being left behind, I'd also become a member of our local fire service. Which I did.

The training's all pretty uniform throughout Tasmania. First you go through the induction, which is where you learn about the fire brigade and its structure. Then you go on to do your basic training where you learn hose and pump skills and all that, and then you move on to the more advanced sorts of training courses.

It was something I really enjoyed. It wasn't just the firefighting side of things. There's also the friendships and connections. I mean, even at the brigade level, like in all walks of life, you have your different personalities. But when it comes to fighting a fire, you all have to work in together. And that was something important because we all knew that if we didn't work as a team, it would never work at all.

As it stands at the moment, the range of our brigade members is between the ages of seventeen and sixty-seven. And that's not including our junior program, which is for kids from ten years old up to seventeen. In the junior program we've currently got a couple of fourteen-year-olds, a twelve-year-old, two eleven-year-olds and a ten-year-old who's just going on eleven and has had a lifelong passion for fire trucks and has always wanted to be a firie. Because the juniors' concentration levels aren't quite up there as yet, we only train them for an hour a fortnight, before us active members do our training.

And over their five or six junior years, similar to the adults, we go through the process of teaching them basic firefighting skills. We instruct them how to use the pumps. How to hold a hose. How to roll a hose. Lots of things. Tying knots is also another part of it because, with firefighting, you have to know how to safely secure all the gear and haul it.

At the end of their junior training, they become what's called an 'underage active'. And with all those basic-level firefighting skills that they've gained along the way, they're given what we call 'a ticket to ride' – which means that they can now come out on the truck with us. As an 'underage active', we put them through what's called Level 1 training. That's where they gain extra skills, like how to put the fire service equipment together and how to use it correctly. As well as that, just like the seniors, they expand the skills they learnt as juniors.

Like in both my husband and my cases, our children are following in our footsteps. Of our two girls and two boys, three are currently involved as volunteers in the fire service. Our eldest is the seventeen-year-old who's recently got her ticket to ride. Then there's the two boys – fourteen and eleven – who are in the junior program. And our youngest – a nine-year-old – is eagerly waiting in the wings to come and join us.

I guess what's kept us involved in volunteering is that it's something useful to the community. And like I said, I'd say that all comes through our parents. So I hope, like our parents, we've been good role models for our children. I mean, the reality is, you never know where they'll end up or what they'll end up doing. But I'm pretty confident that, because it's been such a way of life for them, as it was for us, they'll continue volunteering in one way, shape or form. But you need the role models for that to happen – and a lot of kids these days don't have that.

Note: For information about junior and cadet programs please get in touch with your nearest volunteer fire brigade or contact the head offices of your state's fire service:

Northern Territory Police, Fire & Emergency Services (NTPFES)

Queensland Rural Fire Service (QRFS)

New South Wales Rural Fire Service (NSWRFS)

Victoria Country Fire Authority (CFA)

Tasmania Fire Service (TFS)

ACT Fire & Rescue (ACTF&R)

South Australia Country Fire Service (CFS)

Western Australia Department of Fire & Emergency Services (DFES)

Seven Times Redundant

I was born in north-eastern New South Wales, at Lismore. My parents were on a dairy farm. My mother died when I was two. Apparently, Dad struggled to cope, so me and my sister were sent to a couple of aunties – me to my mother's sister and my sister to one of my father's sisters. That's where I stayed all through my primary school. By the time I was thirteen, my father was on another dairy farm just out of Kyogle. So I went to work part-time with Dad while I attended Kyogle High School. But me and school didn't get on too good. So, on the day I turned fifteen, I left school and went to work full-time with Dad.

Dad had remarried by then so I stayed with them till I was seventeen. Then I joined the railways as a junior porter which led me to becoming a signalman. After doing two years Nasho – National Service – I went to station master's school in Sydney and, at twenty-one, I became the youngest station master in the state for my grade. I then stayed in Sydney till I got a transfer back up to the North Coast, to a place called Raleigh. But when they centralised train control, that job became redundant. So I went up to Murwillumbah, on the branch line there and, when Murwillumbah became redundant, I came back down to Lismore. That's when me and my wife set up house, at nearby Bexhill.

As it turned out I was the last station master at Lismore before they closed that branch line and so that particular job became redundant. I then commuted from Bexhill to Casino till 2000, which was when I got offered the position of network operation supervisor for the North Coast. Basically that's an incident manager who attends everything from stubbed toes to fatalities. But after two years, that job also became redundant, so I went back to Casino. But when centralised train control came through there, that job also became redundant. By then it was 2008. I was fifty-eight. I'd been commuting from my Bexhill home for umpteen years. I'd been made redundant seven times in my railway career and so, after forty years' service, I thought, That's enough, and I retired.

I joined Bexhill Bush Fire Brigade back during my commuting days. In '82 me and my next-door neighbour, Craig, were invited to their AGM by a local butcher, Dave Elliott. Dave had been the brigade's captain almost from its inauguration. So he was getting on a bit. Neither Craig nor me had been to a meeting before so it was, 'Yeah righto, Dave, we'll come along.'

So we went to this meeting. Only half a dozen blokes were there. But with it being their AGM it was when they voted everyone back into their positions. Anyhow, to our surprise, by the time the AGM was over, Craig had been voted in as their new fire captain and me as a fully qualified member. And that's the position both of us still hold today.

My first call-out was to a grassfire, somewhere up a creek near Corndale. We had a box trailer with a 200-gallon water tank on it that was towed by someone's car. Our only other firefighting gear was wet corn bags and rake-hoes. A rake-hoe's a broom-handled type thing with a metal leaf-shaped base that's got a rake on one side of it and a hoe on the other side. There were no uniforms. No boots. We didn't have a hat. We hadn't even done any training. We just learnt on the job.

It wasn't till a couple of years later that we got our first fire truck. It was a big old lumbering Thames that'd come from a town brigade. It was absolutely hopeless for fighting fires in the bush. If you took it off-road, it'd get bogged. And seeing how we didn't have a proper fire shed in Bexhill, Craig kept it at his house.

But over time, we went from being a Bush Fire Brigade to being part of the Rural Fire Service, which was when we became part of the council set-up. So then we started to hound council about helping us with a fire shed. But every time we found a decent block of land, one particular person – who shall remain nameless – would fight tooth and nail against it. Even to this day I don't know why. He just must've had some sort of bee in his bonnet. Like we'd find a vacant block – but no, he was against that. So we'd find another block somewhere else – but no, he was against that too. After that there was a great block down by the railways – but no, he knocked that on the head.

Then we found a block at the bottom of the cemetery which had an open-air cathedral overlooking it. But no, he wasn't going to have a fire shed there neither because it'd be an 'eyesore'. So we kept pushing and pushing and in the end council gave us the okay for the cemetery block. So a lot of us volunteers got to and, with council help, we built the shed at the bottom of the cemetery. And you wouldn't believe it, when we'd finished, the bloke who was so much against it being there acknowledged it wasn't such an eyesore.

Anyhow, over time, Bexhill, Richmond Hill and Numulgi brigades amalgamated. Out of that we gained about ten members – all blokes – and while Numulgi only had a trailer with a small water tank, Richmond Hill had a truck. With the amalgamation, things started to improve. Though we had to buy our own handheld two-way radios, we got uniforms and hats and boots – all that type of thing. And as time went by, the trucks got better – these days we've got a Category 1 Isuzu. It carries 3500 litres of water and it's got everything on it that we need, like with all the pumps and wind-up reels, everything. It even has foam for fuel fires.

One particular highlight of my time with the brigade was that, in the late 1990s both Craig and I were awarded the Australian National Medal for services to the Rural Fire Service.

Now, as for other memories, one that stands out was the time we were called to a house fire at Eltham. We still had the old

Thames back then. Anyhow, at Eltham there's the pub, then there's the general store, then a house that used to be the post office and that was next to the house that'd caught fire.

When we got there it was fully ablaze. And because the old Thames only held five or six hundred gallons of water, we were forever having to drive back and forth to fill the tank. Anyhow, we tried our best, but we lost the house. By then the fire had got onto the house next door. We battled that, but no, we lost that house too. Thankfully, by then the Clunes Brigade had arrived with more water, so we put all our efforts into saving the store. And we did it. Even though it got severely scorched, we saved it.

Anyhow, I got my photo in the newspaper with that one. It was a picture of me with my hat on, standing there in my old army greens, with the house going up in flames behind me and the caption read along the lines of 'Fireman looking for more help.' And I can tell you, at that particular time I needed all the help I could get.

Apart from the house fires, we get called to assist Fire and Rescue with road accidents and we also help fight fires in other districts as backup. We've recently spent a few days out at Tabulam and there's currently some very big fires over Casino–Grafton way.

But around here it's usually grassfires. One time a bloke was slashing the grass in his paddock near the Casino–Murwillumbah railway line. He had the slasher running off the tractor's PTO – power take-off – and, even though he'd covered it, it had somehow caught fire. So he's merrily driving along and when he takes a look back over his shoulder it's, 'Holy mackerel, there's a line of fires chasing me!'

By the time we got there, about sixty acres had already been burnt. But our main worry was that the fires were heading towards the railway line. Now, with this being a floodplain, the railways had built a string of wooden bridges to straddle the lower-lying areas. Like there'd be a hundred metres of bridge, then there'd be dirt, then there'd be another hundred metres of bridge and so on. And with the bridges being built of wood, things were looking pretty grim. What was worse was that, if any of the bridges were damaged by the fire, the property owner had to bear the cost of repairs. And that would've cost him a mint.

So to get this fire under control, we were drafting water out of a waterhole in the nearby river. It took us hours to put the fire out and, thankfully, we did so with only minor damage to one of the bridges.

Anyhow, while we were cleaning up, the owner jumped in his ute. 'I'll be back in a tick,' he said and when he returned, lo 'n behold, his ute was stacked with cartons of beer. 'There you go, fellers,' he said. 'Go for it.' Oh, he was a very relieved man. Because like I said, if the fire had got into the bridges, it could've very well sent him broke.

Other times we get funny sorts of call-outs. Like when we got called to a barbecue fire. When we turned up, there was an old lady out the back of her house, just beside a shed, with a gas bottle on fire. So we turned off the gas and put it out. Anyway, we said to this old lady, 'So what happened?'

She said, 'Well, when I turned the barbecue on, I thought I could smell gas, so I lit a match to it to see if the cylinder was leaking. And that's when it caught on fire.'

I mean, how lucky was she? Instead of pouring soapy water over the gas connection to check for bubbles, it was, 'Oh, I'll just strike a match.'

So yes, I've now been a volunteer firie for thirty-seven years. There's no retirement age, so unlike my seven-times-redundant experience with the railways, I'll continue with the brigade for a good while yet. And anyhow, you know within yourself when you're not up to the more active side of things any more. But, even when it gets to that stage, I'll still stay connected.

We've built the brigade up to about fifteen members. And they're a real good mob. There's great camaraderie. Numbers have never been much of a problem, though about a year ago we were getting a bit low. Then, right out of the blue, six young fellers turned up. All under thirty. And they're keen. With me being one of the older ones, when we go to a fire, I'll be on the back of the truck with the pump, shouting orders to the young fellers: 'Grab those hoses and go.' And off they'll go. Oh, they run up hills. They run here, they run there, they run everywhere. That's how keen they are. They're as keen as mustard.

And now we've got a real young feller who's just turned up. He's on his L plates. See, you've got to be seventeen before you can attend fires and he's got to be trained up first. There's a big facility in Casino now where people go, over a couple months, for training. That includes classroom stuff as well as hands-on. We also have our own training sessions where we practise drawing water out of waterholes. Plus we test all the gear, like the generators, pumps, chainsaws, lighting and so forth, just to make sure it works. Following all that he'll be on six months' probation. But he looks pretty good. He's a real goer.

Our only trouble now is that we're light on for drivers. So we're looking to some of those young fellers. Because see, to drive the fire truck you need a special MR – medium rigid – category licence. Like I'm okay because I got mine when I was driving trucks back in my National Service days.

Also, of course, with being a volunteer organisation, there's the ever-present problem of money. To that end we do a lot of fundraising. Like each year someone gets dressed up as Santa Claus and we put them up on the truck and we do a Christmas run around Bexhill and up through Richmond Hill. And while Santa hands out lollies to the kids, the rest of us carry our hats, taking donations. And the kids really love it. And look, since I joined in '82, I've seen some of them grow from babies into teenagers. And you just hope that, perhaps, somewhere down the track those same kids will think, Hey, I might join the volunteer fire brigade.

Note: Reports on 14 August 2019 had sixty-four fires burning along the New South Wales east coast, with about half of them in the Northern Rivers region. By 16 August, Summerland Way – the road between Casino and Grafton – had just reopened when author Bill 'Swampy' Marsh travelled through there on his way to Taree.

The township of Rappville – just off Summerland Way – was particularly badly hit when two fires, which had already burnt out ninety-two thousand hectares, converged near the town later on in early October. More than thirty homes were either destroyed or badly damaged in the fire. Summerland Way and train lines were again closed. At the height of the blaze a resident said that, due to the 'cyclonic' heat condition of the fire, birds were dropping dead out of the sky.

A large air tanker assisted firefighters as they battled to hold containment lines.

Christmas Island and Beyond

Back in the early 2000s, the federal government got in touch with me. 'Ken,' they said, 'we're going to second you from the Western Australian government and send you over to Christmas Island.'

Basically, they wanted three boxes ticked. First, the Federal Education Department wanted me over there as education and programs manager, teaching adult education to the detainees in the detention centre. So that'd keep those guys happy. They also wanted me to get involved in the Christmas Island Volunteer Fire and Rescue Brigade. So that'd keep those guys happy. Then, because I had a background in safety, they said, 'Can you take a look at the safety standards in the phosphate mine as well?'

This wasn't long after the Tampa crisis in 2001. If you remember, the Tampa Crisis became a big issue during the next federal election when John Howard's Liberals brought in their 'border protection policy'. That all came about after an Indonesian fishing boat's engine failed just outside Australia's international waters, near Christmas Island, with over four hundred asylum seekers on board – including children and pregnant women.

Anyhow, a Norwegian cargo ship, the *Tampa*, came to their rescue. But when the captain wanted to drop the asylum seekers off on Christmas Island, the Australian government put a stop to it. After a lot of toing and froing and politicking, the refugees ended up being shipped to the island country of Nauru, where they were placed in detention centres and were unable to apply for refugee status.

When me and my family arrived on Christmas Island, the population would've been around a thousand. At that time there was only the one Volunteer Fire and Rescue Brigade. They had a large Mazda pumper, which is a fire-apparatus truck with a permanently mounted fire pump and around a 3000-litre water tank plus hoses and all the firefighting paraphernalia. As well as the pumper, they had a light tanker and a rescue trailer. So they were pretty well equipped. And you could understand why too, because with Christmas Island basically being a volcano out in the middle of the ocean, if something big happened, help was a hell of a long way off. And also, with it being an island, it was difficult for just the one brigade to cover the lot and so later on we set up a second brigade on the other side of the island.

We spent near on four years on Christmas Island and, even though there weren't that many major emergencies, there was a lot going on in a political sense. Other than the fallout from the Tampa crisis, the Christmas Island casino was in the throes of being closed down. That's because a new casino had been built in Perth and the owners there didn't want the Christmas Island casino operating in opposition.

See, before the Perth casino came into being, all the high-flyers from Thailand, Bali and Indonesia were coming over to Christmas Island to spend their money. And the Perth casino owners didn't like that. They wanted all the high-flyers to come to Perth. And while the West Australian government was all for closing down the Christmas Island casino, the Islanders didn't like it, not one little bit. Oh no they didn't. It was taking away their jobs. So then the unions got together and said to the government, 'If you're going to close the casino down on us, we want this, this and this.' And they got it.

We thoroughly enjoyed our time on Christmas Island. It was just fantastic. It's where we raised our three daughters. But in 2008, when the detention centre was also closed, my job became redundant. So I came back to Perth for a while. Then I did a stint of teaching out at Kalgoorlie. I joined the fire brigade there. That was when the running competitions started. Running competitions are where the brigades compete to see how fast they can roll out the fire hose from an old-style fire cart to a certain distance. There was also ladder competitions, with volunteer firefighters putting the ladders up and running up the ladders and hitting a target with water. So I was introduced to all that. And it was great fun. I was young and I was fit.

We then moved to Northam, where I worked for the government. Following Northam, I had a change in career direction and got a job as vice president of safety for Australasia Rio Tinto Iron Ore operations. I did that for maybe six years, then this job came up as executive officer for the Volunteer Fire and Rescue Services Association of Western Australia. Basically we're the union who represents our 2500 or so members over the ninety-nine brigades spread throughout WA. To put it simply, we advocate on the members' behalf to the federal, state and local governments, as well as to government departments such as DFES – Department of Fire and Emergency Services.

And that's just Volunteer Fire and Rescue I'm talking about. We're the ones in the red trucks. We're not to be confused with the Bush Fire Brigades – the rural brigades – in the white trucks. See, as well as us in Fire and Rescue, in some of the more rural areas they also have Bush Fire Brigades. And they just fight bushfires. That's all they do. Bush Fire Brigades are predominantly made up of cockies – farmers – who have said, 'Hey, why don't a few of us get together, form a bush fire brigade, get a shed and have a truck or two in there to share around?'

That's what they do, as opposed to us, the WA Volunteer Fire and Rescue Service, who do the lot. We not only fight bushfires, but we've also got all the gear, like the jaws of life, so that we can attend vehicle accidents. We also have BA – breathing apparatus – and so forth so that we can fight structure fires and go into burning houses.

Simply put, I'm the voice for the Volunteer Fire and Rescue Service Association of WA. So if something doesn't go right, or if the members are in need of further training, or extra equipment, or they're after more support in one way or another, or they're having funding troubles et cetera and they've exhausted all their avenues through DFES, they come to me. Then I'll go to the commissioner and say, 'Hey, this's not right. Can we get a shake along?' and he'll go, 'Yep,' or he'll say, 'Sorry, Ken, we haven't got the funding.'

If that happens I'll go to the government minister and try and get an outcome there. Basically, I travel around the state, doing brigade visits, chatting to our members, having a beer with them – listening to their concerns. Trying to help them. It's a great job. I've been in it for a year now and I'm loving it. I mean the pay's not much. But it's rewarding in other ways. Like these days I wake up in the morning and go, 'Shit I love my job. I'm so lucky.'

With having joined my local brigade back in 1991, perhaps the only downside of being a volunteer is that because you're usually working within your own community, when that pager goes off or the phone goes off and it's a vehicle accident, your first thought is, Could it be someone I know, someone close to me? And we have come across a couple of instances where family members have been involved in an accident, and that's hard, very hard, for everyone concerned. So, top of our list is to maintain the welfare of our volunteers. That's why, through both DFES and our association, we've now got a fantastic peer support program up and running.

On the other hand, through being a volunteer firefighter, a real highlight is that every town you go to – and that's a hundred towns in WA – no matter where you've come from, you're instantly absorbed into the Fire and Rescue family. It's a wonderful and very family-orientated organisation. There's the barbecues, with all the kids running around. Family days. Fun days. And that's why the volunteers keep on doing what they do: because of family.

And seeing how I've now been involved in Fire and Rescue for over thirty years, the other highlight for me would be when we go into a burning house and save the life of someone, or I help pull someone to safety from a vehicle accident. There's that thanks and recognition from their family and friends. And that gives us all an overwhelming feeling of a job well done.

Oh, and just on a more personal matter: remember how I said that we raised our three daughters on Christmas Island? Well, they're well and truly grown now. They're eighteen, twenty and twenty-two. One lives in Wyalkatchem, one lives in Northam and one's heading up to Broome, and they've all joined the Volunteer Fire and Rescue Service. And it gives me such a huge buzz when they say, 'Dad, it's just fantastic. They've welcomed us with open arms.'

Note: These days Christmas Island's major tourist attraction is the red crab migration. With the first rainfall of the wet season, millions of large red crabs appear out of the forest and swarm across roads, streams and rocks, making their way to the beaches. In places, crab bridges have been built over the roads.

After their journey to the coast, the crabs take a dip in the sea to replenish the moisture in their bodies. The male crabs then retreat to the lower terraces to dig burrows. The female crabs then join the males to mate. After mating, the male crabs have a second dip in the sea before starting their journey back home, while the females stay behind in the moist burrows as the eggs develop. Each female crab can produce up to 100,000 eggs, which she holds in a brood pouch. With the moon reaching its last quarter, the egg-laden female crabs leave their burrows and gather on the shoreline. When the dawn high tide starts to turn, the female crabs move into the sea and release their eggs before returning to the forest.

Deployment

I come from a place just west of Townsville called Thuringowa. Earlier on Mum and Dad bought some land there. It was more or less a hobby farm with a few fruit trees, a few horses and a few cattle. Anyhow, I loved the place so much that I ended up buying my own block there. If you ever get up this way, our neighbouring township is the beautiful small community of Paluma, which is up in the Mount Spec Ranges with its Paluma Range National Park and its lovely rainforests.

Coming off a farm, I'd experienced fires well before I joined the brigade. But legally you had to be eighteen before you could volunteer, so as soon as I turned eighteen I joined the Thuringowa Brigade. There were thirteen of us members, and they were a fantastic group of people. You couldn't ask for a better bunch.

I'm now forty-nine, so I've got the big five-oh next year. But oh, since I first joined, I've held heaps of different positions. From being a member I worked all the way up to being group officer, where I helped to support all the brigades in the area. I was also first officer in my Thuringowa Brigade, where I also shared positions like secretary and different roles like that, and I've also done a lot of deployments.

A deployment is when there's been some sort of disaster somewhere and the powers-that-be ring you up and say, 'We're looking for this certain sort of role during the crisis. Are you prepared to go and help?' You know, whether it be as part of an Incident Management Team – IMT – or in a firefighting capacity or whatever.

Of course I'd say, 'Yes,' because, to me, it doesn't matter where the fire or the disaster is, I'm one of those people who's always wanted to help and protect my community and/or the environment. Even from way back, I've always had a good head on me. So I had a pretty good knack for incident management and I was also good on the logistics side of an operation. So after Cyclone Larry came through northern Queensland, straight away they got in touch with me and said, 'Kev, look, we need a hand, mate. Can you help us?'

I said, 'Yeah, too easy. What do you want me to do?'

They said, 'We want someone to be part of the first-response IMT clean-up in Innisfail.'

'Yeah, okay,' I said. 'No worries.'

What they were looking for from me was to get together a team of forty volunteers to help the effort up in Innisfail. When I went to my Thuringowa Brigade, they all put their hands up. Then all the other brigades in the area stuck their hands up as well. In the end something like one hundred and eighty people volunteered to go and, because we could only take forty at a time, we decided to send them to Innisfail on monthly rotations.

When we got to Innisfail, we set up a whole sector from the ground up – all the infrastructure and that. First we got in tarps and, for those that needed emergency accommodation, we erected satellite tent-hubs. Then we organised for food and supplies to come in. By the end we'd put in so much support that they were virtually self-sufficient.

Being there as first-response was really an emotional experience because, by living and working within a community that had been devastated by Cyclone Larry, we got to share what they were going through firsthand. In actual fact it proved to be a huge learning and growth period for me. You know, to be able and willing to give so much to that struggling community I, in turn, gained so much out of it. So it proved to be a heart-warming experience, one that forever reminded me of the value of being a volunteer, and I loved it.

I actually received an award for helping out with that one. It's up on my wall here at home. It was presented to me by Prime Minister John Howard and Queensland Premier Peter Beattie. It says, and I quote, 'a special commendation in recognition of outstanding leadership during the Cyclone Larry relief effort of 2006'.

And it's through working in situations like that I reckon a lot more younger ones would get to experience the benefits of volunteering. Because, with it being so hard to get them interested in becoming members, the average age of us vollies is now getting older and older. And that's not the way it should be.

I actually went to a forum last year where they discussed all this and someone said, 'Well, the first thing is, we're making it so bloody difficult to get people in. Like, they're scared to volunteer because they're worried about occupational health and safety issues and litigation and being sued and all that.'

I said, 'Yes, that's all okay, but we've gotta make it more attractive for these younger people.'

As far as I see it, say a brigade ends up with sixty members. With so many members, hardly half of them will get the chance to go out and gain any fire experience, such as taking part in back-burnings. So they get bored. To my mind, the strategy is, no matter how many members you have, share the bloody workload around. Share it around. For example, if you're doing early control burns. Say you've got twenty members and you've only got one truck and that one truck can only carry three people – don't just send out the same three volunteers. Move them around. Get them to go out in a rotation, so that they're not just sitting there, hanging around, waiting for a go. By giving everyone a go, everyone's active.

And another thing, get out and educate the community. That's the way we do it up here and we're getting a lot of younger people interested. And focus on the learning/growth side of firefighting, deployments and rescue, as a human being. Then there's the friendships. I've made heaps of great friends over the years I've been with the volunteer fire service – friends that I would never have met if I hadn't been a member.

See, you've just got to sell the benefits of it. Put forward the positives and leave the negatives. It's amazing how so many people get stuck on the negatives. Mate, over my time, I've found that a positive attitude really helps. I remember when we went down to Brisbane during the big fires back in 2006. That was fourteen years ago and, back then, I would've been one of the youngest ones on the deployment – by a long shot. Then just last year, I led two task forces down south. One was for a fire out west of Brisbane and the other was for a fire down at Bundaberg. And, mate, it was just great to see all these young volunteers putting their hands up, wanting to go. So it sort of shows you that maybe, just maybe, we're starting to see a change.

Note: Cyclone Larry began as a low-pressure system over the eastern Coral Sea on 16 March 2006. Two days later it had strengthened into a Category 4 storm. Larry made landfall close to Innisfail on 20 March as a Category 5 tropical cyclone with wind gusts of up to two hundred and forty kilometres per hour, causing extensive damage to infrastructure and cropping. Approximately ten thousand houses were destroyed and the ensuing flooding cut road and rail access to the area for several days. There was one direct fatality.

Damage-wise, Cyclone Larry was considered to be the costliest tropical cyclone to ever hit Australia – surpassing Cyclone Tracy in 1974 – until Cyclone Yasi in 2011.

Balls

Look, mate, we've heard that you're after some volunteer fire service stories. Well, I've got one here for you that may be true or it may only be partly true. But, as you may have gathered, up here in the Territory, we tend to approach things a little differently than what the southerners do, especially when it comes to tackling life-and-death situations.

Now, the community I come from has a population of less than a hundred. I won't mention the name of the place for reasons that'll soon become obvious. But we do have a volunteer fire service, as small as it is. As far as members go, there's only me, the fire captain, then there's Big Bob, Mad Mick and the McTavishes, John and Jane, who are pretty new to the area. John had been an engineer or something back down south and he and Jane came up here looking for a more relaxed lifestyle.

Now, with being such a small brigade, we haven't got all the fancy gear that the larger brigades have – just the bare basics – though we do have a tray-top Toyota with a small water tank and a pump on it. As for fire training, we don't do much apart from a bit of burning off during the dry season – as you no doubt saw on your way up the highway to visit us. That's a yearly thing, when we get around to it.

So that's pretty much the fire side of things. Then there's the rescue side of it. That's mainly where we help people who have fallen over while they're out bush and may have injured themselves. Or there's those who just get plain lost – like the city slickers. Then, of course, there's the road accidents. They're mostly up and down the highway. We can't do too much there because we don't have the fancy gear to get people out of smashed cars, like the jaws of life and all that. All we've got is crowbars, chisels, hacksaws and stuff. So if things look real bad, we call in one of the more well-equipped brigades and, of course, the Care Flight helicopter is available if anyone's critically injured and needs to be flown up to intensive care at Darwin Hospital.

Now, as far as other sorts of rescues go, we had a pretty ticklish one just the other day. The call came through that there was an emergency around at the Thompsons' place. That's Marj and Jack Thompson. They own a small block just out of town where they run a few head of Brahman cattle and grow a few mangoes and a bit of weed. The thing is that the person who put the call through, and I suspect it might've been Marj, must've been on the giggle-juice or something because her instructions as to what the exact problem was were a bit muffled. The best I could make out was that it had something to do with an incident at a private barbecue function.

Anyhow, I put out the call and everyone turned up, apart from Big Bob that is. But that wasn't too unusual. Big Bob's a busy man. So we had a full crew, almost. So we get into our firefighting gear – or what was left of it after the unfortunate incident we had during our last burn-off – and off we go.

Being fire captain – the boss – I'm driving. In the front with me are the McTavishes. Mad Mick's on the back, which is where he prefers to be. His thinking is that, when we head off to a fire, he likes to get some of the smoke into his lungs before we get there, so that he's fully prepared for the job ahead. But the thing is, with having heard the word 'barbecue' we're fully expecting that a gas cylinder's caught alight. So while I'm driving out to the Thompsons', I've got Jane flicking through the firefighting manual, checking out the procedure with gas fires. You know, how to put them out safely and all that sort of caper.

When we arrived at the Thompsons', we could see a wisp of smoke rising up from their backyard. So we jumped off the truck, grabbed the fire hose and charged in through their front gate. That's when we saw Jack and Marj standing around the barbecue with odd grins on their dials. And right over in the corner, under the shade of the verandah, was our missing member, Big Bob. He's sitting in one of them slatted plastic stacker chairs, looking downright miserable.

Now, I've got to explain something here. Big Bob got the name of Big Bob because we don't like to exaggerate things up here in the Territory. Because, the real truth of it is that Big Bob's a hell of a lot bigger than just plain 'big'. He's massive – an absolute lump of a lad, and that's in all departments.

Now, what'd apparently happened was that when Big Bob squatted himself down on one of those slatted plastic chairs, due to his excess weight, the slats had widened and his testicles had slid out from his shorts and they'd dropped down between the opened slats.

Now, I don't know if you know too much about physics or not but, when he went to get up out of the plastic chair, with the displacement of his weight, the plastic slats snapped shut and his testicles had got caught, dangling under the chair. Oh yes, you could see them all right. Like I said, he wasn't called Big Bob for nothing. So of course we had a problem. One that I, as a veteran volunteer firie of over thirty years, had never faced before and hopefully will never face again. In fact, young Jane McTavish started to go a bit faint, just at the sight.

At first we tried to lift Big Bob out of his situation. But the more we lifted him, the less weight was put onto the chair and so the tighter the slats took their vice-like grip. So I was pretty much stumped as to what we should do and, what's more, Jane couldn't find hide nor hair about such a situation in the advanced firefighting and rescue manual. So, with me being the all-inclusive sort of leader that I am, I opened it up to the rest of the crew. 'Okay,' I said, 'any suggestions?'

That's when Mad Mick piped up. 'I've read about somethin' like this happenin' in a poem or somethin'.'

I said, 'Well, how did they manage to extricate the victim's testicles from out between the slats?'

'I don't know,' Mad Mick said. 'They might'a used the jaws of life or somethin'. I ferget.'

But of course, as I might've already mentioned, we weren't equipped with the jaws of life. But Mad Mick wasn't done yet. If I'll give Mad Mick something, he's a real thinker. Some call him 'the brains of the brigade', which was okay by me because, like I might've said, I'm more one of them inclusive type of leaders where I like to get everyone involved. So Mad Mick says, 'Then how's about we put a blow torch under the seat to melt the plastic, and then we can slide Big Bob's balls out from between the grooves?'

For obvious reasons, Big Bob wasn't too keen on that suggestion. And I had to agree with him. I'd once inadvertently dropped some burning plastic on my finger and I can tell you, I still bear the scar.

'Then how about we rub ice cubes onto his balls so that they might shrink back up through the slats?'

I said, 'Good idea, Mick, but by doing that we could end up doing more damage than good with the shock of them going from balloon-like and swollen to small and frozen like two peas.'

'Anyway,' said Jane, 'there's no way you're going to get me down on my hands and knees, under the chair, rubbing ice on Big Bob's two thingamajigs.'

'Me neither,' said Marj.

'Well, blowed if I know what we can do then,' I said.

That's when Jack Thompson piped up. 'Look,' he said, 'let's not panic. What we need here is a set of calm heads. He's not going to go anywhere, so how's about we just sit down and nut this thing out over a couple of snags and a few beers.'

So that's what we did. We grabbed a few slices of bread, stuffed a couple of snags onto them, squirted on some of Marj's homemade tomato sauce, grabbed a beer and we sat down to have a good calm think about Big Bob's unfortunate situation.

But by gee, I must tell you, them snags of Marj's were bloody delicious. Everyone agreed on that. Apparently, Marj'd made them from an old family recipe. She'd got her hubby, Jack, to knock off one of the next-door neighbour's weaners – a young calf – skin it and hack it up into pieces. Then, as she was shoving the pieces of meat through the mincer, she'd added her family's secret concoction of herbs and spices and mixed it all up before putting it through the sausage maker into one of those real fair-dinkum sausage skins that Jack had saved from the weaner's intestines.

As Marj has always said, 'Waste not, want not.'

'Have some more,' said Jack. 'Help yourselves. Got plenty in the freezer.'

So we did and we washed them down with a few nice icy-cold ales. Actually, it was turning into a perfectly relaxing afternoon. So much so that pretty soon we'd forgotten about Big Bob. That's until our in-depth discussion about the state of play in the current cricket series against Pakistan got interrupted by a strange squeaking sound echoing out from under the verandah.

'Hey, fellers, what about me?'

'Gee, sorry, Bob,' said Marj. 'Completely forgot about you, mate. Do you want a snag? Sauce or not? 'N how's about a beer?'

Anyhow, that's what got us back on track, trying to sort out Big Bob's dilemma. And that's when Mad Mick come up with the idea of how we could turn Big Bob over on his side and cut the offending plastic slats with a knife, which would in turn release the pressure on the big feller's testicles.

'Got me castratin' knife here,' said Jack, with an eager glint in his eye. 'Just sharpened it the other day when I sorted out that weaner yer eatin'.'

When Big Bob heard that one, he almost choked on his snag. His fear was, just one slip of the knife and any chance of him carrying on the family name would be lost.

'Well, the way things are lookin' right now, mate,' said Mad Mick, 'they're pretty much lost already.'

And that's when John piped up. He's the ex-engineer feller I told you about, and this was the first time we'd heard a peep out of him all arvo. He said, 'Look, we mightn't have the jaws of life, but we've got a crowbar in the truck. So how about we roll Big Bob over, chair and all, then we lever the crowbar in between the offending slats and prise them open just enough to release Big Bob's balls? What do yer reckon?'

'Jesus,' said Mad Mick. 'Great idea, mate. Let's give it a crack. We've got nothin' ter lose, ay?'

'Yes we do,' came the squeak from under the verandah.

Anyhow, with me being the inclusive sort of leader that I am, we took a vote on it ... and Big Bob lost. So we gathered around Big Bob and, as gently as possible, we rolled him over on his side, with the plastic stacker chair still intact.

'Easy does it,' squeaked Big Bob.

When that was done, Mad Mick wedged the crowbar in between the offending plastic slats and, on the count of three, we began to prise them open. Now, I've seen some pretty gruesome things in my life, what with car accidents and all that, but they were nothing in comparison. So much so that at one point I had to turn away. And that's when I heard an almighty *ping*, like a giant rubber band being snapped shut, which was followed by an almost simultaneous yelp.

'Oh shit, sorry, Bob,' said Mad Mick.

But there was no response.

'Yer've killed the poor bastard!' cried John.

'No I haven't,' replied Mad Mick. 'He's just out to it.' Then he shouted, 'This's our big chance. John, go 'n get the fuckin' chisel 'n hammer out'a the truck! 'N grab the hacksaw while yer at it!'

Anyhow, to cut a long story short, Mad Mick, John and Jack eventually managed to free Big Bob and his testicles from between the plastic slats. As the doctors up in Darwin Hospital have told us, 'He's doing as well as can be expected, given the circumstances.'

Note 1: The lightweight stackable 'monobloc' chair is reputedly the world's most popular plastic chair. The name 'monobloc' – meaning 'single block' – comes from the process of the chair being injection-moulded from thermoplastic polypropylene, at an extremely high heat, as a single piece rather than it having to be assembled from a number of separate pieces, as a normal chair would be. The lightweight stackable chair usually comes in white and is available at most outdoor garden and hardware centres, and is priced between ten and fifteen dollars.

Note 2: In June 2013, author Bill 'Swampy' Marsh had to be flown to the intensive care unit at Darwin Hospital in the Care Flight helicopter – though for a completely different reason. He fell off a cliff in Kakadu National Park.

Imagine

I've been in the Western Australian Volunteer Fire and Rescue Service – the WAVFRS – for just over twenty years. And while you never know what the future might bring, one thing I'm pretty sure about is that, whatever happens and wherever I go, I reckon I'll always remain involved.

With us living in the sort of flat, remote area that we do up here on the WA coast, we don't have too many bushfires. So unless the local Bush Fire Brigade want some assistance, we pretty much leave that side of things up to them. And because we're not a big town with double-storey buildings, we haven't had to deal with a big structure fire – not for quite a while anyway. Fingers crossed.

Even still, the appliances that we've got carry all the standard equipment like the ladders, the hoses, the pumps, the water tank and all that. We've also got all the hazmat gear for dealing with spilt petrol, escaping gases et cetera. And, just as well, because we do get our surprises.

About eleven years ago we were called up the river to assist our local Bush Fire Brigade. We'd been told that it was a little ten-by-ten-metre first- or second-alarm scrubby – scrub fire. But when we got there, we ended up having to deal with about half a dozen methyl-bromide cylinders venting and exploding. And that went on for a day and a half. I mean, you'll have to check but I believe methyl bromide is injected into the soil to get rid of pests in preparation for the next lot of planting. In this case I'm talking about a banana plantation. The thing was, the farmer wasn't taking safe care with his chemicals.

As for the rescue side of things, we've got all the hydraulic gear, like the jaws of life and parrot's beak, we've got floodlights, extinguishers, self-contained breathing apparatus – BA – and thermal imaging cameras et cetera. Actually, vehicle accidents are our main call-outs and, because of our remote location, that has its difficulties.

If you're looking north, south, east and west from where we are, here on the Indian Ocean, our nearest WAVFRS backup to the west would – obviously – be nothing. Eastwards, Meekatharra's our nearest, and that's over six hundred kilometres away. To the south, our nearest fully equipped WAVFRS is Shark Bay, and that's three hundred and twenty kilometres away. To the north, our nearest brigade is Exmouth, which is three hundred and sixty kilometres away. So we're pretty much it for a very long stretch of the North West Coastal Highway.

So just imagine you've been involved in a vehicle accident. You're severely or critically injured and you're trapped in an overturned vehicle seventy kilometres out along the highway. Being such a remote stretch of road, it could take anywhere up to half an hour before someone comes past. Then, up until not long ago, mobile reception was pretty poor so, unless they've got a satellite phone, they'll have to keep driving until their mobile phone comes into range.

By then another half an hour may well have elapsed. Then, because we're so far away from the scene of the accident, it may be another hour or so before we can get there and start doing our thing. To compound the issue, just imagine it's in the middle of summer, where the temperatures reach up to, and over, fifty degrees Celsius. Just imagine that. It'd be a pretty horrific situation for you to find yourself in, wouldn't it?

Anyhow, touch wood, we haven't had any really serious accidents for quite some time. Maybe people are finally taking heed of all the safety messages that we and DFES – Department of Fire and Emergency Services – keep putting out. Here's hoping, anyway.

But that hasn't always been the case. Back about twenty years ago, when we used to carry all our rescue gear around on a trailer, I remember going to my first big car accident. I'd only been in the WAVFRS for about three months. It was just five days before Christmas, so it was stinking hot and the accident had occurred about a hundred k's south, back down the North West Coastal Highway. It involved a family of six – Mum, Dad and four kids – plus their Rottweiler dog.

The family were in a four-wheel drive wagon and they were towing a boat. From memory, their vehicle might've been an 80 series Toyota, the ones with the bench seat in the front. What made matters worse was that they were overloaded, which is also something else we're forever banging on about. 'Don't overload your vehicle. Don't overload your caravan, and don't overload your trailer.' But these people had.

Other than us, there was the ambos – the ambulance people. Back then they had their old converted Ford F 250, plus one of their new ones. So they would've had two converted Ford F 250s at the time.

It was a similar story to so many I've since experienced. The male driver was fatigued. He'd ended up running off the left-hand side of the highway and he'd hit a guidepost. He then must've snapped awake and had grabbed hard on the steering wheel to try and get back onto the road. In doing so he'd over-corrected and the vehicle had rolled.

By the time we got there, the four kids had found their way outside of the vehicle and were wandering around like walking wounded, suffering from multiple bumps, bruises, scratches and grazes – all sorts of stuff, including shock. The woman – their mother – who must've been sitting in the middle of the front bench seat, had gone out through the windscreen and she was deceased upon our arrival.

In those days they only had the lap-type seatbelts, whereas these days the people sitting in the middle have a sash seatbelt, as well as the lap-style seatbelt. So these days you're a little bit more secure. Then their dog – the Rottweiler – hadn't fared too well either and we ended up burying him beside the highway.

The driver was still alive. But he remained trapped in the overturned vehicle with the driver's side on the ground. The boat was still hooked up to the car, but in such a way that it'd jacked the vehicle up at an awkward angle – which was going to make it even more difficult for us to get to him and get him out.

Because I was only new, I was initially tasked with isolating all the flammable materials. Amongst the wreckage I found three gas bottles and half a dozen jerry cans of fuel. There was also a trail of beer cans strewn for something like two hundred and fifty metres up the road. Amongst the scattered belongings was your usual, plus all the Christmas presents. I mentioned that this was just five days before Christmas, didn't I?

Anyhow, to give us enough space to get to the man and try to get him out, we ended up nudging our light tanker appliance up to the side of his vehicle. So to stabilise it upright, we tied it off to the bull bar. Even then, it still took us quite a while to get him out and, by all the reports, he ended up quadriplegic, with four young kids to look after.

Yet oddly enough, as tragic as it all was, during the time we were out there, I hadn't felt at all traumatised by the event. In actual fact, I remained pretty calm throughout it all. Maybe because it was my first proper rescue job, I don't know. Or perhaps it was because I was so fully occupied with running around cleaning the area up and then being busy helping to get the man out, that I didn't have the time to think about it. But anyhow, it'd been a long night and, when we eventually came back into town, we all congregated at the local Caltex for breakfast. And I remember one of the more experienced boys was sitting there, just shaking his head. Sitting there, just shaking his head.

I said to him, 'What's wrong?'

And his reply was, 'In just five days' time all those Christmas presents would've been sitting under the family tree.'

And that's when it struck me. Imagine, just five days before Christmas and having something like that happen to you.

Note: In rural and remote areas please be mindful that, in the event of an accident, there may well be limited fire and rescue, ambulance and medical services available.

When undertaking a long journey, there are a number of factors to take into consideration.

- *Obey the rules in relation to alcohol and drug consumption, passenger loading and restraint. Drivers from different countries, please note that, in Australia, we drive on the left side of the road and seatbelts are mandatory.*
- *Keep to the speed limit and allow adequate travel time to avoid the urge to exceed the speed limit. Take extra care when driving on dirt, gravel and unsealed roads. Be wary of inconsistent road surfaces, that is, potholes and irregular and poorly maintained road shoulders.*
- *Remain vigilant, particularly at dusk and dawn when visibility is at its poorest. Hazards can appear unexpectedly, for example, wildlife, livestock crossing the road or slow-moving farm machinery.*
- *As fatigue is a major cause of road accidents in rural and remote areas, rest well before beginning a long drive, share the driving if possible, and always take a break every two hours. Travel during the times that you are normally awake, and never drive after a day's work.*
- *Ensure your vehicle has been fully serviced and is in good mechanical condition, complete with a toolkit for changing tyres, radiator hoses, engine drive belts*

et cetera. If experiencing difficulties such as a flat tyre, drive to a safe off-road spot before taking action.

- *Allow plenty of space for road trains et cetera and only overtake when there is adequate space and you feel confident to safely do so.*
- *Consider fitting intelligent transport systems to your vehicle, for example, GPS navigation, or fatigue and speed warning systems. If mobile phone coverage is going to be inconsistent, consider alternative communications such as a satellite phone. If venturing into the more remote areas, consider taking an Electronic Position Indicator Radio Beacon (EPIRB).*
- *It's recommended you do a first-aid course before leaving on a long trip and always carry a well-stocked first-aid kit.*
- *Take note of on-road advisory signs, for example, suggested speed, flood water, rough road ahead, roadworks ahead and impassable when wet signs.*
- *Pre-plan refuelling stops and accommodation, and be mindful of distance and isolation in remote areas.*
- *Continually check road and weather conditions with the relevant state authorities, as well as with other drivers, and tell someone where you are going and roughly what time you're expected to arrive.*
- *Always carry extra water and food plus current detailed road and area maps.*
- *If you break down in a remote area, never leave your vehicle. Remember that vehicles are easier to find than people.*
- *Secure a spare key in an outside, discreet location on your vehicle where it's protected from theft, flood damage, dust and water.*

Travel safe, travel well, and enjoy your trip. Australia is an amazing place.

Meals on Wheels

Mate, the lighter side of the volunteer fire brigade isn't so often reported, so here's a couple of yarns for your new book about us firies.

During one particular fire I'd been out most of the night and my ever-thoughtful wife, Therese, was at home with our young kids, putting me together a lunch of Devon sandwiches and biscuits, which she packed into one of those soft six-pack esky-type things. After she'd done that she drove out to the Rural Fire Service staging area. That's the main gathering spot for the fire services.

The thing was, Therese didn't know where my crew was working. So, when she arrived, she decided to go to the office and ask if anyone was heading out to where I was stationed. Now, before she went over to the office, she placed the lunch pack on the top of the round fuel tank of a nearby bulk water tanker.

So off she went. 'Is there a vehicle going out to where my husband's working? I've got his lunch.'

'Yes,' someone said, 'Con's just about to go out there in the bulk tanker to top up their smaller vehicles. They're almost out of water.'

But by the time Therese got back to the bulk tanker, Con had driven off without noticing the lunch pack perched on his fuel tank. Anyhow, because of the many two-way blackspots in the area, they couldn't get in contact with Con to let him know that Therese had left my lunch pack on top of his fuel tank.

Oblivious to all this, I was having a brief spell during a lull in fighting the fire. Another bloke and me had just come back from a dried-up waterhole where we'd had a bit of a scare. We'd gone down there to try and get some water into our Category 9 tanker. Anyhow, while he was fiddling around, trying to get the pump going, I'd noticed something moving right beside him.

I said, 'What's that down there next to the pump?'

When he turned around, a tiger snake was eyeing him off. So we were out of there like greased lightning.

So anyway, there I was, taking my spell, calming the nerves, when Con turned up in his bulk tanker. Now his trip from the staging area out to our location on the fireground wouldn't have been smooth sailing. It involved driving along several rugged old dirt tracks, across a number of bush paddocks, down into a creek, then finally up a steep gully and further on to where we were.

Anyhow, while Con was busy refilling our vehicles with water, I saw my lunch bag sitting precariously on his fuel tank. Of course I just assumed that Con had put it up there when he'd climbed down from the cab of his truck. So I grabbed the lunch bag, found a log to sit on and I hoed into my wife's freshly made Devon sandwiches and biscuits.

'Con,' I called out, 'thanks for bringing out my lunch.'

'What lunch?' Con replied.

'The lunch that you've just put on the fuel tank.'

'I didn't put it there,' he said.

That's when it twigged. That lunch pack had somehow stayed on top of the fuel tank while it was being driven down tracks, across paddocks, through creek beds and up gullies. And that's a true story. The miracle delivery was later confirmed when we returned to the staging area. From then on, Con got the reputation as being the best off-road driver in the brigade.

So that's a story I'd title Meals on Wheels. But during my years with our local brigade there were many occasions when we were called upon to go and help with 'out of area' emergencies. On these trips we'd not only assist the various brigades fight fires, but we'd also attend to storm damage and flood recovery. During a major outbreak of avian influenza down Newcastle way, we were even involved in a mass chook-culling exercise. Then as far as firefighting went, we'd go to places down the South Coast like Ulladulla or up into the Snowy Mountains to Jindabyne. We also went to a number of places on the Central Coast as well as out west.

I remember being deployed out into the north-west of New South Wales, to Pilliga. That was in the late '90s. It was quite an intense fire and when it burnt through the scrub, it left lots of sharp-pointed stumps. And our hoses were forever getting caught up in and around the burnt trees and stumps. What made it even more difficult was that our hoses were forty metres long and full of water. And that's an awful lot of water-weight to be dragging around. So we had to pace ourselves, and we had to be careful not to trip over and get speared on a stump. Oh yes, that's how sharp they were. They'd even go straight through a vehicle's tyres, no worries.

So these trips were usually hard work, with minimal sleep in, more often than not, uncomfortable beds. I remember being on one particular deployment where, following a thirty-hour shift, we were provided with very comfy motel accommodation. The layout of the motel was typical of most of those places – you know, with the accommodation section being set around a central courtyard, with a swimming pool in the middle.

On our arrival, the motel was already pretty full of firies and most of the parking spaces had been taken up by the big Category 1 fire tankers. The rooms were being occupied in eight-hour shifts, on a three shift per day rotation. So there were crews continually coming and going. Other than us firies there was a family of holiday makers who were having an overnight stay on their way north. Now this family had several young children and, naturally enough, the sight of so many large fire engines was a real highlight.

Anyhow, having found our beds and somewhere to air our blackened PPE – personal protective equipment – it was time for a well-earnt beer and a refreshing dip. So we headed over to the pool to join the other firies who were already in the water. Now, in a winding-down situation, after a hard day's firefighting, there's always the likelihood of some skylarking – letting off steam. And so it was here. The instant we saw the motel owner's sign of '*No bombing in the pool*', the World Championship Pool Bombing Competition was on. And seeing how the motel owner was raking in a fair whack of money from our visit, he wisely ignored our shenanigans and kept his distance.

The World Championship Pool Bombing Competition was well underway by the time the holidaying kids decided they'd like to have a swim as well. Of course, with our lads letting off their pent-up energy, things were getting quite rough in the pool. Now, we could see that the kids' parents were concerned as to how one of their offspring might disappear under this watery onslaught, and with good reason, so a solution had to be found.

And it was. We placed chairs at the end of the pool and, after a brief ceremony, the kids were inducted as official Bush Fire Brigade Water-Bombing Judges. And they had to judge every type of bombing-entry known to man and womankind: from graceful swan impersonations, to triple twisted pikes, right through to the crashing meteorite landings that almost emptied the pool. And these kids had a ball, an absolute ball. I'm sure they'll never forget that stopover. I reckon it would've been the highlight of their holiday.

So that's just another little lighthearted story. But I count the hundreds of hours I spent as a volunteer firefighter as being amongst the most rewarding of my life. I felt part of a fraternity of great people in which I made many long-lasting friendships. There were, of course, the interrupted meals – including one particular Christmas Day – long cold nights, filthy clothes and countless hours sitting by the side of a road, out in the middle of nowhere, waiting.

Firefighting can also be very hard work, and extremely dangerous. Many have made the ultimate sacrifice. Far too many. So there are sad times, yet there's also the fun times. The way I see it, the rural bushfire brigade represents the very best of what it is to be Australian.

Note: In late 2012, more than fifty thousand layer hens were culled due to an avian influenza outbreak at Maitland, near Newcastle.

The 1997 Pilliga scrub fire burnt out near on 1500 square kilometres of remnant woodland forest.

Two Minutes

Now, have I ever been scared or afraid in a fire or rescue situation? That's an interesting question. I've never really been asked that before. I suppose over the years I've gained enough experience to evaluate the risk factors. So, within a given situation, I'll make the assessment, 'Look, I've faced something like this before. I'm pretty confident in my abilities. So I'll be okay.'

Then there are times where, to be honest, you do get scared. And the moment you realise that you're scared, that's the time to realise there's a good reason for being scared. So you'll take a step back. 'No,' you'll say. 'This is too dangerous. Let's get out of here.'

But mostly, you don't have the time to think about being scared or afraid. You just do what needs to be done, and that's all there is to it. And a lot can happen in just a couple of minutes. One time we got called to a fire. On the way there we were informed, via radio, that somebody was trapped inside a structure.

As it happened we were the second appliance to rock up. A fire had broken out in a reasonably large tin shed that'd been converted into a dwelling, with sleeping quarters for two people and a garage attached on the side. The moment we got out of our appliance, we could hear a man screaming, 'My son's trapped inside the shed! My son's trapped inside the shed!'

By that stage, both the shed and the garage were fully enveloped in fire, to the extent where it was almost not survivable. There was flames and smoke and windows were breaking with the heat.

The station officer rushed over to us and said, 'Do what you can. Please.'

We were then informed that the person – the son – was most probably in the nearest of the two bedrooms, in or near the bed. So me and another crew member put on our BA – breathing apparatus – gear, picked up our hose, and we went to the garage entrance, which was where most of the fire was coming from.

We then entered the structure and pushed our way through the flames and smoke. When we came to a window I saw a bed. So I jumped through the window and, in an attempt to cool the area enough so that I could survive the heat, I started spraying water onto the ceiling. Then, as I started searching around, that's when I found him – the boy. But he wasn't going to make it. It's quite distressing to talk about, but it was what it was. He wasn't coming out alive.

To give you an idea of just how quick all this happened, from the time we got out of our appliance, pulled the BAs out of the locker on the side of the truck, put them on our backs, put our masks on, turned it all on, put the flash hoods on, put our structural helmets on, put our gloves on and, because we always go in in pairs, made sure that the backup person was ready to go, then handed over our tally to the entry control officer so that he could keep an eye on how much air and how much time we had available in our tanks, and entered the structure and found the boy, it would've only taken two or two and a half minutes.

But you can only deal with so much of those sorts of events. And so, after that particular incident, we were debriefed. I must say that in recent years the support that's available through DFESWA – Department of Fire and Emergency Services Western Australia – has been excellent. In traumatic cases like that, someone will phone you and say, 'We've been given notice that you've been involved in a critical incident. How are you going? How are you feeling? Are you dealing with it okay? Are there any issues you want to discuss? Is there anything we can do to help?'

Then a couple of weeks later there'll be another follow-up call, where someone will ask you the same thing, just to make sure you're doing okay. And that's not all. There's a whole raft of help that's available. There's the option for counselling. There's chaplains. There's also mental health people who can come out and have a chat with you.

It's the same with road accidents. With our station being positioned near major arterial roads, we deal with a huge number of road accidents. Some are quite horrific, so they do impact on you and you may well need a bit of assistance afterwards. But all that happens after the trauma of the event. There's no use arriving at the scene of a major accident and just standing there, being overcome by it all. Nothing ever gets achieved by doing that.

Lives may well be at stake, so it's more like, Okay, I need to get this door off. And then your total focus is on getting off the door. Or if you need to cut the roof off, your total focus is on cutting off the roof. You never let the fear of it all get in the way. Nor do you focus on the person who may well have passed away in the crashed vehicle. Just focus on the task at hand. It may not be everyone's way of dealing with a traumatic situation, but it's the best way I've found to deal with it – initially anyway. Yet while, at times, situations like that can be extremely challenging, they can also have their rewards.

There was the time a young pizza delivery guy fell asleep at the wheel after his shift and he crashed his car into a power pole, not far from the main entrance to the local hospital.

Now if you can picture the scene: he's hit the power pole with such force that the car's almost completely wrapped itself around the pole. So much so that he's been thrown over onto the passenger seat, with his legs still trapped around the pole. So we got to with the cutters and spreaders, to try and gain access to the poor guy, and we also had a hydraulic ram.

By the time the paramedics arrived, things had gone from bad to worse and this guy was in really serious trouble. At one stage his heart stopped beating. After they revived him, they called for the trauma team to come down from the hospital which, as I said, was literally just at the end of the driveway.

When the trauma team arrived, this guy was in and out of consciousness. But he wasn't really with it. So they made an assessment. If he had any hope at all of surviving, we needed to get him out of the vehicle. The problem was, with his legs being so badly trapped inside, we couldn't get him out. So the doctors made the decision that the only way we'd be able to remove him from the car was to amputate his legs.

Now, to us, that was a shocking concept. We were more used to being able to cut a car away from a person and get them out in one piece, especially if they were still alive – which this young guy was ... just.

Now before the doctors could amputate his legs, they needed to get permission from the guy's parents. So the parents were called down to the scene. They just happened to live nearby. When they arrived, they gave their okay and so the medicos placed the blue mats over the young guy's legs and they painted the incision area. They then laid the saws and scalpels and knives out on the bonnet of the vehicle, ready to cut this kid's legs off.

'Look,' we said, 'can we have just one last go getting him out?'

'Okay,' they said, 'we're not quite ready yet. You've got two minutes.'

Anyhow, very much against protocol, us firies got onto each side of the vehicle and, with one almighty heave, we pulled it just far enough away from the power pole for us to gain a little more access. Then we got to and we spread apart the door so that we were able to free his legs. So we were able to get him out, legs and all, alive and in one piece.

And I remember, just as they were putting the young kid into the ambulance to take him up to the hospital, the parents looked over at us firies and said, 'Thank you.'

There you go. I know it sounded quite traumatic to start with, and it would've been heart-wrenching to have seen this kid lose his legs. But it was a good-news story in the end. Well, as good as it could get within the given situation.

So they're the things that make it all worthwhile, because you know that you did a good job and, in this case, with just two minutes to spare. What's more, I've since heard that the kid kept his legs and he's walking again.

Note: DFES has a free counselling service for all employees, emergency service volunteers and their immediate family. The DFES Peer Support Program also provides initial support and information to help promote positive wellbeing and resiliency.

Your local GP is also available for advice and help in connection in dealing with trauma. Other organisations such as Crisis Care, Lifeline, Beyond Blue, Road Trauma Support (WA), Family Helpline, Mensline Australia, Mental Health Emergencies, The Samaritans, Family Drug Support, Health Direct, Poisons Information and Emergency Services Volunteers' Hardship Assistance Scheme are at hand as well.

Thank You

Kalbarri's near on six hundred kilometres north of Perth, right on the coast, and I've been living here for the past thirty-four years. When I first arrived, we would've had a population of around 1500, and growing. But when the GFC – Global Financial Crisis – hit in 2008, a lot of FIFO – fly-in fly-out – workers left town and moved closer to a city to find employment. And that caused a flow-on effect. With families leaving, school student numbers fell, so we lost a couple of teachers. Then we lost our plumber, then we lost an electrician, and so it went on and on, and we really haven't got back to those pre-GFC numbers.

I'm currently captain of our local Fire and Rescue Brigade, as well as being a deputy chief bush fire control officer. With both of them being volunteer positions, I've worked in and owned a few businesses around town, like the hardware shop, the fuel supply on the fishing jetty, Budget rent-a-car and a few other things.

In 2015, I had the huge honour of going to Perth to receive the Australian Fire Service Medal – AFSM – for services to firefighting. I don't know who nominated me. Perhaps they just drew my name out of a hat. Though, I must say, it was nice to be recognised and thankfully no blood was spilt when the Governor pinned the medal on my chest. Still, it was a humbling experience because, at the same presentation, people far more deserving than me were receiving their Australian Bravery Medals.

Anyhow, back to the beginning: not long after I arrived in Kalbarri, I saw all the guys rushing off to fight a bush fire. When they came back, I went down and said, 'How can I help? How can I join up?'

In those days you had to provide all your own gear, so one of the older guys said, 'If you go and buy a pair of boots and a set of firefighting overalls, you're in.' So I did that, then I did a bit of training and at the next bushfire I got a phone call and off I went.

That was in 1990, and since then Fire and Rescue has emerged from our Bush Fire Brigade. See, in the more remote places you can normally get by with having just a Bush Fire Brigade. But as Kalbarri got bigger and more tourists began visiting the area, the need arose for something more than the Bush Fire Brigade. And because Fire and Rescue dealt with extra stuff like road crash rescue and structural firefighting, we amalgamated the two. And it's worked really well. There's no 'them and us'.

For Fire and Rescue, we're fully equipped with all the hazmat suits and BA – breathing apparatus – and cutters and spreaders, like the jaws of life and defibs – defibrillators – and oxy-vivas, the whole works. An oxy-viva being a steel canister with oxygen in it. Of course, for Fire and Rescue you have to do extra training, but what you generally find is that when someone turns up and says, 'I wouldn't mind joining the Bush Fire Brigade,' we say, 'Would you also be prepared to come along if there's a car crash?'

Of course, some people just don't want to go to car crashes and that's perfectly acceptable. Everyone has the choice. But more often than not they'll say, 'Yeah, I'll come along, but just as a lollipop man or a pump operator.' Then after a few jobs they'll go, 'Wow, this's awesome.' So they'll do the extra training, and all of a sudden they're Fire and Rescue.

To tell you the truth, we try not to focus too much on the car crashes because, even though we are impacted, and we have access to all the debriefs, the counselling sessions and whatever, the actual accident itself involves someone else's pain, suffering or loss. That's why we don't go out of our way to find out the people's names or where they're from.

And only rarely do we get a 'thank you' note for our efforts. I think that's because, after we cut them out of the vehicle, they're rushed out in an ambulance or with the Flying Doctor and taken to a hospital where they may be placed in traction for a while. Following that there's usually a long period of rehab. So really, they just want to put the actual day of the accident behind them and focus on their future.

In saying all that, we once got a written commendation from the Royal Flying Doctor Service. At twenty to eight on the eve of an Anzac Day long weekend, we got a call to attend a single-car rollover out on a station property. Word had it that five people had been seriously injured somewhere near Coolcalaya Station homestead – Coolcalaya being seventy kilometres south of Kalbarri, along the North West Highway, followed by a sixty-kilometre drive east to the station homestead, over a renowned winding and sometimes unkept gravel road.

We took one large truck and our light tanker Land Cruiser. Along the way we got word that a large crowd had gathered for a carnival weekend at the station, with live bands, jet boat races, a rodeo and lots of other events including burn-out competitions. As we got nearer to the homestead we met up with the Northampton Fire Brigade and the two ambulances that'd been dispatched from Kalbarri. On arrival at the homestead, a group of four-wheel-drive campers were waiting to take us to the remote rollover location.

To picture the scene, by this time the partygoer-campers were well into their first-night celebratory blowout. So lots of alcohol had already been consumed. And although no one person seemed to have taken charge, some of the injured had already been brought back to the station homestead while the more seriously injured still remained at the crash scene.

Anyhow, we decided that one ambulance should remain at the homestead to assist the injured there, while us and the other ambulance should be guided to the scene by some of the campers. Now, due to recent rains, the final length of the gravel road out to the location would've normally been impassable for the two-wheel-drive ambulance. But by sheer coincidence, just that very afternoon, a shire grader had made a bypass track.

When we eventually arrived at this fairly isolated spot, one guy was still trapped in an overturned Nissan Patrol, with multiple serious injuries, and, at that stage, the second occupant's injuries were sketchy. Anyhow, all went well and, after we extricated the guys, they were attended to by the ambos and prepared to be driven out.

Then came the first of our many hiccoughs. During our rescue, the ambulance driver had placed his vehicle in park mode and, when he went to start it again, that's where it stayed – stuck in park. Anyhow, as it happened, one of our Kalbarri crew was a mechanic and that particular problem was soon solved.

Due to the extent of the injuries, particularly to the first guy, it was obvious that we were going to have to call in the Flying Doctor. As luck would have it, there was an old airstrip about five kilometres from the station homestead. Good, so we got in touch with the Flying Doctor by satellite phone. 'Yes, okay,' they said, 'we'll be able to land there just as long as the airstrip's eight hundred and fifty metres long and it's in good nick, well lit and with no rubbish or anything on it. If not, the aircraft will have to land at Kalbarri.' Kalbarri being a hundred and thirty kilometres away, and almost a two-hour drive back down that winding gravel track before we even reached the highway.

'Yes,' we said, 'we can meet all those requirements.'

'Good,' they said, 'we're on our way.'

When we went and had a look at the airstrip, it was an absolute mess. It was covered in rubble and fallen branches. To make matters worse, at best it was only eight hundred metres long – fifty metres short of the required distance – with a large wet boggy patch at one end, and of course there was no lighting.

Now, because the bypass track had only been graded that afternoon, we knew that the grader driver would be swagging it out in the bush, somewhere nearby. So we sent someone off to find the grader driver and bring him in ASAP to grade the strip to the required length, plus clear a generous turn-around area at the leeward end.

While this was happening, we had to sort out some form of communications between everyone involved: the grader driver, the fire crews, the station homestead, all the merry campers, the two ambulance crews, the RFDS base and the aircraft. Plus we had to prepare and convey the injured to the airstrip.

After the grader driver, Bom, had been found and was doing his bit, we gave the campers an emergency management course. Sector commanders were nominated and a radio communications plan established. Everyone had a task to do and someone to report to. After one group did an emu-bob – which is where you walk in a line picking up sticks and rubbish – down the freshly graded airstrip to clean away any remaining debris, we ran the light fire tanker down the strip to measure the total length. Great. So far, so good.

By then it was almost midnight. So now we had to organise the lighting of the airstrip so that the RFDS plane could land. To that end, we rounded up about a hundred four-wheel drives with CB radios and got them to park down the length of the airstrip. Mind you, as I may have mentioned, with this being the first evening of what had set out to be a fun long weekend, a lot of these guys were already well into celebration mode. Though I must say, as shickered as some of them were, they were extremely co-operative. And so, via their CB radios, we eventually lined them up, at a safe distance, down each side of the airstrip, facing forty-five degrees away from the aircraft's intended approach and ready to turn their headlights on to high beam for the landing and take-off, and park lights for taxiing.

All was set. We'd sorted out the most injured. We'd done a test run with all the four-wheel drives' headlights. Everything was organised, and the plane was about to arrive. Then the news came through from the homestead that the station manager was having a heart attack. With the RFDS plane only being able to carry two passengers, patient priority had to change. Instead of taking out both the accident victims, we now had to prioritise the station manager.

So then there was another scramble.

Anyhow, it all eventually worked out. The RFDS plane arrived. The lighting system worked. The worst-injured guy and the station manager were flown out to Perth and the other patients were taken by ambulance to Geraldton Regional Hospital.

The whole operation, from our arrival at Coolcalaya Station till the plane took off, would've probably taken about two and a half frantic hours. And so, while the emergency crews headed back home, the partygoers returned to whatever the weekend had in store for them. And Bom – the grader driver – headed back out bush to crawl back into his swag to have a well-earnt rest. Then as I said, the RFDS later presented us all with a letter of commendation for a 'job well done during such an extremely difficult rescue'.

Note 1: The word Kalbarri has been derived from 'Kalbar', the name of an Aboriginal Elder from the local Nanda tribe and/or 'Kalbar', a local edible seed, commonly known as the 'woody pear tree'.

The first Europeans to visit the area were the crew of the ill-fated Dutch East India Company's trading ship *Batavia*, who banished two mutinous crew members ashore just south of where Kalbarri stands today. Nothing more was heard of them.

These days Kalbarri is noted for its spectacular river and coastal gorges, walking trails, swimming bays, dolphins, seasonal humpback whales and over a thousand species of wildflowers. A special feature within Kalbarri National Park's Loop Walk is a natural rock structure overlooking the Murchison River, known as Nature's Window. In 2020, a skywalk was opened that projects two platforms out beyond the gorge rim. In doing so, it provides amazing views over the river, a hundred metres below, plus the gorge and the surrounding bushland.

If venturing out on any of the walking trails, be mindful that daily summer temperatures can reach over fifty degrees Celsius. So make sure you take plentiful drinking water with you, which was something author Bill 'Swampy' Marsh forgot to do during his visit.

Note 2: Bill 'Swampy' Marsh is the author of *Great Australian Flying Doctor Stories*, *More Great Australian Flying Doctor Stories*, *New Great Australian Flying Doctor Stories* and *The Complete Book of Australian Flying Doctor Stories*.

The Man in the Black Hat

What has the most impact on us members of the Western Australian Volunteer Fire and Rescue Service – WAVFRS – is the road rescue side of things. And I'm sure that one of our greatest fears is of us coming across someone we know. Yet, in these smaller communities in particular, where everyone knows everyone, it does happen and it has happened.

I remember going out to an incident one time. A young lady had been involved in a vehicle accident and, when we got there, even though I didn't know her personally, I did know her parents quite well. And that really shook me.

She'd been driving through a small town east of Merredin, called Carrabin, which is in the Central Wheatbelt region of Western Australia. I never found out the full scope of it but, from what I've heard, she was going to turn off the main road, to the left. But according to witnesses, at the last second she turned right to go across to the roadhouse and a truck came through and hit her.

When we eventually got her out of the vehicle, she was alive but she wasn't faring too well, and the volunteer ambos rushed her to Perth. So we had strong hopes for her recovery. But the thing that really hit me was that when I was in town later on in the week, I just happened to bump into one of the local volunteer ambos and she said to me, 'Oh, have you heard that the young woman who was in the accident out at Carrabin has just passed away?'

Anyhow, that was the first incident I attended where I knew someone – or in this case, I knew the parents of someone – who'd died in a vehicle accident. What made it worse was that she was still alive when we got her out of the vehicle. We'd done our job and we thought she'd make it. Well, we very much hoped she'd make it. Then to be told she didn't, well, that really hit me.

Of course, what made the situation even more awkward was having to face her parents at the funeral or at a social gathering or just down the street. What can you say to ease their grief? What can you do to ease their grief? I mean, you'd be at a complete loss, wouldn't you? And with WAVFRS members being some of the last people to have seen that young woman alive, it was definitely something I'll never forget.

That wasn't that long after we'd taken over the role of fire and rescue. As for debriefing, they had a chaplaincy service. And we were very lucky there. The chaplain's name was Ron Wingate. He'd been a chaplain for years. Ron was part of the Salvation Army and he'd basically travel all over the state – not just for the WAVFRS but for anyone who wanted him. Ron was excellent. You could call him twenty-four hours a day and he'd jump in his car to come straight away.

Thankfully Ron was there for me later on in 2013. Because, other than actually being an acquaintance or a friend of someone who's deceased in an accident that you've attended, the greatest fear of any emergency services person is of actually arriving on the scene of an accident where one of your own family has died. And you know, with some people, somehow, they've managed to work their way through it. I don't know how, but it's something that's had a major, major impact on me.

As I said, this all happened in 2013 and it's the main reason why I haven't been as active in Volunteer Fire and Rescue since then.

Look, if you don't mind, I'm just going to stop for a second here. Sorry.

Okay. Thanks. So I'm talking about my son. The night of my son Wayne's accident is something that is, and will always be, etched deep into my memory. Wayne was both president and captain of the hockey club and, because we both played in the same team, I remember speaking to him earlier that day and saying, 'Look, Wayne, I'm not gonna be able to make it to hockey training tonight. I'm a bit rushed and I've already committed to playing squash at 7 o'clock.'

Then I remember being at squash. It was about twenty past seven and I don't know whether you believe in spiritual connectivity or not, like where you'll get some sort of message when something's gone amiss or if something's happened or whatever. Anyhow, while I was at squash, something just popped into my mind telling me to go to my bag and grab my phone. So I went over and I picked up my phone and, because an SMS gets sent to us when there's an incident, there was a message on the phone saying that there'd been a road accident, twenty-two kilometres out of Merredin, on Bullhead Road – the same road that Wayne drives home on.

I did think of Wayne. The thought of him flashed through my mind, so straight away I went down to the station. At that time myself and my partner, Tracy, lived ten kilometres out of town. Tracy was a volunteer as well and so she'd driven in from home. When I got to the station, all the rest of the crew were there, and they must've known something because the captain turned to me and said, 'Oh, how about you follow us out on this one with Tracy, in her vehicle.'

And I remember driving out with Tracy, following behind our appliance. The whole time, I was calling on Wayne's mobile, trying to get him to answer and when there was no answer, I'd do the sign of the cross. So I was ringing and doing the sign of the cross, ringing and doing the sign of the cross and I kept saying to Tracy, 'Look, it can't be Wayne. It just can't be. He would've been home by now.' Because by that time of the evening, he usually would've been home.

Anyhow, when we arrived at the accident site, the whole place was lit up with the lights from the fire brigade, the ambulance and police. And so yeah, I remember Tracy and I, we jumped out of her car and we put our gear on, just like we'd normally do. Then when I walked over to the crew, I noticed how, while some of them were looking at me in an odd sort of way, some of the others had their heads down like they were trying to avoid looking at me. But you know, even at that stage, I was still thinking, Well, it can't be Wayne. It just can't be. Can it? Surely not?

I was totally oblivious to everything else. I was just walking over there. I wasn't even aware that Tracy was right beside me, holding my hand. I had no idea she was doing that. Not until I was told later on. Then when we got nearer to the overturned vehicle, I remember the captain coming over to me and saying, 'Look, we're not sure at this stage but it's a Brookfield Rail vehicle and there's a hockey bag and we've found a black hat.'

Wayne worked for Brookfield Rail and he had one of their vehicles. The hockey bag – obviously he'd been to hockey training. And the black hat – well, if you ask anyone about Wayne they'd describe him as being 'the man in the black hat'. He was a real bushy type, always wearing a black Akubra-style hat. It was then that the pieces fell together and I can still hear myself saying, 'That's my son. I have to go to him.'

Anyhow, as Tracy and I got closer to the vehicle, something suddenly made me look over towards the road. That's when I noticed that my daughter-in-law and my two grandchildren had turned up. So instead of walking to the overturned vehicle, I went straight over to them. To my mind that was Wayne saying to me, 'Hey, Dad, no need to come to see me. My family's just arrived. Go over and see to them.'

And so that's what I did.

As it turned out, Wayne was travelling home from hockey training. And when the coroner's report came back, it said that speed wasn't involved. There was no alcohol. I don't know how they determine fatigue, but they said there was no fatigue. And all the guys who came around over the next couple of days were telling me how Wayne had been in a fantastic mood at hockey training and he was looking forward to the weekend's game. So we've never been given a complete answer as to what the actual cause was.

He lived about thirty-five kilometres out of town and, twenty or twenty-two kilometres on the way out to his place, there was a bend. And instead of going around the bend, he went straight off the road and, unfortunately, there was a small tree, which he hit. On impact it overturned the vehicle. The thing was, if the tree hadn't been there, he would've gone straight through a farm fence and into the paddock and he'd probably be alive today.

Now, I don't know whether your readers are spiritual or not, but a few days after the accident, my mobile phone rang. It was in my pocket and when I picked it up and opened it, Wayne's name just popped up, displayed on the phone. And nobody was on the end of the line. No answer. Nothing. It just lit up with his name on it and, to me, that was Wayne telling me, 'Hey, Dad, it's all right. I'm okay.'

He was such a well-known and much-liked person. He was twenty-seven when he passed away and his funeral was amazing. He was also a member of the Merredin Volunteer Fire and Rescue Brigade and I was completely blown away by the DFES people coming all the way from Perth for the occasion, and most of the vollies from Northam and Kellerberrin and Southern Cross were there as well. So that'll just give you some idea as to his character.

Ever since then I've found it hard to attend call-outs – especially road accidents – and so probably over the last couple of years, I've been quite inactive within the brigade. Even with little things. Like something I've really enjoyed throughout my whole time with the WAVFRS was wearing BA – breathing apparatus. I always loved doing that. But for the first time, I just didn't feel up for doing the qualifying refresher course. So I'm no longer qualified in BA.

And even though I've been a member for thirty-five years, I'm now at the point where I don't know whether I've got the drive, or the want, to stay in the brigade, even just as a support member. We'll just have to see.

In memory of 'the man in the black hat',
Wayne Middleton
14.8.1985–15.5.2013

Cubby House

My name's Emma and I grew up on a two-acre block at Belgrave South, in Melbourne's outer-south-east – sort of near the foothills of the Dandenong Ranges. My parents separated when I was about two, then me and my older sister lived with Mum during the week and we went to Dad's on the weekends.

So this would've happened maybe in mid-February 1983, when I was five and my sister was seven. By then Mum had met my stepdad. Anyhow, me and my sister went off to school in the morning. I was a little preppy. I remember it was a really, really hot day – as hot as. At lunchtime, the teachers got all us kids together in our classrooms and they wouldn't let us outside. They made us stay inside. Our neighbour had two little boys at the same school who were also the same age as my sister and me. We used to play together. Their mum and our mum would take it in turns to come and pick us up after school and take us home.

On that particular day, Mum and our stepfather had gone off to the Ballarat races. When the neighbour picked us up from school, there was all this smoke around. We didn't really grasp what was happening but when we got inside her place she drew all the blinds and wouldn't let us out of the house. We were wondering what all the fuss was about when my sister peeked through the blinds and saw my grandfather. He'd arrived at our place in his car and he was rushing around, looking for us, calling out our names and going frantic.

My sister shouted, 'That's Grandad! That's Grandad!' Then she grabbed me and we ran out of the house, with our neighbour screaming at us to get back inside.

Our house was on a cleared block, on a slope. Above us was all wooded and below us was all wooded as well. That's when we saw the fire all around us and there was flames everywhere.

Grandad was just beside himself – in a real flap. There were no mobile phones or anything like that back then and he couldn't find us anywhere. So when he saw us, he just fell into a mess. A complete mess. Then just as Grandad was about to chuck us in his car, my sister spotted our cat. 'I'm getting the cat. I can't leave the cat.' And so she took off towards our house, with Grandad calling out for her to come back.

Anyway, my sister grabbed the cat and she put it in the car with us. Then Grandad drove us out of there, to his and Grandma's house at Ferntree Gully. The fire was still pretty close to there, but at least we were out of the immediate fire danger zone. Anyway, I remember very distinctly pulling up in our grandparents' driveway and seeing my grandmother standing there just sobbing with relief that we were okay. And, oh, that's right, my sister and I were still in our little school dresses and the first thing our grandmother did was to grab us and chuck us in their above-ground swimming pool, clothes and all. I think the cat must've thought it was about to suffer the same fate 'cause it took off into their house.

The thing was, even with all the smoke and flames, I still didn't fully understand the danger we were in. Perhaps it was because I was so young, I don't know, but it hadn't dawned on me. So then we stayed at our grandparents' place till things had settled down a bit. Maybe it was for a week or something. But we certainly didn't go back home the next day.

While all this was going on, like I said, Mum and our stepfather had gone to the Ballarat races, and that's where they heard that the fires had hit Belgrave. So they took off back towards Melbourne but, because there were fires happening everywhere, they were meeting roadblocks all along the way.

Anyhow, at one stage they got a clear run down the Western Highway, heading back home, and they were doing a hundred and sixty kilometres an hour when the police pulled them over for speeding. Apparently, Mum was really hysterical. She said to the police officer, 'My girls are there, in Belgrave. I need to get to my girls.' And so the police officer gave them a high-speed escort all the way to the Westgate Bridge.

I don't know how, but somehow Mum and our stepfather must've found out that we were at our grandparents' place. So that's where they headed. There was no way they would've got to our house in Belgrave South. All the roads would've been blocked and we found out later that the fires had gone right through the area.

There were a couple of hundred kids at the school that me and my sister went to, and as it turned out a lot of those families were fire-affected. I can't remember if any of the parents died in the fire, but a lot of the houses were completely burnt out. Though we were lucky. Our place survived. But after we got back home I remember, whenever we went outside, everything was so, so burnt black and we'd just come back inside covered in filthy ash and dirt. And oh, the smell. I still remember the horrible smell, and that lasted for like a year or something.

Now I forget how long it was after the fire because chunks of my memory have gone missing. But one of the things I do remember is that, maybe a couple of months or so after the fire, the volunteer fire brigade and some other people turned up asking if we needed help with anything. During the fires we'd lost a lot of our fencing, and part of our garage had gone, as well as our water tanks. And also, during the fire, our little cubby house had got burnt down. And the fire people said to me and my sister, 'Well, what did your cubby house look like?'

And like, it'd just been one of those ordinary old sorts of cubby houses that you see everywhere. Nothing special. But my sister gave me that look of hers that said, 'Emma, just leave this one to me, all right.' Then she started telling them how our cubby house had been this very large, ornately designed two-storey structure, with this, that and the other built into it. And I was like, Hey, I don't remember it looking like that. But she was telling the story. So I just stayed right out of it and kept my mouth shut. Anyhow, later on they came back and they redone our fences and the garage and our water tanks and then they built us this really fabulous cubby house. Oh, you should've seen it.

Note: On 16 February 1983, temperatures in Melbourne reached forty-three degrees Celsius, with near cyclonic winds of over a hundred kilometres per hour and a relative humidity of below ten per cent. At one stage the entire Melbourne metropolitan area was ringed by fire.

The Ash Wednesday bushfires in Victoria burnt out near on 210,000 hectares of land. Over three thousand homes and other buildings were either destroyed or damaged. At the height of the crisis, up to eight thousand people were evacuated and 2680 non-fatal injuries occurred across both Victoria and South Australia. In Victoria alone, forty-seven people lost their lives. This included fourteen Victorian CFA and three South Australian CFS volunteer firefighters. Sheep and cattle losses numbered around thirty-five thousand, plus numerous other animals and wildlife either died in the fire or had to be destroyed later.

An estimated 130,000 volunteer firefighters, defence force personnel, relief workers and support crews were involved in fighting the fires, many from other states. To that time it was the largest number of volunteers ever to attend the one emergency. The Ash Wednesday fires of 1983 proved to be one of Australia's costliest natural disasters to that date.

In the Belgrave Heights–Upper Beaconsfield area, 9200 hectares of land were burnt out, two hundred and thirty-eight buildings were destroyed and twenty-one people lost their lives. In the Dandenong Ranges, twelve volunteer firefighters died after being trapped by a wall of flames when a wind change struck.

The cause was put down to faulty powerlines, arson and negligence after years of extreme drought.

Ash Wednesday One and Two

Part One: The Wife

My husband and I came up to live in the Adelaide Hills in late '78. At first we rented, but we weren't on big incomes so we were struggling. Anyhow, we liked the Bridgewater area. It wasn't overly populated, so it was a lot like being in the country – which was something we both wanted. You could liken Bridgewater to being a poor person's version of Crafers. While the wealthy came up to their nice summer homes in Crafers, Bridgewater was basically the end of the suburban train line – a place where the workers from Port Adelaide and the like would've had their little cottages.

Then suddenly my husband came up with the bright idea that we could afford our own home. This was around the time log cabin kits were coming on the market. He said, 'At a stretch we might just be able to afford a seven-square log cabin. But five would be better.' I mean fuckin' five squares. That's really tiny. It's like a shed.

But we somehow got a loan for a seven-square log cabin. The land cost six thousand dollars and the log cabin was thirteen thousand dollars. The block we got was on the side of a hill, facing east. We've always disagreed over its size. I've always thought it was a hundred and eighty feet by fifty feet, in the old technology, while my husband reckons it was a hundred and sixty-five feet by fifty feet.

But whichever way you look at it, it was a very small block, quite isolated, covered thick with blackberries and bush. Leading down to the block was basically a goat track. The impression we got from the real estate agent was that once we'd built our house, the council would then put in a road. But that didn't happen. Council told us that we'd have to pay for the road out of our own pocket.

We moved into our seven-square log cabin in late November 1978. Everything was tiny. There was an open kitchen area, a lounge room with a pot-belly stove, a bathroom and two bedrooms. By then Toby wasn't quite two and Tess was six months. So the kids shared one bedroom and my husband and I the other. There was no room for a laundry. That had to be outside. We had an ancient washing machine that rocked and clattered. The whole situation was stressful, to say the least. I mean, living in a confined space with two little kids, and with a man who now freely admits that he was a male chauvinist pig, was quite a challenge.

Our first experience of fire happened two years later, on Wednesday 20 February 1980. That was the first Ash Wednesday fire. By then we'd sort of settled into this routine of chaos and when the fire came, it filled the sky. I was pretty calm about it all until the police came along with their megaphone announcing, Dalek-like, 'You will be evacuated.'

It was during the process of our evacuation that I panicked. I remember holding a blanket and thinking, I don't know what to do with this. But people do a lot of weird stuff in a fire. Anyway, we evacuated. I forget where we stayed. It might've been at my parents' place down in the city. And luckily our house was okay. But the strange thing was, when I came back home and walked up to our house, I had the distinct feeling that our front door shouldn't be there. Not even the house should've been there. So perhaps that was some sort of a premonition of what was to come.

Because three years later, on almost the exact same date – Wednesday 16 February – came Ash Wednesday Two. The day began with my husband and I having a big fight. I was three months pregnant and all week it'd been over forty degrees. What made matters worse was that I was madly typing up an author's book because he wanted it done by Friday. And as a young responsible pregnant mum, living on a meagre income, the chance to earn some money for the family was important. And I was getting no help from my husband. He was always off with one of his mates helping him build a mudbrick house.

So it all blew up. I said, 'I can't keep going on like this.'

So we started having this big fight over the division of domestic labour, and mid-argument something in me snapped. 'Well, fuck you!' I said. 'The kids are yours. I'm leaving. I'm going down to Mum's.'

'Good,' he said, 'and don't ever come back.' He said, 'I can't be bothered with all this domestic shit. I've gotta get to work.' And he went off.

The thing was, I half believed him. So I dropped the kids off at Bridgewater Primary School. Our son was in Year 2 and our daughter had only just started. And while I had a strange feeling about the weather, I was more or less ignorant of it. It's like, when you're going through chaos within, you don't really notice the external chaos. Anyhow, our son ran straight to his teacher, but our daughter had heard the argument and she didn't want me to leave her. She was just the saddest little figure. She was clinging on to me. 'Don't go, Mummy. Don't leave us,' and I'm saying, 'It's okay. I'm not leaving forever. I'll be back on Friday,' until finally her teacher came and took her into the classroom.

So I'm off to Mum's. She lived down in the foothills of Adelaide, just off Greenhill Road. And I've got this memory of ferocious winds and the sky being lit up, orange with dust. But I'm still mad at my husband. So I'm driving down the freeway going, 'You fuckin' arsehole. Why don't you understand we're hard up? We're starving. I need to earn some money.'

So I get to Mum's. All I had with me was one of those very early electric IBM typewriters. Oh, and I'd taken two items of ironing in the hopes Mum might do it for me. I just hated ironing. I said to her, 'I have to stay here. I can't go home.'

When she asked why, I told her about the fight I'd had with my husband and how I needed peace and quiet because I had to have this author's book typed up by Friday. Mum was cautiously consoling. Then just as I was about to start typing, the power went off. I said to Mum, 'All right. This's urgent. I'll leave the typewriter on so I'll hear the hum when the electricity comes back on.'

An hour or so later, when the electricity came back on, the very first words I heard over the radio were, 'There's a fire at Bridgewater.'

And I'm going, 'What? Seriously?'

My first thought was to go back and pick my kids up. But the thing was, I had a bomb of a car that always overheated. And because it was so hot and windy, I doubted it'd make it back up to Bridgewater. But I'm in a panic. One moment I'm, 'I have to go and get the kids,' the next, 'But if the car breaks down I'll be stuck.'

Anyhow, I finally decided that I'd go straight up Greenhill Road and on to Bridgewater. I was just about to go to the car when I heard over the radio that some people had been caught in the fire at the top of Greenhill Road and had been burnt to death.

Then, when it struck me that my husband was helping build the mudbrick house on Yarrabee Road, just off the top of Greenhill Road, I was, 'Shit, what if he's in trouble?'

So I started to ring everyone I could think of. But they were all engaged. I tried ringing the school but couldn't get through. I was telling Mum, 'What's wrong with everyone? Don't they know there's a fire?'

It hadn't even dawned on me that the powerlines had gone down and the telephones were out. So I didn't know if my husband was alive and I had no way of getting to my children.

By now the sky was on fire and it was starting to come over the crest of the Adelaide Hills, heading down towards Penfolds Winery. Then the husband of Marie, the woman who lived down the end of our road, got through. He had a son at the same school as my kids. He said, 'Can Marie and our son come and stay with you because she's got nowhere to go?'

I said, 'Of course,' and I gave him Mum's address. I said, 'Where are you ringing from?'

He said, 'The pub.'

I forget which pub it was now, but I said, 'I thought all the lines were down?'

He said, 'Well, I've got through.' He said, 'Marie can't drive, so I'll get someone to pick up her and your kids and my son.'

'And so my kids are okay, are they?'

'Yes,' he said.

'And do you know where my husband is?'

He said, 'He's gone back to help fight the fire.'

'Is he okay?' I asked. 'And what about the house?'

'Oh, didn't you know?' he said. 'Your house is gone.'

I just couldn't believe it. I said, 'What the fuck are you talking about?' And because he had an English accent and his voice sounded a bit slurry, I said, 'It can't be. You must be drunk.'

He said, 'No I'm not. Your house has been burnt down.'

At that, I just slid down the wall and collapsed in shock. So my mother and sister-in-law laid me on my old bed. I'm lying there in kind of a weird, numb state and my young niece came in. She had something in her hand. She said, 'It's moments like these you need Minties.' And she handed me a Mintie. I couldn't have asked for better! It was bizarre. I ate the Mintie and it worked. I actually snapped out of it.

Anyhow, at that time I also had temp work with a transcribing firm. I was rostered on for the next day, the Thursday. So I rang the receptionist. 'Hi,' I said, 'I've just lost my house in the fire and my husband's gone missing, so I probably won't be able to make it in tomorrow. But I can come in Friday.'

She said, 'I think you better take a bit more time off than that, dear.'

Then I don't know how, but the author fellow rang my mum's place. 'Have you finished typing my book up yet? I've got to have it in by Friday.'

I said, 'No, but I'll do my best.' This was on the Wednesday.

So within the hour, I'd gone from collapsing in a heap, then being revived by a Mintie, to carrying on typing. Then Marie turned up with my kids and her son. I don't know who drove her to Mum's. But oh, these little kids were so frightened. Apparently, they were the last kids to leave the school and the teacher had stayed with them right the way through. So there's a lot of stuff I can't forgive myself for. But I have to because that's what happened. And my later logic was that, being three months pregnant, if I'd stayed at home I might've lost my life and lost the child as well.

Anyhow, somewhere along the line, Marie's husband came and picked her and their son up. Then my kids were farmed out amongst the family. 'You're gonna go and sleep with that cousin and you're gonna go and sleep with that other cousin, sharing beds.' Then I think I was taken to my brother's house, over in Kensington.

It wasn't until sometime in the evening that my husband rang and said something like, 'I'm okay but the house's gone.'

And of all the things he could've saved, he saved a concertina file that was full of our bills, and his fuckin' chainsaw. So we were left with just the clothes we were wearing, not even a toothbrush. So we lost all record of our family history. All my stuff from Europe. All my stuff as a child. My own history. My husband's history. The kids' baby photos. Everything was gone.

So these days my life is divided into 'before the fire' and 'after the fire' – BF and AF – and I've lost all those precious trigger things that bring back the BF memories.

Note: The first Ash Wednesday bushfire began in the Adelaide Hills on 20 February 1980. In total, fifty-one homes and twenty-five other buildings were destroyed. Seventy-five farms were affected, forty people were injured and a hundred and fifty people were left homeless. The fire burnt an area of 3770 hectares and caused an estimated $34,000,000 damage. The causes were put down to faulty powerlines, arson and negligence after years of extreme drought.

Part Two: The Husband

Okay. Fire away. So you want to know what sort of day it was? Well, it started with my wife and me having a huge domestic over housework and shit. You know, she reckoned I wasn't doing my fair share while she was busy working to make us some money. So she'd got really upset, threw the kids and a few things in the car, dropped the kids off at school, then nicked off down to her parents' place, in Royston Park. Other than that, weatherwise, it was pretty fuckin' spooky.

At the time I was helping a friend build a post-and-beam house. That's where you've got a grid of posts with a ring-beam that supports the roof load. Then you fill the spaces in between with what was, in this case, mudbrick. It's a type of construction that was quite popular at the time, one I was very interested in.

We were working on Yarrabee Road, Greenhill. Yarrabee Road's pretty exposed along the ridge at the top. By the time I arrived, it was already forty degrees plus with a thirty-five-knot northerly airstream. Anyhow, by midday it was just too hot and unpleasant, so we knocked off and I came back home.

Things are still pretty hazy as to the exact timeline of events, but during the afternoon a fire started from a downed powerline over near the Bridgewater railway track. The first I heard of it were all these explosions – *boom! boom!* – when it roared up through Jarrett's car dealership on top of Germantown Hill. Apparently, it was all the paint drums and stuff going off. So I'm thinking, What the fuck's going on?

Next thing, flames appeared on top of the ridge, just over there to the east-nor-east. The grass was pretty low. But what I soon learnt is that topography has a huge bearing on how fire's going to behave. Because even though the wind was blowing up the gully, the fire started rolling down from the ridge against the wind. Anyhow, there was a patch of scrub about twenty yards down the back of our place. To the left of that there was a thin band of Scottish broom – kerosene weed – which was put there as a barrier between us and our uphill neighbour.

Anyway, the fire came up to the fence line and it got into the grass right next to me. I didn't feel threatened or anything. It was just burning quietly and progressing slowly. Then there was a lot of vegetation in a hollow further down the bottom, and once the fire got into there, it was on. I had a shed in the far corner, and that went up like a fuckin' torch.

Even by that stage I hadn't really connected with the reality of the situation. But I knew that I wanted to stay. There was no question or worry about that. Then the fire moved up into the band of scrub between us and our uphill neighbour, and next thing it got into the eaves of our log cabin.

And there was not one fuckin' thing I could've done about it.

There was no one else around and I had nothing to fight it with. I've got the garden hose and I'm turning on the tap. But there's no water pressure because, as I found out later, the CFS – Country Fire Service – had tapped into all the mains. So

I'm thinking, Fuck, I may as well piss on the fire. So everything's going nuts. Then there's more explosions – *boom! boom!* Smoke and shit everywhere.

Then, once the fire got into the vacant blocks over the road, it sort of started creeping further up the hill. It was still a slow burn. It wasn't an inferno like you'd see in a forest situation. So I didn't feel overly concerned about my life. But the order of things is still pretty hazy. Because somewhere throughout all this, I got back inside our burning house and grabbed what I could, which was a concertina file with some personal papers in it. It was crazy because then I thought, Fuck, I'm gonna need my chainsaw. So I grabbed that as well. The other important thing was my tools, but they were still in my old Peugeot station wagon, which was parked outside. So I chucked the concertina file and my chainsaw into the car.

By then the fire had got up the road a bit and the guy on the corner was freaking out. He's there, trying to pull all the furniture out of his place. There was nothing I could do at my place. I mean, once the fire got into the eaves, it was pretty much fucked anyway. So I went up and started helping the guy on the corner. And, when I looked back down the street, the fire had really taken hold on our place, and it's just fuckin' burning like crazy. So I'm standing in the street watching it go.

The odd thing was, I wasn't freaking out. I don't know what I was thinking. It was like I was in some sort of dreamlike state. Like, Fuck, is this really happening or not? But obviously the house was gone and I couldn't do anything about it. It was gone. So I went back to helping this guy. Then, when the fire started to creep closer to his house, through the low grass, maybe we might've grabbed something and started belting at the flames. I don't know. But then, the wind suddenly changed and the fire started burning back on itself. So his house was okay.

Somewhere along the line the CFS turned up. They were flat-stick. There were fires breaking out all over the fuckin' place. Like they'd rush to one spot to try and put a fire out and, before they knew it, it'd jumped half a kilometre down the road and it'd started up another fire. To make matters worse, their communication set-up was pretty crap. Like, there were no mobile phones or anything back then and I think the CFS network wasn't too efficient.

They eventually did come down to our block – I forget when it actually was – but they took one look at my house and said, 'Sorry, mate, we can't touch it. It's already too far gone and we're not allowed to go near places that're made of permapine because they give off poisonous toxic fumes.'

So that was that. Meanwhile, a dog appeared. I forget what type it was. But it looked lost and it came over to me, probably looking for safety. So I put the dog in my old station wagon and I drove it up to Blackwood Oval. Lots of people had gathered there, so I just dropped the dog off and I went back home – well, I went back to what little was left of my home. And there was an older neighbour of ours who lived over the road and somehow – I forget how now – but somehow I ended up driving her to the Blackwood Oval as well.

Wife: *Can I ask something, because you've never really talked about it? If the place was burning and the council verge has always had those trees, why didn't they catch alight?*

Well, the bark might've been blacked, but I don't think they actually burnt. Like I said, the fire wasn't that intense. It was a quiet burn. The only intense bit was through the patch of scrub and down the hollow behind us where there was a lot of vegetation. Oh, and that's right. We had two one-hundred-pound gas bottles out the front and the safety valves were pointing inward, towards the house, instead of away from the house. When the gas bottles heated up, the safety valves blew. And there was just this huge fuckin' roar as these dual jets of gas blasted into our burning house. And that really stoked things up. The heat was hot enough to melt the enamel on the bath. Fuckin' hell.

But it was all pretty weird. I don't know. I think I just resigned myself to the fact that the house had gone and there was no saving it. Perhaps that's why I ended up helping other people, you know.

In the end, ours was the only house in this small area that got burnt down. But, as you go down the hill into Germantown, a whole swag of houses went there. And you know, if there hadn't been that patch of scrub down in the hollow, it may well have been a different story. But anyway, that's what happened as best I can recollect and eventually everything died down. It wasn't till later that I heard that a lot of houses were lost on Yarrabee Road. And just across from where we were working some people got incinerated in a car.

As for the kids, I just assumed they'd remain at school till the danger had passed. So I had the feeling they'd be okay. Anyhow, as I said, me and the wife had had this huge domestic earlier on in the day. So at about 9 o'clock that night I rang her up and I said, 'Well, the domestic issues have been resolved. We've lost the fuckin' house.'

Note: On Wednesday 16 February 1983 more than a hundred and eighty fires broke out across South Australia and Victoria. Across South Australia, over 200,000 hectares were burnt, three hundred and eighty-three houses were destroyed and twenty-eight lives were lost – the worst affected were in the Adelaide Hills, where fourteen lives were lost. Three CFS volunteers lost their lives fighting fires in the south-east of South Australia and into western Victoria.

The cause of the fires was put down to extreme heat conditions and high winds, sparks from clashing powerlines, tree branches connecting with powerlines, arson and other non-identifiable causes.

Merry Christmas

It was 1984. My husband had died back in 1980 and by that stage my eldest son, Bill, was managing our property, Warrington, which was about thirty miles out of Coonamble, on the Walgett Road. Peter, my other adult son, lived just a bit further down the road. Anyhow, both Bill and Peter had gone away for Christmas, though I forget just who went where. So I was left out on the property with my youngest son, Tim, who would've been about nine, and my eleven-year-old daughter, Kelly.

Then on Christmas morning, a small fire broke out down the back of our property. Whether it'd been a dry-lightning strike or not, I do not know.

Now, the adjoining property to ours had been bought on spec by three men from a place down the line called Collie. They were up here at the time and so they went over to put the fire out.

When they'd finished, they came over to see me. 'Nothing to worry about, Paula,' they said. 'We've put the fire out, so we'll be heading off now, back to Collie for Christmas. See you later.'

'Oh good. Thanks,' I said.

With the worry about the fire now over, I then packed up Tim and Kelly and we drove into town to have Christmas lunch with my other daughter and her husband – my son-in-law – and their six-month-old. And that's what we were doing when I got the call from someone in the local Bush Fire Brigade, 'The fire's started up again. It looks bad. You'd better come back out.'

So we all rushed back out to Warrington. By the time we got there, the fire was roaring through our back paddock and our local volunteer firefighters were trying their best to get some sort of control over it. Anyhow, my son-in-law and a friend of his hooked the water carrier onto the back of the tractor and they, along with my daughter, headed off to help them fight the fire.

Then suddenly I remembered that there was a mob of sheep in the paddock, and they needed to be moved out of there pretty quick-smart before they got incinerated. So I put Tim, Kelly and the baby in the car and I headed out to round up these sheep and get them out of the paddock, up onto the safety of the main road.

And oh, it was frightening, driving flat out across this bumpy paddock, yelling at these blessed sheep, trying to get them to move out of danger and up onto the main road. And if you know how difficult it is to move sheep at the best of times, just add to that their manic panicked state with a fire hot on their heels. And there's me in the car with two young children and a baby, with the fire hot on my heels as well.

Anyhow, we did it. Somehow the sheep must've made the group decision to head for the gate that led out onto the main road.

But oh, we lost so much. Warrington was a long property and the fire had come in from the west and it'd completely burnt out six thousand acres. There was not a scrap of fodder left. Not a blade of grass. We were just lucky that our house was on the other side of the road, so it was safe.

Anyhow, so there I was, looking out over all this burnt-out ground when I saw a bulldozer coming down the road. It turned out to be a very dear friend of ours, Dan Harvey. He said, 'Paula, I've come to help put the fire out.'

Bless him. He'd heard that there was a fire out on my place and he'd driven this bulldozer all the way out from town, just to help.

I said, 'Thank you very much, Dan, but I think we've just about got it under control now.'

'That's okay, Paula,' he said, 'just looking after you.'

I don't quite remember what happened after that. Perhaps I was in shock. I know the kids were. But I think Dan poddled off and went around and graded some firebreaks, just to ensure that the fire would be properly contained.

Anyhow, after Christmas, when my boys Bill and Peter came back home, I said to them, 'Don't you ever leave me out here alone again.'

Which they didn't.

Now, I know there's been other fires since then, but that particular fire is the one that affected me the most. It's still so vivid in my mind, even today. You know, driving across the burning paddock, trying to move those panicking sheep, with two frightened kids and a six-month-old baby in the car.

But oh, I was so cranky with those three men from the neighbouring property who'd told me they'd put the fire out. And I've never let them forget it either. No I haven't. Even today, whenever I see them down the street, I say, 'Remember that big fire we had back in Christmas '84?'

And boy, don't they cringe when I remind them of that, and so they should.

Note: Over the years, author Bill 'Swampy' Marsh has been a frequent visitor to Coonamble where he has run writing workshops and has given performances as a storyteller-songwriter. This is just one of the many stories that has resulted from those visits.

Don't Remember Much

My name is Darlene Addy and I grew up in a picturesque part of
the Adelaide Hills in a small community called Houghton. I don't
remember much about the 1983 Ash Wednesday bushfire that
burnt our house when I was seven. Perhaps it's purposeful, but
I don't think much about it. However, the past few weeks have
put me – and probably most of Australia – in a bit of a funk. The
2019–2020 bushfire crisis has picked at the stitches of my mind,
giving rise to memories I rarely visit.

I remember the smell of our kitten's burnt paws and the
ointment we used on them to help them heal. Even now, I
bristle at the smell of antiseptic. I remember the weird crushing
sound that the burnt grass made when I walked on it, brittle
and snapping easily like singed hair. The black on the soles of
our shoes made marks on the floor of the caravan – one of the
few things Dad managed to save. I had been collecting fifty-cent
coins, and we found the great melted glob of metal in the rubble,
still warm. Fair call to say that it was the most memorable show-
and-tell item my classmates had all year.

Some days later, after the fires, when I returned to school,
kids gathered at the library and pointed up at the scorched
corner of the building where the black monster had dared to lick
the eaves. That was as far as the fire managed to trespass as,
thankfully, the primary school was saved by the Country Fire
Service – CFS.

I remember seeing kindness in people's faces. We received a
big box of donated books from parents at the primary school,
and maybe even the school itself. I was delighted because we

didn't have many books before the fire. I remember teachers, friends and parents being generous and gentle. I remember whispers and a lot of silence.

I have one memory that – pardon the pun – burns bright. We went to the Salvation Army to pick out a few clothes to keep us going. I was pint-sized, and things were too big and dripped off me. A lovely woman made a bit of a fuss of us, asking what our names were. We hardly have common names, my siblings and I, yet this woman proudly produced brand-new towels that were lovingly stitched with each of our names on them, as if it was such a stroke of coincidence.

I know it's quite likely that at that age, I would have been awestruck to receive any items with personalised stitching regardless of any fire. However, in that moment, when I had nothing that was mine, nothing that felt like mine, smelt like mine or looked like mine – the sensory starvation for a seven-year-old – to have something that was unarguably mine, something that was clean and soft and given to me so lovingly, well, it's a memory that will always make me smile.

While we were building a new house on our Murphy Road property, we moved a few kilometres away to a small rental. But I remember very little about the rest of that year. The sum of memories could fit on two hands. I remember the garden, the road, the water pipeline, the forest. Basically, the outdoors. I remember walking every weekday morning to a neighbour's house for a lift to school. I remember the short time we spent in their house like it was yesterday. Yet, for the life of me, I cannot remember a single morning in the rental. I remember going to our property and watching excitedly as the new house emerged.

I can only assume my memory dent during that time is on account of things being pretty tough and strange. My world was small; my sense of place, belonging and safety was a patch of land around the corner and down the road. Not far at all – the cats kept going back there. Yet far enough for my memory to go on strike.

To me there were positives out of the experience, though these were perhaps less apparent to my parents who had lost almost everything. Our old home was mouldy and mildewy, and I grew into severe asthma, which possibly fared better in the new build than it might have done in the old. And the books – there was something about being given that box of books that made my heart sing. Even to this day, when all else feels tough, books and stories and characters – real or imagined – are still my friends. I attribute my love of literature to that precious box of charity.

So in a funk I am, and in a funk I will be, like many Australians watching this beautiful land burn, animals perishing and suffering, memories turned to ash, people being displaced, even if only temporarily. Yet I am heartened by all the positivity people are showing: the kindness, generosity and elbow grease. I'm encouraged by the acknowledgement that this will impact on mental health.

Mental health wasn't really a thing in 1983. The Addy household held true to the era, and as kids, we kept quiet and got on with it. The getting on with it part was helpful, though the keeping quiet part, not so much. Trauma impacts us in many weird and wonderful ways and, like a bushfire itself, the outcomes can be both positive and negative. I know it helped 'build my character' – a cliché, I know – in beneficial ways. Yet it also gave me a few quirks that are bothersome to this day. It's in those quirks that we all have, in some form or another, for whatever reasons, that we are ourselves. We are us. I am me. And it's in the unconditional love and acceptance we receive from friends and family that we can show our raw selves without apology.

Many stories will emerge from the horrific fire season of 2019–2020. Every story will be unique – a mix of positives and negatives and everything in between. Along with better bushfire prevention and response, I hope a big positive to come out of this will be a collective shake-up of complacency around climate change, and what actions we can do – big or small – to rein it in and to hopefully stop it. I know I can do better on both fronts.

I have no reason to write this story at all, other than it being a method of de-funking myself during these current times. A friend recently told me, 'Play to your strengths,' so I am. In telling a small bit of my story, I'm welcoming others to do the same. Write your story. It might be just a sentence, a word or even a picture. But it's through the telling of our stories that we share recognition, connection and compassion. They're the stuff that keeps us going.

Note: Darlene Addy was a student of Bill 'Swampy' Marsh's in the now defunct Professional Writing Unit at Adelaide Institute of TAFE.

Aftermath

Husband: It was a completely surreal situation to actually stand there and watch your house burn down. At the time I didn't comprehend it. I just followed my inner instincts and I did what I did and helped a few people. But as for getting over something like that, I'm not sure if you ever really do. In our case we dealt with it differently. Though one thing's for sure: I certainly learnt a lot about myself.

Wife: *But it's never just the fire or the losing of the house or the losing of everything. While the fire's the drama, dealing with the shit that follows in the aftermath can take years and years to come to grips with. So it's sort of started a whole new phase in life for us.*

See, as individuals, none of us know how we'll respond to a trauma, not until the moment arrives. But something I did learn through the process of the fire was that I'm actually quite good in threatening situations. For instance, we've had a few serious fires since we lost our house. One of the more recent ones got into that big patch of reserve scrub, down the back there, not that far away. It was fanned by a south-westerly so it was burning like crazy and an elderly neighbour of ours was really freaking out. But I'm just standing here, looking at the flames through the trees and I'm thinking, No need to panic just yet. When it gets a bit closer we might think about doing something.

*We were only in our early thirties when the first fires came through.
And the learning thing for me was that our uphill neighbours
stayed calm. The husband went back to watch the cricket and his
wife went on drying her apricots. And psychologically that's what
helped me hold it together. I now tell anyone who's freaking out
with fires that we'll assist them. Like, with last Wednesday being
a catastrophic fire day, our new neighbours were freaking out. So
we said to them, 'Look, stay calm. We're here to help you if things
get tough. You don't have to run.' Anyhow, in the end they booked
a room in the city and took off with their twins.*

*But what saved me on a more personal level was that one
day, when I was heavily pregnant with our third child, I heard
this inspirational voice come out of wherever and say, 'Go to
university.' And I heeded it. I went to university as a mature-age
student.*

In my case I'd been working on houses of a certain type of
construction and my first thought was, You fuckin' beauty.
Here's an opportunity to have a go at building my own house. So
I turned a traumatic event into something positive which, rightly
or wrongly, then led on to a whole string of other issues.

How it all came about was that, after the fires, our then
state premier put a lot of pressure on the insurance companies
to settle claims expediently. And they did. We had a $19,000
mortgage and we were insured for $24,000. So we immediately
paid out the mortgage. And I clearly remember, right when I was
handing the cheque over to the bank to pay out our mortgage,
the arsehole was saying, 'Well, thank you very much, and now
would you like to borrow some more money to rebuild?' And this
was at the time when interest rates were around seventeen per
cent. So we said, 'No, I don't think so.'

But then through the Lord Mayor's Appeal we got a couple
of thousand. And somewhere further down the track the
government, to their credit, made loans available to the victims

of the fires at just four per cent interest. That's what enabled me to begin building the house. So then I became completely obsessed with the whole 'building-the-new-house' thing. In doing so, I was able to channel my energy into the project – though, unbeknown to me at the time, it was to such an extent that I left no space to inwardly deal with the trauma from the fact that we'd lost everything we owned. And I do mean 'everything', because we came out of it with just the clothes we were wearing on the day.

I've since found out of course that, among a myriad of other things, the owner builder's journey is fraught with danger. Just for starters, while I was cleaning up all the ash and shit from our old house, I didn't realise that I was breathing in all this residual highly toxic permapine shit. No one told me that.

But of course, as it always does, life intervenes. There's all these other considerations that have to be accounted for. There's bills to be paid. There's the care of the children. And also you have to deal with the stresses of living in such close proximity to each other. But then to suddenly lose your house and find yourselves living on top of each other in a caravan, kids and all, it's utter chaos. And for some people that's intolerable, so they split up.

But look, a whole string of issues emerged during the building of the house. We had five moves in two years. My wife was at uni, during which time she gave birth to our third child. We'd virtually run out of money. And understandably, over time she just got fed up with it all. You know, 'I'm sick of showering in archaic conditions. I want a complete bathroom so I can have a decent shower.' Then one day she just snapped. 'This is fucked,' she said. 'I just can't do this any more. We've gotta move into the new place.' So we moved into our half-built house.

Yes, and so most of my writing career was in a half-built house.

So, I don't know, maybe it affected me more than I realised. Though I can say with absolute certainty that, before the fire, my beard was brown and, during the building of the house, my beard turned white. Then, years later, I was listening to the radio. And this guy's going on about stress and the symptoms of stress and suddenly the penny drops. 'Fuck, he's talking about me.' I didn't realise how wound up I was.

In fact, the terminology of post-traumatic stress disorder – PTSD – hadn't been used until the '83 fires. A doctor was looking into it and, after the fires, he sent us forms to fill in and be part of his research. But we were too traumatised to do it. So in a way we missed out on being part of that early research into PTSD. So, yes, we suffered it.

Then later on we had free counselling through a guy called Michael White under the condition that we allowed ourselves to be shown on video to his students around Australia and other countries. Michael White was fabulous. At that time he was developing what's called 'narrative therapy', which is where storytelling is used as a tool to deal with your traumas. In doing so, we got to understand that we didn't have to be so angry.

Yeah, he did. But I was angry for a myriad of reasons. When I was younger I just had all this fuckin' energy that I didn't know what to do with. Like, I didn't know how to channel myself and utilise my time in a satisfactory way. The one thing that saved me was surfing. And I'm extraordinarily grateful for that, because every time I went surfing, it mellowed me out.

But hey, fuck, we used to fight and argue like you wouldn't believe. And me wife could've easily pissed off. And I wouldn't have blamed her. See, because I'd taken on the building of this house, the alpha male in me imagined I'd be waited on hand and foot by this 'earth-mother' figure who'd cater to my every whim and need. Well, I can tell you right now that that did not happen. Instead of that, she's off at university studying women's studies of all things. So I continually get bombarded with all this dialogue about how fuckin' dreadful men are and how they're responsible for everything that's gone wrong in the world. And so, fuckin' hell, mate, things got pretty feisty, I can tell you.

Yeah, and so we all moved into this half-built house. But somehow it all worked even though we had an open-air kitchen for a couple of years.

It was more like ten years. It was a running joke at uni: 'Is the kitchen finished yet? What about the bathroom?'

But look, all that aside, I can't really praise the CFS – Country Fire Service – enough. My hubby didn't want me to come back home for a couple of weeks after the fires because he thought it'd be too much for me. And when I did and I saw the devastation, not only at our place but throughout the whole Hills area, I just went up to the CFS and said, 'Look, we lost our house in the fires and I know you couldn't help us. But you're just amazing people for all the other stuff you done.'

And have you heard of the Emergency Services Levy? It's money that everyone has to pay to cover the costs of any future emergencies. Well, that came in soon after the fires. And do you know what the most disgusting thing is? The volunteer firies have to pay the emergency levy, and the volunteer ambos. And to think that these volunteer people put their lives on the line to save others and they still have to pay it. Well, I think that that's just plain wrong. What's more, they don't even get a concession.

Anyhow, what I'm on about is that either of us, at various times, could've said, 'Fuck it. I can't do this any more.'

But the good thing that came out of it was that, in spite of what befell us and everything else we went through – it was an extremely chaotic, arduous, traumatic and difficult time –

somehow we managed to survive all that and we came out the other end and here we are, still married after forty-six years.

Note 1: Post-traumatic stress disorder – PTSD – is a mental health condition that's triggered by a terrifying event or events. A number of organisations can assist with those who are suffering PTSD. They include betterhelp.com, beyondblue.org.au, helpguide.org, headtohealth.gov.au, blackdoginstitute.org.au, plus many others.

Note 2: Michael White, an innovative physiotherapist, social worker and family therapist, passed away suddenly in 2008. He has written a number of books on narrative therapy.

Bless 'em

Hang on, I'll just sort out my cigarette before we begin. Ah, good. That's better. Right, so you'd like to hear about the fire I had in my house, correct? Okay, here goes.

I was at the stove cooking dinner so it would've been around sevenish. Now the kitchen-dining area in my place is separate from the lounge room. Being winter I had the wood fire going in the lounge room. Next thing the kitchen starts filling up with smoke.

The odd thing was, the hardwired fire alarm, which had a new battery, didn't go off, which it normally does at the first hint of smoke. *Beep, beep, beep.* Drives me bloody crazy. So something just didn't seem right. I was cooking a stir fry, which yes, was giving off a bit of smoke, but I wasn't burning the food. So where's all this smoke coming from?

So I turned the stove burners off and, when I stuck my head through the door into the lounge room, holy fuckin' Jesus, the place is so full of smoke that I couldn't even see the four or five metres over to the fireplace. What the fuck's going on? Then I saw flames coming out of the ceiling from where the flue from the firebox goes through into the roof.

I thought, This's not lookin' good. So I went off to find the fire extinguisher that my partner had bought several years ago off some fly-by-night salesman. And because we were down on our arses at that time, I'd given her curry about buying it too. But now it's, Thank Christ she bought it.

So I grabbed the fire extinguisher and I started spraying up into the ceiling, where the flames were. I thought I was getting somewhere but when I looked out the lounge room windows and saw flames reflecting off the leaves of my banana patch it was, Jesus, this's not looking good. The fire's got into the friggin' roof. I'd better go and get some help.

A mate was renting my cabin, so off I go. It's only down the ramp and five metres away. But it's the first time I've run since I've had two collapsed discs. I get there in a flash and I start thumping on his door. 'Phil! Phil! No matter what yer drinkin' or smokin', get yer arse out here, the fuckin' roof of me house's on fire!'

So Phil comes out in a bit of a daze. 'Hey, what's goin' on, mate?'

I said, 'Me fuckin' roof's on fire.'

He takes a bit of a look and says, 'Yeah, yer right. So it is.' Then he adds, 'I reckon yer in a bit of strife, mate.'

'Too fuckin' right I am,' I say. 'Can yer grab the hose that's hooked up to the rainwater tank?' It had a pressure pump on it. I said, 'Stick a nozzle onto it so that I can get a decent spray of water up through the eaves and onto the fire.'

Which he did. But no matter how much water I put up there, the flames still kept coming out.

I said, 'Jesus, Phil, we're really in the shit here.'

He said, 'Have yer got a manhole cover somewhere?'

'Yeah,' I said, 'just off the verandah. It's the opposite end of where the fire is.'

So Phil grabs my ladder and, being the bloke he is, he climbs up and takes the cover off the manhole. And because the trusses for the ceiling were made of treated pine – of which one ingredient is arsenic – when he sticks his head up into the ceiling area he starts coughing and going on. 'Fuck,' he says, 'I can't breathe. I'm likely to die up here.'

I said, 'Well, get down off the ladder and give me a go.'

So I go up the ladder with the bloody water hose. And that's when I see there's a fully blown blaze going on. Anyhow, being down on my arse as I was at that time, I hadn't paid my house insurance. So there's no fuckin' way I'm gonna let this bloody house burn down on me. That house was very precious to me. I'd built it myself out of forty-year-old seasoned pine timber. Every bit of it. I'd cut the wood. I'd milled the wood. I'd shaped the wood. I built the whole fuckin' thing, nails and all. So I'm up there with a hanky over my nose to try and stop the fumes getting to me and I'm frantically spraying water around.

Then it dawns on me – if the fire burns the electrical wiring and the water gets onto it, I'll get well and truly cooked. I'll not only get fried through electrocution, I'll suffocate from the arsenic smoke and I'll still lose my house – the one I haven't insured.

So I call out to Phil, 'Phil, ring triple zero and get the fire brigade out here.'

After Phil rings the fire brigade, he comes back and says, 'It'd be better if we had more than just the one point of access, mate.' Which I thought was a good idea, so he runs downstairs into the workshop and comes back with a crowbar. He then starts to punch holes through the eaves so that we can get more water into the fire.

Amongst all this carry-on he calls out, 'Get down from there, mate, or you'll die from breathing arsenic smoke.'

I said, 'Shut the fuck up, Phil! My lungs are already well and truly stuffed from years of smoking. So stop worrying about me and let's focus on getting this fire under some sort'a control.'

So there's me spraying water all over the place, while Phil's punching holes in the eaves. Water and shit everywhere ... and the smoke's getting to me. Then, within my panic, I have a moment of clarity. I say to Phil, 'Go downstairs to the workshop. Scrounge around me safety gear. I've got some face masks and there's two type of filters, one's for dust and the other one's for gas.' I said, 'Get me one and don't forget to put the filter on it that reads "gas".'

So he scoots down to the workshop and he comes back with the mask with the gas filter on it. Now I can crawl further into the ceiling, closer to the seat of the fire. And that's when I run into another problem. A couple of years previous to this, I'd put insulation into the ceiling. It was that cellulose and wool stuff – a hundred per cent guaranteed to be flameproof. Well, the fuck it is! It's burning like a compost heap. So I'm up there spraying this stuff down with the hose while Phil's still punching holes in the ceiling with the crowbar, and eventually we get the fire down to the smouldering stage.

That's when the firies turn up. There's about half a dozen of them. I later worked out that, from the time of the emergency call, it'd only taken them twenty minutes to get out to my place. Which was very impressive considering they were volunteers who lived in far-flung parts of the district. So they would've got the call, then they had to get to the fire station, jump in the truck and drive out to my place, ten k's out of town.

Anyhow, with being such a close-knit village, I knew most of them. So when they rocked up they're like, 'G'day, mate. How yer goin'?'

And there I am, shaking all over, trying to recover from the biggest panic I'd ever had, apart from the time I was stabbed and shot at. So I said, 'How do yer fuckin' think I'm goin'? I almost lost me house.'

Then the boss of the brigade takes a bit of a look around. 'Well,' he says, 'seems like yer might'a pretty much put it out yourselves. But I'd better just go up into the ceiling and double-check there's no smouldering embers.'

Any rate, he grabs a fire extinguisher and he goes up and he sprays around here and there. When he crawls back down he says, 'It's safe now, but you're gonna have to replace a couple of those melted roof panels.' Then he tells me how the fitting over the flue, which was supposed to be bolted down onto the roof, hadn't been installed properly by the plumber – and, mind you, I'd forked out a fair whack of money to him to do the job properly.

Any rate, I was so grateful for them to have given up their time to come out that I offered them a contribution. But the boss of the brigade said, 'We don't do it that way. If you want'a make a donation, pop into the station on our open day. And whatever you put in the kitty will be divvied up amongst all the brigades in the state.'

I thought, Jesus Christ, not only are they volunteers but they share around whatever donations they're given, bless 'em.

Then, as they were about to leave, the boss feller said, 'I must say you two blokes did a great job. So good in fact that have yer ever thought about joining up with us?'

'No thanks,' I said. 'If it's anything like tonight, I wouldn't be able to handle the stress.'

In memory of my great mate and storyteller,
Terry Beltrame
20.11.1948–28.9.2020

Memories of the Bangor Fire

My name is Dr Annette Marner and the Southern Flinders Ranges of South Australia is my home. The area is divided by the range, with Port Pirie, Port Germein, Napperby, Nelshaby and Weeroona Island on one side, and Wirrabara, Laura, Murray Town, Melrose and Booleroo Centre on the other. In 2014, I was the presenter of ABC Radio's statewide *Late Afternoons* program in Port Pirie. In doing so I was part of the local radio emergency broadcast team who covered what became known as the Bangor fire. Bangor is a small town with a population of less than fifty, and is a touch less than half an hour's drive south of Melrose, which sits at the foot of Mount Remarkable.

The Bangor fire hit both sides of the range with such ferocity that it took thirty-one days before it was finally declared as 'controlled'. Ironically, with changing weather conditions, the rain came and we went from fires to floods.

It all started with a week-long scorching heatwave. Then on Tuesday 14 January, dry lightning strikes ignited several fires throughout the southern Flinders. One of them was a small fire in inaccessible land near Bangor. In the following days, soaring temperatures and high winds presented perfect bushfire conditions. By 17 January, the situation had gone from bad to worse and on that evening, the Bangor fire was dangerously out of control and travelling at incredible speed towards several towns.

Then on 30 January, the fire was declared 'contained' and on 6 February it was declared 'controlled'. But two days later, fanned by ferocious winds and temperatures rising to over forty degrees Celsius, the fire broke control lines in the south-western corner. The Bangor fire just wouldn't go away and kept threatening us over and over.

Like thousands of people that month, I lived on high alert. I evacuated five times in the knowledge that my house might not be there when I got back. My most important possessions stayed safe in the boot of my car. But the three places I loved most on this earth, and that have nurtured me from birth, were changed forever: our family farm; The Old Nursery, which was started by my great-great-grandfather in 1877; and Port Germein Gorge.

From my diary entries I now reflect on those days.

Thursday 16 January. My evacuation plan is on my phone. And I need it. An hour from airtime the conditions escalate and the emergency warnings ring out for Telowie, Nelshaby, Napperby. In my mind I say goodbye to my house and all my precious books. Before I turn on the microphone to alert Adelaide and the state, Petria Ladgrove, my producer on that day, and I are desperate to know if our loved ones are safe.

Just moments before airtime, someone calls out, 'They're okay!'

At 6.05 p.m. we're off air. It's too dangerous to go home. I have the things I need to start all over again: my mother's watch, my signed Ondaatje from my library. I tell Peter Goers on his Adelaide *Evenings* program how I grew up with my father telling me about the 1960 Southern Flinders fire. It too was started by lightning and a wild south-westerly took it over the top of the range and into Wirrabara Forest. I tell Peter, 'That's the last thing we want to see happen this time.'

Friday 17 January. I go home. It's still there. I want to kiss the bathroom taps and hold my library of beloved books in my arms. By mid-morning I'm back on air at the Port Pirie ABC studio, reading out yet more emergency warnings, checking weather reports and watching the wind through my office window.

Early evening. A powerful wind squall hits the river oaks outside my office. It's vicious. I leave my desk and hurry outside. The wind's coming from the south-west. Thinking of the 1960 Wirrabara Forest fire, I worry that this one might also be going over the top of the range. I run back inside to my desk, saying to myself, 'Think. Think. Who can I call in Wirrabara Forest? Yes, Denise and Paul Kretschmer.'

Denise says, 'Can't talk, Annette. We're fighting it now, out in the orchard.'

I rush to the studio, slap on my headphones, fade down the cricket, take a deep breath and say, 'I now have reports that the fire is in Wirrabara Forest. I'll bring you more information as soon as I can.'

Then to myself I say, 'Hurry. Think. Who can tell me what's happening? Yes, my brother Paul in Wirrabara. He'll be able to see the forest from his place.'

I ring Paul. 'You have to come on air. Now. We need to let people know what's going on. Just tell me what you can see.'

Then, just as I have done tens of thousands of times, my hand brings up the volume control for the phone line. Though never like this. I'm putting my own brother to air because a huge bushfire is hitting the forest and I don't know if everyone's going to be all right.

Paul says, 'I'm standing in Wirrabara looking west ... The wind's just changed and I can't see the hills ...' Then he breaks the frightening news. 'We've just been told to leave and that's what we'll do ... The wind's sprung up from the west, so we're evacuating.'

I tell the listeners to my broadcast, 'Wirrabara has just been told to evacuate ... I'll let you go, Paul. Thank you. Good luck to everyone there. And stay safe.'

Nimbus clouds of fire and smoke and ash are bursting over the area. I know those dirt roads. Those high trees. How will people get out? When the update comes through from the

South Australian Country Fire Service – CFS – I play the studio's emergency siren warning. I try to hold the piece of paper still so that I can read it clearly for the listeners. 'This is a bushfire emergency warning from the CFS ... Wirrabara Forest, Beetaloo Reservoir, Laura Township, Stone Hut, Wongyarra and Wirrabara Township ...'

My boss in Adelaide calls to see how I'm coping. I say, 'I'm staying on.'

A voice from Wirrabara cries over my phone: 'Where do we go? What do we do?'

I say, 'Choose three things you love and leave the rest!'

When I hand over to Peter Goers in Adelaide, he continues to broadcast warnings. I go home and stay up until 2 a.m. I listen. I wait for news. I call my family. 'Is everybody safe?' I keep watch over the burning hills.

Sunday 19 January. I go to our farm at Wirrabara Forest. The buildings of my ancestors are still standing and so in my heart I thank the CFS for saving my family's history.

But all else is an underworld of grey. The ground is leaking smoke and black wire. The trees that I have known all my life are still burning. The ancient red gums on Bentley's Hill are white shadows of ash, like X-rays seared into the stones and earth. The grey box trees that we played under as children are on fire. Their boles are red ovens of coals. The old blue gum by the stable is a smashed and broken giant lying on the ground. In 2010 we wore its leaves in the black lapels of our funeral coats and placed its flowers on the coffin of our father. Some things are not meant to die in your lifetime.

Wednesday 22 January. Telowie, Nelshaby and Napperby are in danger. Petria Ladgrove and I, along with our producer Angela Smallacombe, broadcast throughout the night. During a 2 a.m. interview with the CFS the news is grim. I look over at Petria and, in that single glance, we acknowledge that our homes may well be gone by morning.

Friday 24 January. Though some events are lost in the blur of days and adrenaline, I do remember an afternoon, about ten days into the fire, a woman coming up to me on the street. 'You're Annette Marner, aren't you? Tell them. Tell them, so they'll know in Adelaide that we're really hurting up here, and we're going to hurt for a long time.'

'Yes,' I said, 'I'll tell them.'

Week after week I play the emergency siren over the radio and read out warnings for places that are home to me: Wirrabara, Bangor, Laura, Telowie, Napperby, Nelshaby, Stone Hut, Murray Town and Wirrabara Forest. But there is no time for sorrow.

Saturday 8 February. The winds whip up from the north-west and the temperature soars to forty-three degrees Celsius. Then it breaks. The fire escapes the control line and explodes up a hill-face, north of the Napperby Scout Camp. I tweet photographs and ask my Adelaide colleague, Suzy Ramone, to put me to air so that I can send out warnings that the fire's on the move again.

A few hours later and the fire is bearing down on Laura, Wirrabara, Stone Hut and the community of Beetaloo. I broadcast updates into the night.

Over those thirty-one days I do not know how many times I played the emergency siren to our radio audience and read out those terrible words: 'bushfire emergency ... out of control ... risk to lives and homes'. And throughout the entire duration of the fire, our Adelaide-based presenters, Sonya Feldhoff and Peter Goers, put me to air whenever I wanted to report fire updates. I am very grateful to them.

The Cartography of Fire: Somewhere there's a black island on a map. It's the fireground of the Bangor fire. Thirty-five thousand hectares. But there are no roads for sorrow on that map. It cannot tell you about the grief we feel for what we've lost, and for what's changed. There are no lines on that map to show where people stood in fear and with courage, and travelled into the deep parts of themselves so they could endure day after day, until the rains came.

In all, the Bangor fire destroyed the homes of six families, burnt out a number of farms and killed much livestock and wildlife. Yet the community spirit and camaraderie that surfaced from this awful event is something to be very proud of. Community fundraisers were held to raise money for those who lost their homes. Our local footy club helped pull up kilometres of burnt fencing. BlazeAid brought in nearly two hundred volunteers to help us get back on our feet. And a huge number of firefighters volunteered to come from interstate to assist our own local and regional CFS volunteer brigades.

I cannot tell you how many signs and banners I saw around the Southern Flinders that said 'Thank you!' to the CFS and all the volunteer firefighters for what they did in saving lives and homes.

For all the power of the Bangor fire, not a single human life was lost. And for that, there is no map that can measure the depth and breadth of our gratitude.

Note: Dr Annette Marner is a writer and photographer. Her latest book is called *A New Name for the Colour Blue* and her photographs have been shown in many state and national exhibitions.

A Firie's Prayer
Author unknown

When I am called to duty, God
Wherever flames may rage
Give me strength to save some life
Whatever be its age.

Help me embrace a little child
Before it is too late
Or save an older person from
The horror of that fate.

Enable me to be alert
And hear the weakest shout
And quickly and efficiently
To put the fire out.

I want to fill my calling and
To give the best in me
To guard my every neighbour and
Protect their property.

And if according to my fate
I am to lose my life
Please bless with your protecting hand
My children, my partner, my husband or my wife.